COACHING PRINCIPLES
CLASSROOM
STUDY GUIDE

Third Edition

**Official Course of the
NFHS Coaches Education Program**

American Sport
Education Program

HUMAN KINETICS

D1088072

Coaching Principles Classroom Study Guide, Third Edition

ISBN: 0-7360-5176-7

Author of Classroom Units: Christine M. Drews
Acquisitions Editor and Author of Self-Study Units: Scott Parker
Managing Editor: Kathleen D. Bernard
Copyeditor: Patsy Fortney
Graphic Designer: Fred Starbird
Graphic Artist: Kim McFarland
Cover Designer: Keith Blomberg
Photographer (cover): Dan Nierling
Printer: Edwards Brothers

Printed in the United States of America   10 9 8 7 6 5 4 3 2

HUMAN KINETICS
Web site: www.HumanKinetics.com

United States: Human Kinetics
P.O. Box 5076
Champaign, IL 61825-5076
800-747-4457
e-mail: humank@hkusa.com

Canada: Human Kinetics
475 Devonshire Road Unit 100
Windsor, ON N8Y 2L5
800-465-7301 (in Canada only)
e-mail: orders@hkcanada.com

Europe: Human Kinetics
107 Bradford Road
Stanningley
Leeds LS28 6AT, United Kingdom
+44 (0) 113 255 5665
e-mail: hk@hkeurope.com

Australia: Human Kinetics
57A Price Avenue
Lower Mitcham, South Australia 5062
08 8277 1555
e-mail: liaw@hkaustralia.com

New Zealand: Human Kinetics
Division of Sports Distributors NZ Ltd.
P.O. Box 300 226 Albany
North Shore City
Auckland
0064 9 448 1207
e-mail: blairc@hknewz.com

Contents

Preface   v

CLASSROOM UNITS

Unit 1   Introduction to Coaching Principles (25 minutes) 1

Unit 2   Developing Your Coaching Philosophy and
          Determining Your Coaching Objectives (30 minutes) 9

Unit 3   Selecting Your Coaching Style and
          Refining Your Coaching Philosophy (25 minutes) 24

Unit 4   Coaching for Character (20 minutes) 32

Unit 5   Coaching Diverse Athletes (25 minutes) 44

Unit 6   Communicating With Your Athletes (30 minutes) 58

Unit 7   Motivating Your Athletes (30 minutes) 68

Unit 8   Managing Your Athletes' Behavior (25 minutes) 78

Unit 9   Coaching the Games Approach Way (20 minutes) 86

Unit 10   Teaching Technical Skills (25 minutes). 93

Unit 11   Teaching Tactical Skills (30 minutes). 99

Unit 12   Planning for Teaching (20 minutes) 106

Unit 13   Training Basics (20 minutes) 124

Unit 14   Training for Energy Fitness (20 minutes) 128

Unit 15   Training for Muscular Fitness (15 minutes) 132

Unit 16   Fueling Your Athletes (15 minutes) 136

Unit 17   Battling Drugs (15 minutes) 149

Unit 18   Managing Relationships (25 minutes) 155

Unit 19 Managing Risk (15 minutes) 161

Unit 20 Coaching Principles Wrap-Up (20 minutes). 163

SELF-STUDY UNITS

Unit 1 Introduction to Coaching Principles Self-Study. 171

Unit 2 Developing Your Coaching Philosophy. 174

Unit 3 Determining Your Coaching Objectives 176

Unit 4 Selecting Your Coaching Style 179

Unit 5 Coaching for Character. 184

Unit 6 Coaching Diverse Athletes 188

Unit 7 Communicating With Your Athletes 193

Unit 8 Motivating Your Athletes 199

Unit 9 Managing Your Athletes' Behavior 205

Unit 10 Coaching the Games Approach Way 214

Unit 11 Teaching Technical Skills 219

Unit 12 Teaching Tactical Skills 224

Unit 13 Planning for Teaching 229

Unit 14 Training Basics. 236

Unit 15 Training for Energy Fitness 244

Unit 16 Training for Muscular Fitness. 252

Unit 17 Fueling Your Athletes 260

Unit 18 Battling Drugs 266

Unit 19 Managing Your Team 274

Unit 20 Managing Relationships 277

Unit 21 Managing Risk 287

Unit 22 Coaching Principles Self-Study Wrap-Up 302

Preface

Welcome to the Coaching Principles course! The goal of this course is to help you become the most successful coach that you can be. The classroom course and self-study activities are designed to help you develop your coaching philosophy, motivate your athletes, teach techniques and tactics, develop training programs, plan for the season and each workout, and manage your team and your relationships with all of the people with whom you work.

The *Coaching Principles Classroom Study Guide* has two sections: classroom units and self-study units. You'll use the classroom units during the classroom course. Follow along in this part of the study guide as your instructor leads you through activities, videos, and discussions. All of the resources you need for the classroom course are in these classroom units, and plenty of space has been left for you to write notes.

After you've completed the classroom course, you'll use the self-study units to learn additional coaching information. You'll read the course text, *Successful Coaching*, as you work through these self-study units. Become familiar with the book so that you can refer to it as you face new coaching challenges. At the end of many self-study units, you'll find solutions to the activities so that you can check your responses and clarify your understanding.

Attending the classroom course, working through the self-study units, and reading *Successful Coaching* will prepare you for the Coaching Principles Test. Participating fully in the classroom course and diligently studying the self-study units should improve your score on the test and, more important, enhance your likelihood of becoming a successful coach.

The Coaching Principles Classroom course is a component of the NFHS Coaches Education Program. Since 1990, ASEP has been working with the National Federation of State High School Associations (NFHS) to develop and deliver coaching education courses through this program. Numerous state high school associations currently use the NFHS Coaches Education Program in qualifying high school coaches. More than 25,000 coaches are credentialed through the Coaching Principles course each year.

COACHING PRINCIPLES CLASSROOM UNITS

Unit 1	Introduction to Coaching Principles (25 minutes)	1
Unit 2	Developing Your Coaching Philosophy and Determining Your Coaching Objectives (30 minutes)	9
Unit 3	Selecting Your Coaching Style and Refining Your Coaching Philosophy (25 minutes)	24
Unit 4	Coaching for Character (20 minutes)	32
Unit 5	Coaching Diverse Athletes (25 minutes)	44
Unit 6	Communicating With Your Athletes (30 minutes)	58
Unit 7	Motivating Your Athletes (30 minutes)	68
Unit 8	Managing Your Athletes' Behavior (25 minutes)	78
Unit 9	Coaching the Games Approach Way (20 minutes)	86
Unit 10	Teaching Technical Skills (25 minutes)	93
Unit 11	Teaching Tactical Skills (30 minutes)	99
Unit 12	Planning for Teaching (20 minutes)	106
Unit 13	Training Basics (20 minutes)	124
Unit 14	Training for Energy Fitness (20 minutes)	128
Unit 15	Training for Muscular Fitness (15 minutes)	132
Unit 16	Fueling Your Athletes (15 minutes)	136
Unit 17	Battling Drugs (15 minutes)	149
Unit 18	Managing Relationships (25 minutes)	155
Unit 19	Managing Risk (15 minutes)	161
Unit 20	Coaching Principles Wrap-Up (20 minutes)	163

Introduction to Coaching Principles

(25 minutes)

PURPOSE: To introduce you to the Coaching Principles course, including the course purpose, learning objectives, agenda, and resources.

LEARNING OBJECTIVES

In this unit you will learn

- the purpose, learning objectives, and agenda for the Coaching Principles course;
- how you might use the course text and study guide; and
- some of the reasons other coaches have for taking the Coaching Principles course.

Unit Overview

Topic	Activities	Time (minutes)
A. Welcome and Introductions	Introduce yourself to the class.	5
B. Overview of the Coaching Principles Course	Learn about the purpose, objectives, and agenda for the course. Review the course resources. Discuss housekeeping details (rest rooms and so forth).	5 to 8
C. Am I a Successful Coach?	Complete Activity 1.1 Coach Self-Assessment, and discuss reasons for taking the Coaching Principles course.	10 to 15
D. Unit Summary	Review key unit points.	2

UNIT CONTENT

A Welcome and Introductions (5 minutes)

- Be prepared to introduce yourself by giving your
  - name,
  - present position,
  - sports coached, and
  - length of career.

Check that you have all of the contents of the course package, including the following:

- The course text, *Successful Coaching, Third Edition*
- A *Coaching Principles Classroom Study Guide*
- A Coaching Principles Classroom Test Package, including
  - an ASEP Bronze Level Evaluation Form to evaluate the course,
  - a Coaching Principles Classroom Test,
  - an ASEP Test Answer Form A to record test answers,
  - the Coaching Principles Test Instructions,
  - a preaddressed ASEP mailing envelope in which to mail the completed ASEP Test Answer Form A, and
  - a cardboard insert to ensure that the test form is not damaged in the mail.

B Overview of the Coaching Principles Course (5 to 8 minutes)

The purpose of the Coaching Principles course is to help you reflect on the skills needed to be a successful coach. Some of what we discuss today will confirm what you already know, but some information will be new and will help you refine your skills. In addition, you'll likely gain new insights from the other coaches in our class. This course has been designed to help you

- examine your goals as a coach,
- develop your abilities to communicate with and motivate your athletes,
- teach the techniques and tactics of your sport using the games approach,
- understand how to develop a training program for your sport,
- manage your team and your coaching relationships, and
- learn how you can increase your athletes' safety and reduce your legal liability.

Coaching Principles Classroom Course Agenda

Unit number	Unit title	Time (minutes)
1	Introduction to Coaching Principles	25
	PRINCIPLES OF COACHING	
2	Developing Your Coaching Philosophy and Determining Your Coaching Objectives	30
3	Selecting Your Coaching Style and Refining Your Coaching Philosophy	25
4	Coaching for Character	20
5	Coaching Diverse Athletes	25
	BREAK	**15**
	PRINCIPLES OF BEHAVIOR	
6	Communicating With Your Athletes	30
7	Motivating Your Athletes	30
8	Managing Your Athletes' Behavior	25
	PRINCIPLES OF TEACHING	
9	Coaching the Games Approach Way	20
	BREAK (LUNCH)	**30**
10	Teaching Technical Skills	25
11	Teaching Tactical Skills	30
12	Planning for Teaching	20
	PRINCIPLES OF PHYSICAL TRAINING	
13	Training Basics	20
14	Training for Energy Fitness	20
	BREAK	**15**
15	Training for Muscular Fitness	15
16	Fueling Your Athletes	15
17	Battling Drugs	15
	PRINCIPLES OF MANAGEMENT	
18	Managing Relationships	25
19	Managing Risk	15
20	Coaching Principles Wrap-Up	20
	TOTAL TIME:	**8 HOURS, NOT INCLUDING LUNCH**

Course Resources

Coaching Principles Classroom Study Guide

- You'll use the first part of the study guide today as we do activities together.
- We can't cover everything in this classroom portion of the course, so the second part of the study guide includes self-study exercises that you can do on your own to prepare for the test. It's filled with activities to help you examine your own situation and improve your coaching skills.
- Finally, as appropriate, the study guide includes answers to the self-study activities so that you can check your work.

Successful Coaching

- The book is divided into five parts: Principles of Coaching, Principles of Behavior, Principles of Teaching, Principles of Physical Training, and Principles of Management.
- Each chapter integrates the latest sport science research with practical knowledge acquired by highly experienced coaches. Dozens of references from leading experts bolster each chapter's content.
- You'll find plenty of illustrations, photos, tables, and forms to help you examine your own situation and plan for the future.
- Chapters 12 to 15, especially, include many tables and forms that you can use to plan your practice sessions and fitness testing.
- The appendix includes a detailed explanation of this and other ASEP courses.

The Learning Environment

- Feel free to ask questions at any time. There are no dumb questions. Be assertive about what you need to understand the topic better.
- Use the study guide in whatever way makes it easier for you to learn. Take notes, make check marks, underline important things—do whatever you need to do to make it a worthwhile resource.
- Relax. Enjoy yourself. Be open. Participate. We're all here to learn together.

Housekeeping Details

- Where to put coats
- Seating arrangements

- Rest room locations
- Refreshments
- Other

C Am I a Successful Coach? (10 to 15 minutes)

Activity 1.1 Coach Self-Assessment

Introduction

Coaching education organizations have found that the most successful coaches are knowledgeable and skilled in certain areas and share some common attitudes about coaching. Before learning about each topic in the remaining units, let's take some time to find out how you rate yourself as a coach.

Resources

- The Coach Self-Assessment Inventory (provided after the following instructions and activity outcome)

Instructions

1. Work individually.
2. Read each item on the inventory, and rate yourself as accurately as you can. Circle the rating that best matches your knowledge, skills, or attitudes in the area. For instance, if you don't know much about the tactical skills of the sport you coach, you would circle "1" for being "Weak" in that knowledge area.
3. Be honest. You will not need to share your results publicly.
4. Once you've circled your responses, total your points. Calculate your subtotals for the three areas of the inventory: knowledge, skills, and attitudes.
5. Then calculate your grand total and write it in the space provided at the bottom of the inventory.
6. Finally, compare your grand total with the rating scale to see what your goal for today might be.
7. You'll have 8 minutes to complete the inventory.

Activity Outcome

When you're done, you should have completed the inventory and totaled your points.

Coach Self-Assessment Inventory

This inventory will help you assess your knowledge, skills, and attitudes, which are important to fulfilling your duties as a coach. Read each item and rate yourself as accurately as you can. Circle the rating that best matches your knowledge, skills, or attitudes in the area. For instance, if you don't know much about the tactical skills of the sport you coach, you would circle "1" for being "Weak" in that knowledge area. Be honest. You will not need to share your results publicly.

	WEAK	AVERAGE	STRONG	
KNOWLEDGE _Rate your knowledge in the following areas._				
Rules of the sport	1	2	(3)	
Technical skills needed to play the sport	1	2	(3)	
Tactical skills of the sport	1	2	(3)	
Methods to motivate athletes	1	(2)	3	
Cardiovascular and muscular demands of the sport	1	2	(3)	
Science of conditioning and training	1	2	(3)	
Physical and mental characteristics of the people I coach	1	(2)	3	
Sport nutrition and hydration	1	(2)	3	
How to prevent and treat injuries	1	(2)	3	
Risk management—legal duties, informed consent, appropriate insurance, minimizing athlete risk	(1)	2	3	
Subtotals for Knowledge section (Total the Points Circled in Each Column)	1	8	15	**Total Knowledge Score:** 24
SKILLS _Rate your ability to do the following._				
Teach the technical skills of the sport (the specific procedures to move one's body to perform the task that needs to be accomplished—e.g., passing, blocking, executing a gymnastics movement, running or rowing efficiently)	1	(2)	3	
Teach the tactical skills of the sport (the decisions and actions of athletes to gain an advantage over the opposing team or athletes)	1	(2)	3	
Make tactical decisions for the team during the contest	1	(2)	3	
Plan the instructional program for the season and practices	1	2	(3)	
Prepare athletes for competition	1	2	(3)	

	WEAK	AVERAGE	STRONG	
Communicate with, *including listening to,* athletes	1	2	③	
Communicate with, *including listening to,* parents, officials, other coaches, and administrators	1	2	③	
Manage athletes' behavior by using positive discipline	1	2	③	
Coach for character	1	2	③	
Manage the details of coaching—medical records, contest schedules, transportation, budgets, and so forth	1	②	3	
Subtotals for Skills section (Total the Points Circled in Each Column)		8	18	**Total Skills Score:** 26
ATTITUDES *Rate your likelihood to do the following.*				
Emphasize athlete development over winning	1	②	3	
Continually incorporate newly learned beliefs, values, and insights into my coaching philosophy	1	②	3	
Treat others as I would like to be treated	1	2	③	
Incorporate fun into practices	1	2	③	
Involve athletes in decision making	1	2	③	
Convey empathy to athletes	1	2	③	
Instill a joy of participation and a positive attitude toward sport	1	2	③	
Actively prevent drug and alcohol use among athletes	1	2	③	
Develop positive, collaborative relationships with parents and colleagues	1	2	③	
Enjoy being a coach (overall level of motivation)	1	2	③	
Subtotals for Attitudes section (Total the Points Circled in Each Column)		4	24	**Total Attitudes Score:** 28
				Grand total: 78

Rating Scale

30 to 50 points: Hold on to your hat because you're going to learn a lot today!
51 to 75 points: Listen for the finer, more subtle points today because you're on your way to becoming a great coach!
76 to 90 points: Help coach your classmates today because you've got a lot to share!

Some inventory items are based on the 8 Domains of Coaching Competencies, from *Coaching Education: Designing Quality Programs,* NASPE. www.aahperd.org/naspe/template.cfm?template=coaching.html. Accessed December 2, 2003.

D Unit Summary (2 minutes)

- The Coaching Principles course is designed to help you reflect on the skills needed to be a successful coach.
- The course is 8 hours long, not including lunch or breaks.
- The primary course resources are the *Successful Coaching* book and the *Coaching Principles Classroom Study Guide*.

Developing Your Coaching Philosophy and Determining Your Coaching Objectives

(30 minutes)

PURPOSE: To help you consider your coaching philosophy and objectives and to introduce you to the Athletes First, Winning Second philosophy.

LEARNING OBJECTIVES

In this unit you will learn

- the importance of knowing what kind of coach you want to be and
- ASEP's perspective on winning as an objective in sport.

Unit Overview

Topic	Activities	Time (minutes)
A. Unit Introduction	Hear about the unit's purpose, objectives, and agenda. Get into groups by the sport you coach.	2 to 5
B. Your Coaching Philosophy and Objectives	As a class, complete Activity 2.1 Making the Tough Call, in which you discuss a scenario that will challenge you to think about your coaching philosophy.	12 to 15
C. Athletes First, Winning Second	• Watch DVD segment 1, "Athletes First, Winning Second." • In teams, complete Activity 2.2 Athletes First, Winning Second: From Principle to Practice, in which you discuss scenarios that challenge you to make an Athletes First, Winning Second decision.	12 to 15
D. Unit Summary	Review key unit points.	1

UNIT CONTENT

A Unit Introduction (2 to 5 minutes)

- What kind of coach you want to be
- Your coaching philosophy and objectives
- ASEP's perspective on winning as an objective in sport
- Organize into groups by the sport you coach

B Your Coaching Philosophy and Objectives (12 to 15 minutes)

Activity 2.1 Making the Tough Call

Introduction

A philosophy consists of (1) your major objectives (the things you value and want to achieve) and (2) your beliefs or principles that help you achieve your objectives.

Your coaching philosophy and objectives affect your actions on the court or playing field. If you place a high value on fairness, you probably treat your athletes and the other team fairly. If you believe in developing athletes' leadership skills, you likely give your athletes many opportunities to step into leadership positions.

Your coaching objectives will help you to form your philosophy. The three major objectives of sport are

- to have a winning team;
- to help young people have fun; and
- to help young people develop physically, psychologically, and socially.

In this activity and throughout this unit, we'll take a hard look at how much emphasis you put on winning and the other objectives.

Resources

- The Wildcats scenario (provided after the following instructions and activity outcome)

Instructions

1. Work in teams of two to four, preferably grouped by the sport you coach.
2. Read the scenario and answer the questions posed.
3. You'll have 10 minutes for this activity.

Activity Outcome

When you're done, you should have read the scenario and answered all five questions about making a tough call.

▶ *Wildcats Scenario* -

Coach Mitchell's football Wildcats are down 14 to 10 with one minute to play. The fans scream as "Recordbook Rodney," his star tailback, spins away from two tackles, dodges another, then lunges forward, tackled six yards short of the end zone. Cheering teammates surround Rodney, who—unseen by the officials—takes a cheap shot to the kidney of his tackler. When Rodney gets to his feet, he spits toward the tackler, who is in obvious pain, and then glances to the sidelines to find Coach Mitchell's eyes fixed on him. It's obvious to both of them that his actions have flown square in the face of the team's philosophy and rules. This is not Rodney's first offense with conforming to Coach Mitchell's philosophy and rules.

The refs call in the chains while the other team's trainer assists the injured tackler. The crowd roars as the signal is given: first down and goal. Coach Mitchell calls a time-out. Several players slap Rodney on the back as they run to the sidelines, and the PA system announces, "This is it, Wildcat fans! Six yards away from the first playoff season in 15 years of Huntsville football."

Think about the incredible amount of pressure that Coach Mitchell is under because of the importance of this play. And now the coach is under even more pressure. Rodney has displayed flagrant and dangerous unsportsmanlike conduct and knows that the coach has witnessed it. If the coach lets Rodney stay in, which is his best chance of getting this critical first down, he's sending a message that Rodney's behavior is OK. But if the coach makes Rodney sit out, he'll likely lose the game.

1. How would you respond if you were the coach? What would you do?

   I would leave Rodney in for the remainder of the game but talk to him about his behavior. Explain that it is not ok to do what he did and if he ever did it again there would be consequences.

2. Who will your decision affect? List all possibilities.

fans
Rodney
the team
The coach himself
parents
the other team
Scouts
The integrity of the school

3. How will your response affect Rodney?

- morals

if you leave him in & never explain that
its wrong he may think its ok

if you take him out he may be angry &
lead to neg. consequences

4. How will your response affect the rest of the team?

if you take him out the team may
lose but also be able to teach the team
a life lesson

if you leave him in the team may
win & achieve their goal

5. ASEP's philosophy, which you'll learn more about in a
   moment, is Athletes First, Winning Second. How do you
   think Coach Mitchell will respond if he follows ASEP's
   philosophy of Athletes First, Winning Second?

Take Rodney out.

C Athletes First, Winning Second (12 to 15 minutes)

On the DVD Segment, "Athletes First, Winning Second"

- The relationship between how you coach and the significance you give to winning
- Society's objectives for sport
- ASEP's philosophy of Athletes First, Winning Second
- The Bill of Rights for Young Athletes
- Keeping winning in perspective

Activity 2.2 Athletes First, Winning Second: From Principle to Practice

Introduction

Athletes First, Winning Second is a simple, straightforward philosophy, and few coaches disagree with it when asked. On the other hand, few coaches consistently put this philosophy into practice.

When confronted with the question of prioritizing winning and development, many coaches contend that they want both and that they coach to achieve both. They rightfully point out that winning can help athletes develop by giving them self-confidence and that it's often easier for athletes and coaches alike to feel like they're having fun when they're winning. On the other hand, at times you will have to choose one over the other. Discerning which action places the athlete before winning, or vice versa, is not always easy.

In this activity you'll work individually to decide how you would respond in difficult situations.

Resources

- The Athletes First, Winning Second scenarios (provided after the following instructions and activity outcome)

Instructions

1. Work individually.
2. Read the Athletes First, Winning Second scenarios, and answer the questions posed.
3. You'll have 8 minutes for this activity. Complete as many scenarios as you can during that time.

Activity Outcome

When you're done, you should have responded to as many scenarios as possible and be prepared to share your answers with the entire group.

▶ *Athletes First, Winning Second Scenario 1: Playing With an Injury* - - - -

It's the state basketball championship. Margie, your star center, has sprained her knee. The trainer suspects a Grade II sprain, which means the ligament is stretched and has some tearing but portions of it are still intact. Margie can function at only about 65 percent. However, if she plays, your chances of winning are much better. Being a competitor, Margie desperately wants to play because the championship is the culmination of three hard years of training for her. The trainer advises you not to play her; he says she has a good chance of injuring herself even more seriously if she plays.

Do you let Margie play? Select one of the options here, or write an alternative decision in the space provided.

   a. Let Margie play for as long as she can bear the pain.
   b. If her parents approve, let Margie play as much as she can.
   c. Let Margie play, but only briefly, only late in the game, and only if the outcome of the contest is in question.
   d. Do not let Margie play under any circumstances.

▶ *Athletes First, Winning Second Scenario 2: Problem Athlete* - - - - - - -

Fred is a problem athlete with great potential and an awful attitude. He's also one of the stars on your team. You've counseled Fred a few times about the rules and the consequences of breaking them, but so far nothing has changed. He disrupts practice, and his negative attitude is adversely affecting some of his teammates. As you are contemplating whether to cut Fred from the team, you run into his mother. She tells you that Fred really wants to be a part of the team, and that his involvement is making a positive difference in his life.

Do you keep Fred on the team? Select one of the options here, or write an alternative decision in the space provided.

(a.) Tell Fred what he needs to do to improve his attitude and that you're giving him one more chance. If he continues to misbehave, bring his mother in with him, and cut him from the team.

b. Cut Fred from the team now.

c. Try to let the problem iron itself out and keep Fred on the team regardless of his behavior problems.

d. Tell Fred what he needs to do to improve his attitude and that you care about him and his future. Bench him whenever his misbehavior warrants it, but keep him on the team.

▶ *Athletes First, Winning Second Scenario 3: Academic Problems* - - - - -

Kevin, one of your starters on the team, has been in constant academic trouble. You happen to overhear in the locker room that two other members of the team sat next to Kevin in class and gave him the answers on a midsemester geometry examination. Without this help, Kevin would have flunked the course and been ineligible to play on the team. You confront the two about what you overheard, and they admit they did it because it would help the team.

How do you respond? Select one of the options here, or write an alternative decision in the space provided.

a. Bench all three players for the season.

b. Notify the teacher of the cheating, and let her take the action she deems appropriate.

c. Notify the teacher and jointly decide the appropriate action, which at minimum would be to declare Kevin ineligible and to bench the two players who helped Kevin for three games.

d. Discuss with the athletes why they should not have done this, but let all three athletes continue to play because Kevin didn't officially fail the exam.

▶ Athletes First, Winning Second Scenario 4: Playing Time - - - - - - - - -

It's late in the fourth quarter against your cross-town rival. Tina, a young reserve point guard, has been in for several minutes, resting your starter. She's played well enough, but now with the score tied and a time-out called, your starter could come back in. Like all players on your team, Tina can benefit from more playing time, but she may not have the presence on the floor that you need right now to win the game.

Do you keep Tina in the game? Select one of the options here, or write an alternative decision in the space provided.

a. Let Tina stay in for the rest of the game. She needs the experience to develop as a player.

b. Put your starter back in for Tina. It's the end of the game, and you need to do all you can to win at this point.

c. Tell Tina you'll give her another minute to see if she can do something special out there and that you'll be replacing her if she does not.

d. Tell Tina she's played well, but you don't let backups play at the end of games.

D Unit Summary (1 minute)

- Examining who you are and what you believe will help you develop your coaching philosophy.
- Defining your coaching objectives will help you to form your philosophy. The three major objectives of sport are
    - to have a winning team;
    - to help young people have fun; and
    - to help young people develop physically, psychologically, and socially.

- The significance you give to winning will play a vital role in determining how you coach.
- Your coaching decisions affect your athletes, the team, the school, and the community.
- ASEP's philosophy is Athletes First, Winning Second because this ensures the best long-term outcome for athletes.

Unit 2 Activity Outcomes

1. How would you respond if you were the coach? What would you do?

The best response, because it follows the Athletes First, Winning Second philosophy:

- *Remove Rodney from the game and later explain to the team in the locker room why you made the decision you did, win or lose.*

Consider these coaching points:

- *In such a situation, you would need to be prepared to have one of your assistant coaches take Rodney aside and defuse him. Rodney may react in a way on the sideline that will make a bad situation a disaster for him, the team, and yourself. Head coaches need to coach their assistant coaches to be buffers in certain situations.*

- *The explanation to the team should not be intended to humiliate Rodney in front of his teammates. Instead, the message to the team should be constructive criticism and reinforcement of the team's philosophy and rules. If Rodney needs further discipline, it should be done in private.*

Other possible responses, all of which make winning a higher priority than athlete development, safety, ethical behavior, or sportsmanship:

- *Leave Rodney in the game and ignore the situation.*
- *Leave Rodney in the game but later address the situation privately with him.*
- *Take Rodney out of the game and chew him out in front of everyone, but then put him back in the game for the final set of downs.*
- *Leave Rodney in the game, but don't give him the ball. Address the team and Rodney after the game in the same fashion as found in the "best response." One could argue that this would send Rodney a message that his actions are unacceptable and that by using him as a decoy you are giving the team an opportunity to win. However, this response compromises your values and the values you have tried to instill in your players.*

2. Who will your decision affect?
- *Rodney*
- *The team*
- *Rodney's backup: Leaving Rodney in the game is telling his replacement that the coaching staff has no confidence in the backup's ability.*
- *The school*
- *The community*
- *The safety of your athletes and the safety of the athletes on the opposing team*

3. How will your response affect Rodney?

Your response will communicate volumes to Rodney. If you let him stay in the game, you're communicating to him that although you say you want athletes to show good sporting behavior, when it comes right down to it, you'll accept some unsportsmanlike conduct to gain a win. If you take Rodney out of the game, you're letting him know that you mean what you say and will stand by your word, even if that means the team loses. Whatever you do, you're communicating a set of priorities and values to Rodney, which he will likely model because he probably looks up to you as his coach.

4. How will your response affect the rest of the team?

Your response will communicate the same message to the team as it does to Rodney, but the implications on the team as a whole could be profound. What you do will send a message about what you truly value. Your actions will communicate to the team what you see as acceptable and unacceptable means of attaining a win and could affect their behavior in future games.

In addition, your response may have far-reaching implications for athletes' development. The athletes on the team will think about this decision in the days and weeks following the game. Each athlete will decide, consciously or not, whether to incorporate the value you displayed into his own value system. Not every athlete will follow your example, but many will because as the coach you are viewed as a respected authority figure.

5. ASEP's philosophy, which you'll learn more about in a moment, is Athletes First, Winning Second. How do you think Coach Mitchell will respond if he follows ASEP's philosophy of Athletes First, Winning Second?

Following the ASEP philosophy, Coach Mitchell would have established—from the beginning of the season—that this sort of behavior would not be tolerated. Furthermore, he would have reinforced the importance of sportsmanlike behavior throughout the season. Coach Mitchell would pull Rodney out, and he would explain why he made this decision (win or lose) to the team in the locker room. He'd explain that he understands how emotions run high in situations like this, but that he will not allow his players to commit flagrant or dangerous acts of unsportsmanlike conduct—regardless of how important the win might be to the team. A victory won under those circumstances would be hollow and shameful.

▶ **Athletes First, Winning Second—Activity 2.2 Outcome** - - - - - - - - -

ATHLETES FIRST, WINNING SECOND SCENARIO 1: PLAYING WITH AN INJURY

Do you let Margie play?

a. Let Margie play for as long as she can bear the pain.

Your response shows an emphasis on winning. This could put the athlete at risk of a greater injury to have a better shot at winning the game.

b. If her parents approve, let Margie play as much as she can.

You're most likely thinking about winning more than what's best for Margie. Parental approval might seem like a good reason to play her, but it shouldn't replace your responsibility as her coach to make a decision.

c. Let Margie play, but only briefly, only late in the game, and only if the outcome of the contest is in question.

You're trying to minimize Margie's risk of injuring herself, but are still willing to risk it if it could mean winning the game.

d. Do not let Margie play under any circumstances.

Keeping Margie out of the action for the state championship will be tough on you and on her. In addition, your chances of winning the game will be lessened. However, this choice eliminates the risk of further injury and thereby focuses on Margie's long-term development and well-being.

ATHLETES FIRST, WINNING SECOND SCENARIO 2: PROBLEM ATHLETE

Do you keep Fred on the team?

a. Tell Fred what he needs to do to improve his attitude and that you're giving him one more chance. If he continues to misbehave, bring his mother in with him, and cut him from the team.

Talking to Fred about the problem is a good step, and one that could lead to improvement of his attitude as well as his personal development. Remember, though, that if you cut him, you won't have much of a chance to influence him.

b. Cut Fred from the team now.

You might not make any strides toward winning or Fred's development with this choice. You won't have much of a chance to influence him, and his potential to contribute will obviously be lost. Disciplining an athlete is certainly necessary at times, but cutting Fred at this point isn't likely to do him much good.

c. Try to let the problem iron itself out and keep Fred on the team regardless of his behavior problems.

With this choice you seem to be saying that winning is more important than dealing with Fred's problem. Letting him stay on the team could help you to win some games, but left unchecked, Fred's attitude will continue to hurt your team in the long run.

d. Tell Fred what he needs to do to improve his attitude and that you care about him and his future. Bench him whenever his misbehavior warrants it, but keep him on the team.

Talking to Fred about the problem is a good step, and letting him know you're interested in his welfare could help him to change. Your team might suffer on the field if Fred is on the bench, but you'll be sending a message to him and his teammates that there are consequences for breaking rules. This choice shows that you place athletes first and winning second!

ATHLETES FIRST, WINNING SECOND SCENARIO 3: ACADEMIC PROBLEMS

How do you respond when the two players admit they helped Kevin on the exam?

a. Bench all three players for the season.

Wanting to take action is good, but by benching all three players, you're unlikely to have any impact on their development throughout the season.

b. Notify the teacher of the cheating, and let her take the action she deems appropriate.

Certainly the teacher should be notified, but in your role as a coach, you also have a duty to be involved in your athletes' development. Letting the teacher take action skirts your responsibility, and you'll have to live with whatever the teacher decides, whether it's good for the athletes or not.

    c. Notify the teacher and jointly decide the appropriate action, which at minimum would be to declare Kevin ineligible and to bench the two players who helped Kevin for three games.

Involving the teacher is a good step, and jointly deciding action ensures that you'll have a say in a decision that will affect your athletes' development. Declaring Kevin ineligible teaches him responsibility and shows him and the team that you place a higher priority on their academic development than on winning. Benching the two players for a short time teaches them this same priority yet doesn't exclude them from the good development they may experience as part of the team for the rest of the season. This is a great Athletes First, Winning Second choice.

    d. Discuss with the athletes why they should not have done this, but let all three athletes continue to play because Kevin didn't officially fail the exam.

Selecting this option shows that you may place more importance on winning than on teaching your athletes responsibility. In fact, because they know you know of their cheating, letting all three athletes continue to play sends a clear signal that you don't mean what you say when you tell them to respect authority and work hard. Your decision diminishes the authority of the administration in setting eligibility rules and demonstrates that you don't care if athletes don't work hard for their grades.

ATHLETES FIRST, WINNING SECOND SCENARIO 4: PLAYING TIME

Do you keep Tina in the game?

    a. Let Tina stay in for the rest of the game. She needs the experience to develop as a player.

You're definitely putting an emphasis on athlete development, possibly at the risk of losing the game. That's a choice you'll have to make as a coach.

    b. Put your starter back in for Tina. It's the end of the game, and you need to do all you can to win at this point.

This choice shows that you want to win the game and are willing to play your best athletes at the end to do so. That's not a bad decision, especially if you coach at the competitive level. Striving to win a contest in the short term is the goal of all coaches and competitors.

c. Tell Tina you'll give her another minute to see if she can do something special out there and that you'll be replacing her if she does not.

It may seem at first that this decision focuses on Tina's development, giving her the chance to prove herself in a pressure situation. However, by requiring her to perform or be benched, you could actually be sending the message that winning is paramount.

d. Tell Tina she's played well, but you don't let backups play at the end of games.

By telling Tina that you don't play backups in crunch time, you're removing a potential goal from her and possibly damaging her confidence. In the long run, this could hurt your team's chances of winning as well!

Selecting Your Coaching Style and Refining Your Coaching Philosophy

(25 minutes)

PURPOSE: To introduce you to three coaching styles and help you refine your coaching philosophy.

LEARNING OBJECTIVES

In this unit you will learn

- the characteristics of three coaching styles and how these styles affect athletes,
- the qualities of successful coaches, and
- more about your coaching philosophy.

Unit Overview

Topic	Activities	Time (minutes)
A. Unit Introduction	Hear about the unit's purpose, objectives, and agenda.	1
B. Coaching Styles	Watch DVD segment 2, "Qualities of Successful Coaches."	4
C. Coaching Philosophies	Complete Activity 3.1 Refining Your Coaching Philosophy, in which you fill out a form that helps you think about your coaching objectives and principles.	18
D. Unit Summary	Review key unit points.	2

UNIT CONTENT

A Unit Introduction (1 minute)

- Three possible coaching styles
- Qualities of a good leader
- Putting your coaching philosophy in writing

B Coaching Styles (4 minutes)

On the DVD Segment, "Qualities of Successful Coaches"

- Three coaching styles:
    - Command style (the dictator)
    - Submissive style (the baby-sitter)
    - Cooperative style (the teacher)
- Leadership defined
- What leaders do

Additional Points About Coaching Styles

Being a cooperative style coach does not mean that you aren't sometimes quiet, observing your athletes in action or letting athletes develop leadership skills. And it doesn't mean that you don't make decisions, giving athletes direct instructions. But as a cooperative coach, you take these actions with the athletes' best interests in mind, always looking out for their long-term development and well-being, which is different from the submissive or command style coach.

C Coaching Philosophies (18 minutes)

Activity 3.1 Refining Your Coaching Philosophy

Introduction

This activity will help you put in writing your philosophy of coaching. Your coaching philosophy consists of

- your major objectives as a coach, which are those things you value and want to achieve, and
- your principles that serve as guides to achieving your objectives.

In this activity you'll first write notes about your objectives, and then you'll be presented with some issues that will help you determine your coaching principles.

Resources

- The Coaching Philosophy form (provided after the following instructions and activity outcome)

Instructions

1. You will work through the Coaching Philosophy form as a class, but answer individually.
2. Your instructor will introduce the first part of the form—Your Coaching Objectives—and give you some time to write notes in that section.
3. Then your instructor will introduce the second part of the form—Your Coaching Principles. You'll read and briefly respond to as many of the principles as you can during this unit. You'll revisit the form in later units to see if you want to modify your responses in any way.
4. You'll have 15 minutes for this activity.

Activity Outcome

When you're done, you'll have a rough draft of your coaching philosophy, which will eventually include statements regarding your objectives and key principles by which you intend to coach.

Coaching Philosophy

Part A. Your Coaching Objectives

Part of your coaching philosophy includes your major objectives as a coach, those things you value and want to achieve. Remember that the three major objectives of sport are

- to have a winning team;
- to help young people have fun; and
- to help young people develop physically, psychologically, and socially.

Finish each of the following sentences by stating your position, and then in the space provided add any additional comments you wish to make. For example, your first sentence might be, "My objective with regard to winning is that winning isn't the most important thing, and yet I can't ignore it. I will strive to help my athletes win whenever possible, but not at the expense of their physical health or emotional well-being." This is only an example. You should write your own philosophy in the space provided.

My objective with regard to winning is . . .

My objective about helping athletes have fun is . . .

My objective about helping athletes develop physically, psychologically, and socially is . . .

When situations arise in which I must choose among these three objectives, my priorities will be . . .

Additional comments about your coaching objectives:

(continued)

Coaching Philosophy (continued)

Part B. Your Coaching Principles

Your coaching principles are the set of beliefs you have that serve as general guidelines in helping you make the many decisions you must make when coaching. Some of the principles are likely to be well established in your mind, but you've probably not had a chance to think much about other principles.

In this part of the form, you'll think about your position on seven key issues in coaching. Consider each of the issues carefully and read the two positions presented. Then indicate your position. You can agree with one of the positions stated, modify one of these statements, or state an entirely different position. Our goal is not to prescribe your principles but to bring to your consciousness the principles that you now hold and to help you think further about them.

Issue 1: Winning Versus Participation

Among your toughest decisions is deciding who gets to play in contests. Do you play the best players because you believe they have earned the right to play or because it increases the team's chances of winning, or do you believe that everyone who is a member of the team should get to play in contests?

Position 1: Teaching young people to win—to pursue excellence—by committing themselves to mastering the skills is the goal of sports and my coaching. The best players will play most of the time, with other players getting to participate when winning is secured.

Position 2: Whether the team wins or loses is far less important than my players' participation in the contest. By playing, regardless of winning or losing, they will not only have fun, but will learn many valuable lessons that will benefit them throughout their lives.

Your Position:

Issue 2: Athlete-Centered Versus Coach-Centered

Athlete-centered coaches involve their athletes in making decisions about the team goals and season activities, whereas coach-centered coaches believe they know what is best and as the leader of the team they have the right and responsibility to make all decisions.

Position 1: I like to share the decision making with my athletes to the extent that they are prepared to make such decisions. It's their team too, and sharing the decision making increases their commitment to the team.

Position 2: I know what is best for my athletes, and they can learn more if I make the decisions necessary to be successful.

Your Position:

Issue 3: Ends Versus Means

As a coach, you'll often have to make judgments regarding ethical issues. To what extent do you believe the "end justifies the means" in achieving success as a coach?

Position 1: Although I won't break the rules as a coach, I'll stretch them, find ways around them, and do whatever it takes within the letter of the rules to produce a winning team.

Position 2: I'm cognizant not only of the letter of the rules, but of the spirit of the rules, and although I want a winning team, coaching ethically is more important to me.

Your Position:

Issue 4: Family Versus Sport

Coaching is a very time-demanding profession. You will most likely have to choose between commitments to your family and commitments to the sport you coach.

Position 1: My family always comes first.

Position 2: During the season the demands of coaching require me to give the team more time than I give to my family. But after the season I'll give my family more time. And of course if there is a problem or emergency at home, that will be my first priority.

Your Position:

Issue 5: Quantity Versus Quality

Coaches differ in their views about the amount of time devoted to practice and the number of contests in which they compete. As a coach, do you emphasize quantity or quality?

Position 1: Excellence is achieved by hard work. You can't practice too much, and the more games we play, the better we'll be.

Position 2: Well-organized, efficient practices that focus not just on repetition of the skill but on mastering it through carefully designed drills and games are far better than long practices. More gets done in less time, and the athletes don't get bored. Likewise, I want to carefully select how many and which competitions we enter to give my athletes well-rounded competition but not burn them out.

Your Position:

(continued)

Coaching Philosophy *(continued)*

Issue 6: Coach Versus Guardian

As a coach, do you believe it is your responsibility to be a mentor to your athletes only when they are participating in the sport, or do you also believe you should serve in this role outside of sport?

Position 1: It is my responsibility to help my athletes both on and off the field (court, track, pool, etc.). That's why our team policies include rules not only about athletes' behavior when involved in the sport, but also about their behavior in school and elsewhere.

Position 2: I'm their coach, not their guardian. I'm responsible for my athletes during their participation on my team. Although I certainly will help counsel my athletes on issues outside of sport, it is not my role or place to set rules about their behavior outside of sport or to be responsible for their actions when they are not under my supervision.

Your Position:

Issue 7: Sport-for-All Versus Sport-for-the-Gifted

Many coaches face the decision of whether to keep all athletes that come out for the team or to cut the less gifted players to keep the team number limited. (Sometimes this is not the coach's decision, but a policy of the school or sport organization, and sometimes cutting players is required because of limited facilities, equipment, or coaching staff.) If the decision is within your control as a coach, what is your position on eliminating the less gifted players?

Position 1: I will find a place for every young person who wants to be a member of my team.

Position 2: Sport at this level is for the gifted athlete. I and my assistant coaches can only coach so many players effectively. Players who lack sufficient ability will be cut. Players who are cut can find opportunities to play in intramural and community recreational sport programs.

Your Position:

Additional Coaching Principles

You will certainly face many other issues in sports as a coach. Begin noting these as you experience them, add them to this list, and write down your position. Can you think of any other major principles at this time? If so, record your position on these in the following space.

1.

2.

3.

4.

5.

D Unit Summary (2 minutes)

- Most coaches lean toward one of three coaching styles—the command style, the submissive style, or the cooperative style—but only the cooperative style of coaching fosters the Athletes First, Winning Second philosophy.

- Leadership is action designed to influence others toward set goals. Effective leaders cast a vision, create a positive team culture, instill values, motivate their athletes, resolve conflicts assertively, and communicate effectively.

- Your coaching philosophy consists of your coaching objectives and certain principles that guide your actions. Your philosophy will shift over time as you think on it more and as you develop as a coach.

Coaching for Character

(20 minutes)

> **PURPOSE:** To introduce you to the value of character education and how you can help your athletes develop good character.

LEARNING OBJECTIVES

In this unit you will learn

- the definitions of character and sportsmanship,
- why character education is an essential duty of coaches, and
- how to help your athletes develop good character.

Unit Overview

Topic	Activities	Time (minutes)
A. Unit Introduction	Hear about the unit's purpose, objectives, and agenda.	1
B. Coaching for Character	Watch DVD segment 3, "Coaching for Character." In teams, complete Activity 4.1 Ethical Dilemmas, in which you decide how you would respond to situations that present ethical dilemmas.	12 to 15
C. Coaching Philosophy Revisited	Review your responses to part B of the Coaching Philosophy form and make any changes you desire.	2 to 3
D. Code of Ethics	Read the NFHS Coaches Code of Ethics.	2
E. Unit Summary	Review key unit points.	1

UNIT CONTENT

A Unit Introduction (1 minute)

- Character and sportsmanship
- Coach's responsibilities
- How to teach character and sportsmanship
- Ethical dilemmas as opportunities to demonstrate good character

B Coaching for Character (12 to 15 minutes)

On the DVD Segment, "Coaching for Character"

- Character and sportsmanship defined
- Why character education is important and why it is a coach's responsibility to help athletes develop good character
- What leading organizations promote as the key points of character
- How to teach character and sportsmanship

Activity 4.1 Ethical Dilemmas

Introduction

Often when coaching, you encounter situations in which you have an ethical decision to make. Your athletes watch how you make these decisions and learn about your character as you do so. Coaches are role models, and athletes often follow what their role models teach them, so how you approach these ethical dilemmas has a significant impact on your athletes' character education.

Resources

- The Ethical Dilemma scenarios (provided after the following instructions and activity outcome)

Instructions

1. Work in teams of two to four, preferably grouped by the sport you coach.
2. Read the Ethical Dilemmas scenarios, and answer the questions posed.

3. For each scenario, you can select one of the options given or you can write in a different approach.
4. You'll have 8 minutes for this activity.

Activity Outcome

When you're done, you should have responded to all of the scenarios assigned and be prepared to share your answers with the entire group.

▶ Ethical Dilemma Scenario 1: Being Respectful - - - - - - - - - - - - - - -

In the locker room at halftime your athletes are complaining about poor officiating. You honestly have the same assessment. What should you do?

a. During the second half, complain loudly from the sideline so that the official knows that the team disagrees with the calls.
b. Encourage your athletes to concentrate on their play rather than on the calls. Tell them you're going to concentrate on coaching and let the official worry about officiating.
c. Tell the team that this is a rookie official who shouldn't be taken too seriously.
d. Before the second half starts, privately tell the official that he's doing a lousy job and that you expect him to give your team a break.
e. Other:

▶ Ethical Dilemma Scenario 2: Being Responsible - - - - - - - - - - - - - - -

During the third inning, your first-string pitcher injures his shoulder and has to sit out for the rest of the game. Unfortunately, the relief pitcher is having some trouble with his grades and is ineligible to play. Jason Williams, your only other pitcher, knows that he has a chance to show what he's made of, but after five runs are scored against your team in the next inning, he wants to quit. "I can't do this," he exclaims in frustration. "Get someone else to pitch." Which response would best teach responsibility?

a. "All right, I'll put Harding in for this game and work more closely with you at the next practice. Sound good?"

b. "What?! You're not giving up on us just because you had a bad inning! Now get in there and pitch!"

c. "Williams, the important thing here is that everyone on this team has a responsibility to the rest of the team. If you give up now, you'll let the whole team down. All we ask is that you do your best."

d. Other:

▶Ethical Dilemma Scenario 3: Being Caring - - - - - - - - - - - - - - - - -

As you head out to practice, you notice that one of your athletes looks distressed. "Is anything wrong, Robin?" you ask. "I really need to talk to you," Robin says with a look that appears close to tears. How should you respond?

a. "Robin, I'd be happy to talk with you after practice today if it doesn't take too long."

b. "If you'd like, I could ask Jana to start practice without us while we talk."

c. "Well, let's get out there and have a great practice, then. That'll make you feel better."

d. Other:

▶ Ethical Dilemma Scenario 4: Being Honest - - - - - - - - - - - - - -

You saw potential in John and so you put him on the football roster this year, but so far he hasn't met your expectations. Although you thought he'd make a good defensive lineman, he misses a lot of tackles and doesn't seem to read the plays well. John's dad approaches you and asks you why his son isn't getting much playing time. How should you respond?

    a. Change the subject and ask John's dad how his business is going.

    b. Tell John's dad that you haven't seen any improvement and you don't expect John to be able to play at all this season.

    c. Tell John's dad that you didn't realize you hadn't been playing John very much and that you'll try to put him in more.

    d. Tell John's dad that you see potential in John but that you haven't seen the improvement needed before it's safe and appropriate for him to get a lot of playing time. Discuss the areas you're concerned about and how you might partner together to help John improve. Ask what other athletic skills John's dad sees in his son.

    e. Other:

▶ Ethical Dilemma Scenario 5: Being Fair - - - - - - - - - - - - - - - - -

You're the head volleyball coach at a midsized high school. For several years you've been close friends with the school's athletic director (AD), Carol Pilke. This year Carol's oldest daughter, Ellie, is on the volleyball team despite the fact that she is a mediocre player. When Carol saw that you weren't playing Ellie in the first few games, she approached you and asked you to let Ellie start in the next contest. Should you allow Ellie to start? Why or why not?

a. Yes, because you need to be loyal to the friendship with Carol.

b. Yes, because the request came from the AD.

c. No, because that would be unfair to the better players.

d. No, because it might cause a rift in the team.

e. No, because it might cause the team to lose.

f. Other:

▶Ethical Dilemma Scenario 6: Being a Good Citizen- - - - - - - - - - - - -

An elderly man who lives close to the practice field, and who is known for complaining, calls you to tell you that he can't tolerate any more early-morning practices. The athletes are too loud, he says, and wake him up. He also complains that the athletes leave behind towels and cups, which blow onto his property. How should you respond?

a. Ignore the complaint. None of the athletes heard the phone call, and the neighbor is just a grumpy old man.

b. Tell the neighbor they're just teenagers. You'll see what you can do, but he shouldn't expect a big change.

c. Report the incident to the athletic director and ask him or her to deal with it.

d. Apologize to the neighbor. Let him know that you can't change the practice times, but you'll start workouts on the other end of the field and make sure the athletes pick up all towels, cups, and so forth, after practice.

e. Other:

C Coaching Philosophy Revisited (2 to 3 minutes)

1. Refer back to the Coaching Philosophy form on page 27.
2. Look especially at issues 3 and 6 in part B of the form.
3. Review your responses and make any changes that you would like to make at this time.

D Code of Ethics (2 minutes)

1. Refer to the NFHS Coaches Code of Ethics on page 47 in *Successful Coaching*.
2. To coach for character you must be of good character. As coaching continues to become a respected profession, several organizations have developed codes of ethics for coaches. These are guidelines arrived at by coaches and sport administrators prescribing what is acceptable and unacceptable behavior by coaches. The National Federation of State High School Associations (NFHS) has developed a coaches code of ethics, and you'll find it on page 47 of *Successful Coaching*.
3. Read the NFHS Coaches Code of Ethics.

E Unit Summary (1 minute)

- Good character consists of knowing what's right, desiring to do what's right, and doing what's right. Sportsmanship is simply good character when participating in sports.
- The essential elements of character-building in sports can be summed up in these core principles: be respectful, be responsible, be caring, be honest, be fair, and be a good citizen.
- Coaches have a duty to promote sportsmanship and foster good character by teaching, enforcing, advocating, and modeling these ethical principles.
- You can help athletes develop good character by creating a moral team environment, setting rules for good behavior, and modeling moral behavior and ethical decision making.

Unit 4 Activity Outcomes

ETHICAL DILEMMA SCENARIO 1: BEING RESPECTFUL

    a. During the second half, complain loudly from the sideline so that the official knows that the team disagrees with the calls.

This is not the best choice. This reaction is disrespectful and sends the wrong message to the athletes and spectators.

    b. Encourage your athletes to concentrate on their play rather than on the calls. Tell them you're going to concentrate on coaching and let the official worry about officiating.

Yes! With this response, you model the principle of respect and help your athletes to keep their focus in the right place. Your job is to coach; the official's job is to officiate. Officials have a tough job to do, and they deserve respect, even when they're not performing as well as some people think they should. Coaches who expend a lot of energy complaining to the officials send the message that it's OK to be disrespectful in certain circumstances.

    c. Tell the team that this is a rookie official who shouldn't be taken too seriously.

This is not the best choice. This reaction is disrespectful and sends the wrong message to your athletes.

    d. Before the second half starts, privately tell the official that he's doing a lousy job and that you expect him to give your team a break.

Talking privately with the official is a good step. However, this conversation seems disrespectful. If you're going to talk privately with an official, you can still be polite about it.

    e. Other:

ETHICAL DILEMMA SCENARIO 2: BEING RESPONSIBLE

 a. "All right, I'll put Harding in for this game and work more closely with you at the next practice. Sound good?"

It's not a good idea to let Jason out of his commitments so easily. Take advantage of the opportunity to teach a principle of character.

 b. "What?! You're not giving up on us just because you had a bad inning! Now get in there and pitch!"

That's not the best response. This could be seen as an example of the command-style coach we discussed in unit 3. This difficult moment provides a great opportunity to teach the principle of responsibility.

 c. "Williams, the important thing here is that everyone on this team has a responsibility to the rest of the team. If you give up now, you'll let the whole team down. All we ask is that you do your best."

Because team sports are all about working together, this comment allows you to teach Jason the importance of following through on his responsibilities. Young people, and sometimes even adults, often forget how their actions affect others, so these types of gentle reminders are an important part of your job of coaching for character.

 d. Other:

ETHICAL DILEMMA SCENARIO 3: BEING CARING

 a. "Robin, I'd be happy to talk with you after practice today if it doesn't take too long."

You might want to rethink your approach. This response gives the impression that you really don't have time to be bothered with Robin's concern, or that you just don't care. The other team members will be watching to see how you respond. In some cases it may be appropriate to wait until after practice, but if Robin is close to tears, you might be better off to find out right away what the problem is.

 b. "If you'd like, I could ask Jana to start practice without us while we talk."

Great choice! This approach lets Robin know that you are there for her if she really needs you. She may simply want to tell you about a challenge at home that's preventing her from performing her best on the field, or she may just need reassurance that she's doing a good job. In the extreme case, she could even be suicidal, and a few minutes with you could save her life. It never hurts to show your athletes that you care. If you do spend a few minutes with Robin, you should keep in mind that you're giving up practice time with the team, a trade-off that you should evaluate carefully.

    c. "Well, let's get out there and have a great practice, then. That'll make you feel better."

This is a fairly callous approach that doesn't validate Robin's concern. A more caring approach is called for.

    d. Other:

ETHICAL DILEMMA SCENARIO 4: BEING HONEST

    a. Change the subject and ask John's dad how his business is going.

We might all be tempted to respond in this way, but it's not a response of integrity.

    b. Tell John's dad that you haven't seen any improvement and you don't expect John to be able to play at all this season.

Although you could consider this an honest response, it's certainly not the best one. If you don't expect John to be able to play and offer no positive steps to take, John's likely to fulfill your low expectations. How would your response be different with an Athletes First, Winning Second philosophy?

    c. Tell John's dad that you didn't realize you hadn't been playing John very much and that you'll try to put him in more.

This type of answer seems to slip out more often than we intend, but it's not an honest answer, and it sets you up to break a promise. You knew you weren't giving John much playing time. Do you really intend to play John more? On both counts, this response lacks integrity.

d. Tell John's dad that you see potential in John but that you haven't seen the improvement needed before it's safe and appropriate for him to get a lot of playing time. Discuss the areas you're concerned about and how you might partner together to help John improve. Ask what other athletic skills John's dad sees in his son.

Great answer! It's truthful and forthright—you're telling John's dad exactly why you haven't given John much playing time—and it's productive in that you open up a dialog with John's dad. By discussing how you can partner together to help John improve, you show genuine interest in John and demonstrate an athlete-centered philosophy. By asking John's dad what other athletic skills he sees in his son, you learn more to help you make better coaching decisions. It's possible John has talents that would be better used in a position other than defensive line-man.

e. Other:

ETHICAL DILEMMA SCENARIO 5: BEING FAIR

a. Yes, because you need to be loyal to the friendship with Carol.

Loyalty is a good thing, but it shouldn't dictate the course of action in this case.

b. Yes, because the request came from the AD.

On the face of it, this conclusion seems reasonable. However, the AD of all people should understand the importance of fairness. It's important that you model fairness to all those around you.

c. No, because that would be unfair to the better players.

That's it! The main reason you shouldn't bend to Carol's request, whether Carol spoke as a parent or as the AD, is because it would be unfair to the better players. You can still be loyal to your friendship with the AD while upholding your coaching objective of fairness.
This doesn't mean that you should never allow an athlete with a lower skill level to compete. Creative coaches know that there are ways to give a hardworking but less skilled athlete some playing time.

    d. No, because it might cause a rift in the team.

That result is a possibility, but it's not the primary reason for letting Ellie sit on the bench.

    e. No, because it might cause the team to lose.

That result is a possibility, but it's not the primary reason for letting Ellie sit on the bench.

    f. Other:

ETHICAL DILEMMA SCENARIO 6: BEING A GOOD CITIZEN

    a. Ignore the complaint. None of the athletes heard the phone call, and the neighbor is just a grumpy old man.

Even though you can probably get away with it, this response will not help your athletes learn the principle of citizenship.

    b. Tell the neighbor they're just teenagers. You'll see what you can do, but he shouldn't expect a big change.

This response communicates low expectations of athletes and does not demonstrate goodwill toward the community.

    c. Report the incident to the athletic director and ask him or her to deal with it.

You can probably get away with this response, but the golden opportunity to teach your athletes good citizenship will be lost. You're abdicating your responsibility to the team and the neighbor.

    d. Apologize to the neighbor. Let him know that you can't change the practice times, but you'll start workouts on the other end of the field and make sure the athletes pick up all towels, cups, and so forth, after practice.

By taking these steps, your athletes will see that you are willing to show respect to others, even people who aren't particularly liked. You'll communicate that being a good neighbor, cooperating with the community, and protecting the environment are all important ways of showing good citizenship.

    e. Other:

Coaching Diverse Athletes

(25 minutes)

PURPOSE: To help you know how to accommodate athletes with disabilities and be responsible in dealing with sexual issues.

LEARNING OBJECTIVES

In this unit you will learn

- factors to consider in coaching with athletes with disabilities and
- about some of your responsibilities regarding sexual relationships with athletes.

Unit Overview

Topic	Activities	Time (minutes)
A. Unit Introduction	Hear about the unit's purpose, objectives, and agenda.	1
B. Coaching Athletes With Disabilities	In teams, complete Activity 5.1 Coaching Athletes With Disabilities, in which you respond to scenarios that will help you think about whether and how to accommodate athletes who have disabilities.	8 to 10
C. Sexual Relationships	• Watch DVD segment 4, "Sexual Relationships." • Complete Activity 5.2 Crossing the Line, in which you fill out a questionnaire that will help you know if you are potentially crossing the line with an athlete.	7 to 10
D. Coaching Philosophy Revisited	Review your responses to part B of the Coaching Philosophy form and make any changes you desire.	2 to 3 minutes
E. Unit Summary	Review key unit points.	2

UNIT CONTENT

A Unit Introduction (1 minute)

- How to accommodate athletes with disabilities
- Sexual relationships with athletes
  - Crossing the line
  - Self-assessment

B Coaching Athletes With Disabilities (8 to 10 minutes)

Activity 5.1 Coaching Athletes With Disabilities

Introduction

Most of us don't have formal training in dealing with people with disabilities, and so we might not feel comfortable or qualified to work with an athlete who is disabled.

- However, the law requires that you provide comparable opportunities to people with disabilities.
- No sport program may discriminate against players or coaches with disabilities; you must make reasonable accommodations to ensure that athletes with disabilities have equal access to sports.

Of course, you probably want to provide this equal opportunity; it's more that you might not be sure how to do so. In this activity we'll explore ways you can accommodate athletes who have disabilities.

Resources

- The Athlete With Disability scenarios (provided after the following instructions and activity outcome)

Instructions

1. Work in teams of two to four, preferably grouped by the sport you coach.
2. Read the Athlete With Disability scenarios, and answer the questions posed. The scenarios are not sport specific, so that you can apply them to the sport you coach. This means that different groups may come up with different, yet appropriate, responses.
3. For the first question under each scenario, you can select

one of the options given or you can write in a different approach.

4. While working through these scenarios, keep in mind these principles of dealing with athletes who have disabilities:

   a. You must make reasonable accommodations to help people with disabilities play on the team.

   b. It is unreasonable, however, if the accommodation
      - puts the able-bodied members of the team at risk or at a disadvantage,
      - represents substantial risk to the well-being of the athlete with disabilities, or
      - requires unreasonable cost or assistance.

   c. After you have made reasonable accommodations, athletes with disabilities should be expected to play at the same level as all members of the team to earn a position on the team.

5. You'll have 7 minutes for this activity.

Activity Outcome

When you're done, you should have responded to all of the scenarios and be prepared to share your answers with the entire group.

▶ Athlete With Disability Scenario 1: Athlete Who Is Deaf- - - - - - - - - -

Jackson shows up for your first preseason workout and wants to try out for your team. You see Jackson signing with his parents, and you ask his parents the degree of his hearing loss. His mom tells you that Jackson has complete hearing loss in his left ear and a 70 percent loss in his right ear. You have no idea how to communicate with Jackson. However, when Jackson figures out how to participate, you can tell that he's quite skilled. His mom tells you that Jackson's been playing your sport on a hearing-impaired team for seven years, but he'd really like to play on a more competitive team such as yours.

1. How should you respond to Jackson's wanting to try out for and play on your team?

   a. Tell his mother that you're sorry, but you simply have no idea how to work with Jackson. He cannot try out for your team.

   b. Let Jackson know that he can try out for the team, but his chances aren't good because he won't be able to hear all that happens on the court or field.

    c. Allow Jackson to try out for the team, but give him minimal playing time during the season because he cannot hear what the other athletes are saying.

    (d.) Ask Jackson what the best ways are for you and his teammates to communicate with him. Incorporate those accommodations in the preseason workouts, and allow Jackson to try out for the team. If he plays at the same level as the other members of the team, keep him on the team.

    e. Other:

2. What reasonable accommodations in equipment, training, communication, or rules do you think you should make for Jackson?

    Signs

▶ Athlete With Disability Scenario 2: Athlete Who Uses a Wheelchair - - -

Andrea approaches you about trying out for the sport you coach. Andrea has paraplegia: Her lower body is paralyzed, but her upper body is fully functional. Andrea has been practicing your sport by herself, but because there is no wheelchair league in your area, she has no fellow athletes to compete with.

1. How should you respond to Andrea's request to try out for your sport?

    a. Thank Andrea for showing interest, but tell her that she won't be able to play your sport. People in your sport must have full use of their legs.

    b. Discuss the request with Andrea's parents, and let them make the decision about her participation.

    (c.) Set up a time to meet with Andrea and her parents to discuss this further. Explore together whether she and the other athletes would be safe and what accommodations you would need to make. If it's not safe for her to compete with your team, or if her skills are not up to par, discuss alternate ideas for how Andrea could participate in the sport or improve her skills.

d. Let Andrea try out for and make the team, even if she is less skilled than your other team members.

e. Other:

if she doesn't make the team to give her a small role

2. If Andrea were to compete in your sport with able-bodied peers, what reasonable accommodations in equipment, training, communication, or rules do you think you should make for her?

talk about safety w/other players

▶ Athlete With Disability Scenario 3: Athlete With Cognitive Disabilities - -

Brian shows up at your preseason practices overenthusiastic and ready to respond to your every command. The problem is, he doesn't follow directions very well because he has several learning disabilities and attention-deficit/hyperactivity disorder (ADHD). During practices, Brian shows some pretty good skills, but you can tell that he often either doesn't appear to understand the strategy of the sport or fails to execute strategy correctly.

1. How should you respond to Brian's desire to play your sport?

a. Ask Brian's special education teacher to decide whether Brian should be part of your team.

b. Coach Brian just as you would anybody else, but make sure you have his attention when instructing, repeat the instruction several times, and invite Brian to summarize what you just said. Try teaching him some basic strategy, and see if he catches on. If he plays as well as other members of the team, allow him to make the cut; if not, cut him from the roster just as you would any other player.

c. Cut Brian from the team. He's going to demand a lot more energy than usual from you this season, and if he doesn't understand the strategy of the game, he simply can't play on your team.

d. Allow Brian to try out for and make the team, even if his skills are far below those of the other athletes on the team.

2. What reasonable accommodations in equipment, training, communication, or rules do you think you should make for Brian?

More direct instructions to him

Coaching Athletes Who Have Disabilities

- The decision to permit a person with a disability to try out for a nondisability sport should be made jointly by the athlete, the athlete's parents, medical consultants, the sport organization, and the coach. These decision makers should consider any special accommodations for the athlete, the safety of the athlete with the disability, and the safety of the other athletes.

- When coaching athletes with disabilities, your first obligation is to understand how their disabilities will affect their participation. Research the disabilities in question so that you know all that you can about them, and consult with educational specialists who have expertise related to the disabilities of interest.

- Remember that the same disability will affect different people in different ways. You should meet with the athlete and his or her parents to get a complete and accurate picture of the athlete's capabilities and needs and ideas about how to adapt activities.

- Develop reasonable skill progressions based on the disability.

- Assist athletes when requested, but do not become overbearing and smother them.

- Allow athletes to experience risk, success, and failure. Do not overprotect them.

- Do not underestimate what athletes with disabilities can do.

- Have a smaller coach-to-player ratio when coaching athletes with disabilities.

- Find ways to match athletes with comparable abilities.

Reference for bullets 4 to 9: DePauw, K. and S. Gavron. 1995. *Disability and Sport.* Champaign, IL: Human Kinetics, p. 171.

C Sexual Relationships (7 to 10 minutes)

On the DVD Segment, "Sexual Relationships"

- Sport naturally builds close relationships
- Carefully evaluate relationships so that you don't cross the line

Activity 5.2 Crossing the Line

Introduction

Coaches sometimes cross the line from appropriate behavior to inappropriate behavior with an athlete without even realizing it. In this activity you'll complete a questionnaire that helps you gauge your relationship with the athlete you are closest to.

Resources

- The Crossing the Line Questionnaire (provided after the following instructions and activity outcome)

Instructions

1. Work individually. You will *not* be asked to share your responses with the class.
2. Circle "Yes" for each statement that reflects your behavior or attitude toward the athlete that you are closest to. Circle "No" if the statement does not reflect how you behave or feel.
3. You'll have 4 minutes to complete the questionnaire.

Activity Outcome

When you're done, you should have answered all questions on the questionnaire.

Crossing the Line Questionnaire

Coaching is an emotionally intense profession, and strong bonds and emotions are part of the job. The line between appropriate and inappropriate behavior is often a matter of intent and context. The following list of questions is intended to help you know when you may be extending the boundaries of your role as coach and potentially crossing the line with an athlete.

Circle "Yes" for each statement that reflects your behavior or attitude toward the athlete that you are closest to. Circle "No" if the statement does not reflect how you behave or feel.

1.	I often tell my personal problems to this athlete.	Yes	No
2.	I want to be friends with this athlete when his or her career ends.	Yes	No
3.	To be honest, my physical contact with this athlete is motivated by desires that go beyond an attempt to support and motivate the athlete.	Yes	No
4.	I find myself thinking of ways to work individually with this athlete and in special practice sessions that run before or after practice.	Yes	No
5.	There is something I like about being in the office with this athlete when no one else is around.	Yes	No
6.	I often listen to this athlete's personal problems.	Yes	No
7.	I find myself wanting to coach practices when I know this athlete will be there, and I'm unusually disappointed when this person is absent.	Yes	No
8.	I find myself saying a lot about myself with this athlete (for example, telling stories and engaging in peerlike conversation).	Yes	No
9.	This athlete has spent time at my home (other than for a team function).	Yes	No
10.	I find myself looking at this athlete's body in a sexual way.	Yes	No
11.	I find myself making sexual jokes around this athlete.	Yes	No
12.	To be honest, I feel jealous when this athlete spends time with other people.	Yes	No

Because coaching involves intense emotional and complicated relationships with athletes, making blanket statements about what is appropriate and inappropriate behavior is difficult. If you are unsure whether your behavior is ethical and professional, discuss it with colleagues. Self-assessment and peer supervision can help you avoid trouble before it starts.

If you circled "No" to all questions: Your responses indicate that your behaviors and attitudes are in line with your coaching responsibilities.

If you circled "Yes" to one or more of questions 1 to 9: You may have crossed the line between coach and friend and may be using the athlete to meet your own need for acceptance or companionship.

If you circled "Yes" to question 3 or 12: You may be using the athlete to meet your own sexual or romantic needs in addition to your need for companionship.

If you circled "Yes" to question 6: You are potentially extending the coaching position into the role of counselor. You may be out of your league, and you might suggest that the athlete seek professional advice.

If you circled "Yes" to question 10: You may be looking at the athlete as a sexual object rather than as a human being.

If you circled "Yes" to question 11: You may be contributing to a hostile environment (sexual harassment). Some abusive coaches assess the likelihood that an athlete will report a sexual advance by judging an athlete's response to sexual remarks.

Adapted by Dr. Todd Crosset from *Are You in Trouble With a Client?* by Estelle Disch, BASTA!, Cambridge, MA.

Crossing the Line

- Because coaching inherently draws coaches close to athletes, it's difficult to provide guidelines about what is appropriate and inappropriate in every situation.

- If you're not sure if you are crossing the line with an athlete, consider consulting with a trusted colleague. Doing so may help you prevent inappropriate behavior.

- You can use this questionnaire throughout your coaching career to help keep yourself on track.

- If at any time you sense that a relationship is becoming inappropriate, remember that your role is to be the responsible adult with a larger perspective. The athletes you are working with are young and impressionable. It is up to you to correct the relationship and behave appropriately.

- You can read more about the legalities of sexual relationships on page 85 of *Successful Coaching*.

D Coaching Philosophy Revisited (2 to 3 minutes)

1. Refer back to the Coaching Philosophy form on page 27.
2. Look especially at issues 1 and 7 in part B of the form.
3. Review your responses and make any changes that you would like to make at this time.

E Unit Summary (2 minutes)

- By law, you must make reasonable accommodations to help people with disabilities play on the team.

- It is unreasonable, however, if the accommodation puts the able-bodied members of the team at risk or at a disadvantage, it represents substantial risk to the well-being of the athlete with disabilities, or the cost or assistance required is unreasonable.

- After you have made reasonable accommodations, athletes with disabilities should be expected to play at the same level as all members of the team to earn a position on the team.

- It is illegal to have sex with your athletes if you coach for an *educational organization,* regardless of the age of the athlete or whether the athlete consents to having sex.

- Having sex with a minor is harmful emotionally to the player; it can destroy a coach's career; it can lead to legal action against the coach and sport organization; and it usually devastates a team's cohesiveness.

- It is up to you to be the responsible adult in such situations. If you've crossed the line, it's up to you to correct the relationship and behave appropriately.

Unit 5 Activity Outcomes

▶ *Coaching Athletes With Disabilities—Activity 5.1 Outcome* - - - - - - - -

ATHLETE WITH DISABILITY SCENARIO 1: ATHLETE WHO IS DEAF

1. How should you respond to Jackson's wanting to try out for and play on your team?

   a. Tell his mother that you're sorry, but you simply have no idea how to work with Jackson. He cannot try out for your team.

   Not only is this response insensitive, but it is also illegal. You must give Jackson equal opportunity to try out for your team.

   b. Let Jackson know that he can try out for the team, but his chances aren't good because he won't be able to hear all that happens on the court or field.

   This reaction may demotivate Jackson and will show your halfheartedness. It also illustrates that you aren't willing to make reasonable accommodations for his disability, and this is against the law.

   c. Allow Jackson to try out for the team, but give him minimal playing time during the season because he cannot hear what the other athletes are saying.

   You're on the right track, in that Jackson should be allowed to try out for the team. However, giving him minimal playing time without considering accommodating his hearing loss is demotivating and not legal.

   d. Ask Jackson what the best ways are for you and his teammates to communicate with him. Incorporate those accommodations in the preseason workouts and allow Jackson to try out for the team. If he plays at the same level as the other members of the team, keep him on the team.

Yes! Talking directly with Jackson is the best way to start. If you don't know how to sign, ask someone to interpret for you or ask your initial questions in writing. If reasonable accommodations can be made, his participation doesn't impose any safety risks, and his skills are as high as those of other team members, he should make the team. If any of these conditions can't be met, it is reasonable for you to cut him from the team.

    e. Other:

2. What reasonable accommodations in equipment, training, communication, or rules do you think you should make for Jackson?

No equipment, training, or rule modifications need to be made for Jackson. But you need to accommodate his needs for communication. You should consider obtaining the services of an interpreter and communicate team, training, and safety rules in writing and via the interpreter. Make sure that athletes who are deaf know their roles before going onto the playing field to minimize uncertainty during competition.

Use visual communication as much as possible: Develop a name sign for the athlete who is deaf and each of the athletes on the team to facilitate communication; emphasize visual demonstrations over verbal instruction; develop visual and tactile cues to promote rapid communication on the court or field; use videotape of practices and games to communicate and reinforce instructional points; be sure that verbal and nonverbal messages are consistent; and refrain from using sarcasm, which can be misinterpreted by athletes who are deaf.

You should do all that you can to make sure the athlete who is deaf sees and understands all instructions: Communicate important instructions during warm-up periods and timeouts; face the athlete and enunciate words clearly and precisely when speaking to athletes who rely on lip reading; face the sun when practicing or playing outdoors so that athletes who are deaf can see the attempt to signal or communicate; use light signals (e.g., turning the lights on and off in the gym) to get the athlete's attention during practice; use flags or other visual signals to assist in communication during ongoing play; and have the athlete restate directions or instructional content to show full understanding.

ATHLETE WITH DISABILITY SCENARIO 2: ATHLETE WHO USES A WHEELCHAIR

1. How should you respond to Andrea's request to try out for your sport?

    a. Thank Andrea for showing interest, but tell her that she won't be able to play your sport. People in your sport must have full use of their legs.

It actually might be possible that for your sport, Andrea cannot compete on an able-bodied team. However, even in that situation, a more tactful response is called for, and you may need to do some research to find out what opportunities are available to Andrea in your community. It's also possible that you could invite Andrea to work out with your team even if she cannot compete as a member of your team.

b. Discuss the request with Andrea's parents, and let them make the decision about her participation.

You're on the right track with discussing this with Andrea's parents. However, the decision should be a joint one among Andrea, her parents, and you and take into account the safety of Andrea and the other athletes.

c. Set up a time to meet with Andrea and her parents to discuss this further. Explore together whether she and the other athletes would be safe and what accommodations you would need to make. If it's not safe for her to compete with your team, or if her skills are not up to par, discuss alternate ideas for how Andrea could participate in the sport or improve her skills.

This is a great idea. Especially if you're not familiar with Andrea's disability, her skills, and how to incorporate her on the team, discussing this openly with Andrea and her parents is a great way to start. If her skill level is not high enough, you can discuss ways Andrea can train (or ways you can help her to train) so that she can try out in the future. If it's not safe for her or the other athletes for Andrea to compete on your team, you can explore other sports that might be safer for her to participate in. On the other hand, if her skills are good and if it is safe, there is no reason Andrea shouldn't be part of your team.

d. Let Andrea try out for and make the team, even if she is less skilled than your other team members.

Although this sounds like a caring response, it actually shows disrespect for other athletes who also tried out but didn't make the team. In addition, Andrea may perceive this as patronizing, which will not help build her self-esteem.

e. Other:

2. If Andrea were to compete in your sport with able-bodied peers, what reasonable accommodations in equipment, training, communication, or rules do you think you should make for her?

In a competitive integrated sport with able-bodied peers, rules of play for the most part cannot be substantially altered. For example, a wheelchair tennis player typically would not be allowed to take two bounces to play a ball in a high school varsity tennis match as he or she would be afforded in USA Wheelchair Tennis sanctioned competition. On the other hand, a golfer with a severe mobility impairment may be allowed to use a golf cart to travel between holes because the mode of travel between holes is not deemed to be a substantial alteration of the rules of play.

You would be expected to include the athlete in any practice activities that the athlete could perform in a wheelchair and that would not create a greater-than-usual risk of injury to any party. Specialized equipment would vary by sport. You would be expected to devote time to learning wheelchair movement mechanics to better understand how to effectively teach the techniques and tactics of the sport.

ATHLETE WITH DISABILITY SCENARIO 3: ATHLETE WITH COGNITIVE DISABILITIES

1. How should you respond to Brian's desire to play your sport?

   a. Ask Brian's special education teacher to decide whether Brian should be part of your team.

Talking with Brian's special education teacher is a good step, but leaving the decision to this person is not appropriate. You might consult with the teacher and with Brian's parents as you decide what to do.

   b. Coach Brian just as you would anybody else, but make sure you have his attention when instructing, repeat the instruction several times, and invite Brian to summarize what you just said. Try teaching him some basic strategy, and see if he catches on. If he plays as well as other members of the team, allow him to make the cut; if not, cut him from the roster just as you would any other player.

This response demonstrates your willingness to make reasonable accommodations. It also shows a fairness to your other team members. Despite Brian's learning disabilities and ADHD, he may be a very skilled athlete, and you might be the one to help him reach his full potential.

   c. Cut Brian from the team. He's going to demand a lot more energy than usual from you this season, and if he doesn't understand the strategy of the game, he simply can't play on your team.

It's true that Brian will demand a lot of energy from you, but this is not a reason to cut him from the team. If you coach an elite-level team, it is possible that at your level of play you cannot accommodate Brian because of his lack of understanding of strategy. However, in a high school setting, you must make reasonable accommodations, which would involve evaluating whether Brian can learn strategy. It's possible that he's simply not been taught these skills before.

> d. Allow Brian to try out for and make the team, even if his skills are far below those of the other athletes on the team.

Although this sounds like a caring response, it actually shows disrespect for other athletes who also tried out but didn't make the team. In addition, Brian may perceive this as patronizing, which will not help build his self-esteem.

> 2. What reasonable accommodations in equipment, training, communication, or rules do you think you should make for Brian?

No equipment, training, or rule modifications need to be made for Brian. However, several accomodations in communication should be made:

- *In offering instruction or performance feedback, always make sure you have the athlete's attention before beginning.*
- *Keep instructional or coaching points brief.*
- *Repeat central instructional or coaching points.*
- *Ask the athlete to repeat instructional points.*

Communicating With Your Athletes

(30 minutes)

PURPOSE: To help you evaluate and improve your communication skills.

LEARNING OBJECTIVES

In this unit you will learn

- eight communication problems common to the coaching profession and
- how to improve your communication skills.

Unit Overview

Topic	Activities	Time (minutes)
A. Unit Introduction	Hear about the unit's purpose, objectives, and agenda.	1
B. Evaluating Your Communication Skills	Individually, complete Activity 6.1 Evaluating Your Communication Skills, in which you rate yourself on several coaching communication skills.	12
C. Effective Communication	• Watch DVD segment 5, "Communication." • In teams, complete Activity 6.2 Becoming a Better Communicator, in which you match communication tips with problem coaches.	15
D. Unit Summary	Review key unit points.	2

UNIT CONTENT

A Unit Introduction (1 minute)

- Rating your own communication skills
- Verbal and nonverbal communication
- The communication styles of command coaches, submissive coaches, and cooperative coaches
- Improving your listening skills
- Improving communication with your athletes

B Evaluating Your Communication Skills (12 minutes)

Activity 6.1 Evaluating Your Communication Skills

Introduction

Coaches need certain communication skills to do their job well. In this activity you'll rate yourself in eight areas of communication that are especially applicable to coaches.

Resources

- The Communication Survey (provided after the following instructions and activity outcome)

Instructions

1. Work individually.
2. Read the description of each mythical coach and then rate yourself on the skill discussed. Circle the number that best describes you.
3. If you have not coached before, answer according to how you communicate in a leadership position.
4. Once you've rated yourself in every area, total your score and see where you land on the rating scale.
5. You'll have 10 minutes for this activity.

Activity Outcome

When you're done, you should have completed the Communication Survey.

Communication Survey

Coach Incredible

Never admitting to an error, Coach Incredible finds he doesn't get the respect he demands because he doesn't show any for his athletes. He often doesn't follow through on what he says he will do, he thinks he's far more knowledgeable about the sport than he is, and he's very self-centered. When he speaks, he preaches rather than coaches so his athletes tune out because what he says never amounts to much. Coach Incredible has not yet learned that he cannot demand respect; instead it must be earned. Hence he has no credibility with his athletes.

Think about how you communicate with your athletes and others. Does it add or detract from your credibility? Rate yourself on how credible your athletes perceive your communication.

1   2   3   ④   5

Very low   *Very high*

Coach Naysayer

Most of the words and actions of Coach Naysayer are negative, sometimes almost hostile. She frequently criticizes her athletes, which increases their self-doubts and destroys their self-confidence. Coach Naysayer is slow to praise, as though she believes it is not "coachlike" to say a kind word, and when she utters an infrequent kindness, she usually overshadows it with other negative comments.

Think back to your recent communications with your athletes. Are you primarily positive in the messages you deliver, or are you like Coach Naysayer? Rate the degree to which your messages are positive or negative.

1   2   3   4   ⑤

Negative   *Positive*

The Judge

The Judge continually evaluates his athletes instead of instructing them. When a player errs, the Judge places blame rather than providing feedback or information about how to correct the error ("Who screwed up here?" "Why can't you get this right?" "You cost us the game with that dumb move."). When the players do well, the Judge cheers them on but doesn't know how to instruct them to achieve advanced skill levels. The continuous judgments, even when they are occasionally positive, cause athletes to feel uncertain and uncomfortable around the Judge.

Reflect a moment on the type of messages you send to your athletes. Do you give ample feedback and instructions, or are you like the Judge? Rate the extent to which the content of your communication is high in information or high in judgment.

1   2   3   ④   5

High in judgment   *High in information*

Coach Fickle

You are never sure what Coach Fickle will say next. Today it's one thing, tomorrow another. Last week she punished Janeen for fighting but not Sara, her star goalie. She tells players not to argue with the officials, but she does so regularly.

It's not easy to detect our own inconsistencies, but ponder for a moment how consistent you think you are in the messages you send and between what you say and what you do. Is your message consistent, or are you more like Coach Fickle? Rate the consistency of your communication.

1   2   3   ④   5

Inconsistent   *Consistent*

Coach Glib

Coach Glib is the most talkative person you ever met. He gives instructions constantly during practice, and when he's not yelling advice to his players during the contest, he's muttering to himself on the sidelines. He's so busy talking that he never has time to listen to his athletes. It has never occurred to him that his players might like to tell him something rather than always being told.

Are you a good listener, or are you like Coach Glib? Rate how good a listener you are.

1   2   3   4   ⑤
Not good   Very good

Coach Stone

Coach Stone never shows emotion. She doesn't smile, wink, or give her athletes pats on the back. Nor does she scowl, kick at the dirt, or express disgust with them. You just don't know how she feels, which leaves her players feeling insecure most of the time.

Do you communicate your emotions effectively both verbally and nonverbally, or are you like Coach Stone? Rate how effective you are in expressing your emotions constructively.

1   2   3   4   ⑤
Weak   Strong

The Professor

The Professor is unable to explain anything at a level understandable to his players. He talks either above their heads or in such a roundabout way that they are repeatedly left confused. In addition, the Professor, who is used to dealing with abstractions, is unable to demonstrate the skills of the sport in a logical sequence so that the athletes can grasp the fundamentals.

Are you able to provide clear instructions and demonstrations, or are you like the Professor? Rate your ability to communicate instructions.

1   2   3   ④   5
Weak   Strong

Coach Skinner

Coach Skinner just doesn't seem to understand how the principles of reinforcement work. Although he gives frequent rewards to his athletes, he reinforces the wrong behavior at the wrong time. When faced with misbehavior, he either lets the infraction pass or comes down too hard.

Do you understand the principles of reinforcement, or are you like Coach Skinner? Rate your skill in rewarding and punishing athletes.

1   2   3   ④   5
Not good   Very good

Rating Scale

36-40   Golden Tongue Award—You are destined for success!

31-35   Silver Tongue Award—Good, but you can be better. See what you can learn from this unit today.

26-30   Bronze Tongue Award—OK, but you have plenty of room for improvement. Carefully take in what the rest of this unit offers.

21-25   Leather Tongue Award—The prize given to those who frequently place their feet in their mouths. Listen up! You'll learn a lot about communication in this unit.

8-20   Muzzle Award—You've got a lot to learn. Listen carefully during this unit to find out how you can improve your communication skills.

Additional Points About the Survey

- The coaches on this survey are extremes, but hopefully you see the point: How you communicate with your athletes directly affects how they perceive you and how they feel about themselves.

- Regularly evaluate yourself with this survey to see if you need to work on a certain communication skill.

- Later in this unit you'll learn how you can improve if you have one of these communication problems.

C Effective Communication (15 minutes)

On the DVD Segment, "Communication"

- Verbal and nonverbal communication
- The communication styles of command coaches, submissive coaches, and cooperative coaches
- Improving your listening skills

Activity 6.2 Becoming a Better Communicator

Introduction

When you took the Communication Survey, you read about eight coaches with poor communication skills. You may have identified with one of those coaches or at least have been able to see some of the same characteristics in your own communication style. If you're like most people, you can improve in some area of communication, and in this activity we'll learn how to improve our communication with athletes.

Resources

- The Help the Coach form (provided after the following instructions and activity outcome)

Instructions

1. Work in teams of two to four.

2. The coaches who don't communicate very well are listed under "Coach Names" before the table. Several lists of ways coaches can improve their communication are included in the second column of the table under "Communication Tips."

3. Using the table, determine which list of communication tips would help each coach become a better communicator. Write the name of the coach in the blank provided in the

corresponding left-hand column of the table. For instance, if the first list in the table seems to be the improvements that Coach Incredible needs to make, you'd write "Coach Incredible" to the left of the first list.

4. You'll have 8 minutes to complete this activity.

Activity Outcome

When you're done, you should have filled in all of the coach names in the table.

Help the Coach

Coach Names: Coach Incredible—Not credible; doesn't admit when he is wrong
Coach Naysayer—Negative, critical, slow to praise
The Judge—Gives feedback that is high in judgment rather than high in information
Coach Fickle—Inconsistent in what she says; also, what she says is different from what she does
Coach Glib—Often talking, rarely listening
Coach Stone—Seldom shows emotion
The Professor—Doesn't communicate clearly; talks above the athletes' heads
Coach Skinner—Doesn't know how to use the principles of reinforcement correctly

COACH	COMMUNICATION TIPS
glib	**1** • Show the person speaking to you that you're interested in listening and trying to understand. • Once someone has spoken to you, check that you understand what was said by paraphrasing the message, not only the content but also the emotion behind it. • Express empathy, not sympathy, by showing that you care and respect what the person speaking to you has to say.
judge	**2** • Provide athletes with specific information that helps them correct mistakes rather than general information that judges their performance. • Be certain that you understand the reason for your athletes' actions before you judge their behavior. • Avoid making evaluative comments when athletes know they've made a mistake. • Focus your comments on the athletes' behaviors, not on them as people to avoid damaging their sense of self-worth.
naysayer	**3** • Provide honest, direct, and constructive messages. • Embrace an attitude in which you look to catch your athletes doing good or right, and then tell them they've done so. • Avoid sarcasm and put-downs, but at the same time don't sugarcoat athletes' behaviors by falsely putting a positive spin on them. • Emphasize what can be done, not what cannot be done, and avoid language that dwells on problems; instead, use language that focuses on solutions. • Seek to build character rather than destroy it.

(continued)

COACH	COMMUNICATION TIPS
Skinner	**4** • Before the season begins, define for yourself what you will reward and how you will reward your athletes. Stick to this plan during the season. • Develop team rules with your athletes so that they know what is expected and what the consequences will be if they misbehave. • When an athlete misbehaves, follow through with the consequence that is listed in your player handbook. • Don't let your mood dictate how you treat athletes. The athletes' performance and behavior should dictate your use of rewards and consequences. • Reward athletes only when they have earned it. • Use positive discipline, which uses instruction, training, and correction, rather than negative discipline, which uses punishment.
Fickle	**5** • Strive hard to be consistent in your verbal messages and to ensure that your nonverbal actions are consistent with your verbal messages. • When you promise to do something, be sure to follow through. • Avoid gossiping, and discourage your athletes from gossiping. • Develop a sense of trust with your athletes by being consistent and positive. Through trust you become a coach of character.
incredible	**6** • Become a cooperative-style coach. • Become knowledgeable about the sport or at least honest about whatever knowledge you possess. • Be reliable, fair, and consistent. • Follow through on what you say you'll do. • Express warmth, friendliness, acceptance, and empathy. • Be dynamic, spontaneous, and open. • Remain calm under pressure. • Use the positive approach.
Professor	**7** • Use language that your athletes will understand. Keep your vocabulary simple and straightforward. • Think through your demonstrations before you present them. Break skills down into a step-by-step process and then present them in an organized sequence. • Keep cues short and simple, such as "Stay on your man" or "Arms in the air." • Use analogies that your athletes can relate to. "It's like keeping a rudder steady on a plane" won't work very well because few of your athletes have piloted a plane.
Stone	**8** • Recognize how much of what you communicate is in the form of nonverbal messages. • Learn how to both send and receive messages by effectively using and reading body position, body motion, voice characteristics, and touching behaviors. • Remember that it's not so much what you say but what you do that influences your athletes.

D Unit Summary (2 minutes)

- How you communicate with your athletes directly affects how they perceive you and how they feel about themselves.

- Over 70 percent of communication is nonverbal. Your gestures, body positions, facial expressions, and actions are more important than what you say.

- Cooperative-style coaches show respect to athletes and others. They communicate in a straightforward, positive, and confident way and allow and encourage others to do the same.

- You can continually improve your communication skills. Doing so will help your athletes communicate appropriately with you as well.

Unit 6 Activity Outcomes

Help the Coach

Coach Names: Coach Incredible—Not credible; doesn't admit when he is wrong
Coach Naysayer—Negative, critical, slow to praise
The Judge—Gives feedback that is high in judgment rather than high in information
Coach Fickle—Inconsistent in what she says; also, what she says is different from what she does
Coach Glib—Often talking, rarely listening
Coach Stone—Seldom shows emotion
The Professor—Doesn't communicate clearly; talks above the athletes' heads
Coach Skinner—Doesn't know how to use the principles of reinforcement correctly

COACH	COMMUNICATION TIPS
Coach Glib	**1** • Show the person speaking to you that you're interested in listening and trying to understand. • Once someone has spoken to you, check that you understand what was said by paraphrasing the message, not only the content but also the emotion behind it. • Express empathy, not sympathy, by showing that you care and respect what the person speaking to you has to say.
The Judge	**2** • Provide athletes with specific information that helps them correct mistakes rather than general information that judges their performance. • Be certain that you understand the reason for your athletes' actions before you judge their behavior. • Avoid making evaluative comments when athletes know they've made a mistake. • Focus your comments on the athletes' behaviors, not on them as people to avoid damaging their sense of self-worth.
Coach Naysayer	**3** • Provide honest, direct, and constructive messages. • Embrace an attitude in which you look to catch your athletes doing good or right, and then tell them they've done so. • Avoid sarcasm and put-downs, but at the same time don't sugarcoat athletes' behaviors by falsely putting a positive spin on them. • Emphasize what can be done, not what cannot be done, and avoid language that dwells on problems; instead, use language that focuses on solutions. • Seek to build character rather than destroy it.

COACH	COMMUNICATION TIPS
Coach Skinner	**4** • Before the season begins, define for yourself what you will reward and how you will reward your athletes. Stick to this plan during the season. • Develop team rules with your athletes so that they know what is expected and what the consequences will be if they misbehave. • When an athlete misbehaves, follow through with the consequence that is listed in your player handbook. • Don't let your mood dictate how you treat athletes. The athletes' performance and behavior should dictate your use of rewards and consequences. • Reward athletes only when they have earned it. • Use positive discipline, which uses instruction, training, and correction, rather than negative discipline, which uses punishment.
Coach Fickle	**5** • Strive hard to be consistent in your verbal messages and to ensure that your nonverbal actions are consistent with your verbal messages. • When you promise to do something, be sure to follow through. • Avoid gossiping, and discourage your athletes from gossiping. • Develop a sense of trust with your athletes by being consistent and positive. Through trust you become a coach of character.
Coach Incredible	**6** • Become a cooperative-style coach. • Become knowledgeable about the sport or at least honest about whatever knowledge you possess. • Be reliable, fair, and consistent. • Follow through on what you say you'll do. • Express warmth, friendliness, acceptance, and empathy. • Be dynamic, spontaneous, and open. • Remain calm under pressure. • Use the positive approach.
The Professor	**7** • Use language that your athletes will understand. Keep your vocabulary simple and straightforward. • Think through your demonstrations before you present them. Break skills down into a step-by-step process and then present them in an organized sequence. • Keep cues short and simple, such as "Stay on your man" or "Arms in the air." • Use analogies that your athletes can relate to. "It's like keeping a rudder steady on a plane" won't work very well because few of your athletes have piloted a plane.
Coach Stone	**8** • Recognize how much of what you communicate is in the form of nonverbal messages. • Learn how to both send and receive messages by effectively using and reading body position, body motion, voice characteristics, and touching behaviors. • Remember that it's not so much what you say but what you do that influences your athletes.

Motivating Your Athletes

(30 minutes)

PURPOSE: To help you learn how to motivate your athletes.

LEARNING OBJECTIVES

In this unit you will learn

- what motivates athletes and
- what doesn't motivate athletes.

Unit Overview

Topic	Activities	Time (minutes)
A. Unit Introduction	Hear about the unit's purpose, objectives, and agenda.	1
B. What Athletes Need: To Have Fun	• As a class, complete Activity 7.1 Why I Play Sports, in which you list reasons for playing and quitting sports. • Watch DVD segment 6, "Fun and Flow." • In teams, complete Activity 7.2 Go With the Flow, in which you brainstorm ways to help athletes achieve optimal arousal.	17 to 20
C. What Athletes Need: To Feel Worthy	• Watch DVD segment 7, "Winners and Losers." • As a class, complete Activity 7.3 Think Like a Winner, in which you list attributes of athletes who are success-oriented and failure-oriented.	10 to 12
D. Unit Summary	Review key unit points.	2

UNIT CONTENT

A Unit Introduction (I minute)

- Why you play sports, and if you've quit any sports, why you quit
- The importance of having fun and what you can do to keep sports fun for your athletes
- How your success-oriented athletes think and how your failure-oriented athletes think
- What you can do to help your athletes be more success-oriented

B What Athletes Need: To Have Fun (17 to 20 minutes)

Activity 7.1 Why I Play Sports

Introduction

Most of us have played a variety of sports, but at least some of us have also quit some sports along the way. In this activity we'll discuss why we've played sports and why we've quit some.

Instructions

1. We'll work together as a class.
2. First we'll list the reasons we have played sports.
3. Then, if any of us have quit any sports, we'll discuss the reasons we did.
4. We'll record our responses on the whiteboard or flipchart.
5. We'll have 3 to 5 minutes for this activity.

Activity Outcome

When we're done, we should have a thorough list of reasons we play sports and reasons we've quit, and we'll look for a common thread.

On the DVD Segment, "Fun and Flow"

- Why athletes quit sports
- What was missing? Fun!
- Optimal arousal
- The flow experience

Activity 7.2 Go With the Flow

Introduction

We learned on the DVD that if athletes have too low a level of arousal in practice or game settings, they get bored. If athletes have too high a level of arousal, they can become fearful or anxious and not perform well. But if athletes experience optimal arousal, they are experiencing just the right level of stimulation to have fun and play well. This will enhance not only an individual athlete's performance, but also that of the entire team. In this activity you'll work in teams to identify what coaches can do to help athletes experience optimal arousal.

Resources

- The Optimal Arousal worksheet (provided after the following instructions and activity outcome)

Instructions

1. Work in teams of two to four, preferably grouped by the sport you coach.
2. Think about your own sport experiences and the testimonials you heard on the DVD.
3. On the Optimal Arousal worksheet, list the ideas you have for
   - keeping athletes from getting bored,
   - limiting athletes' anxiety or fear of failure, and
   - helping athletes experience optimal arousal and flow.
4. This is a competition, and the team with the most ideas wins.
5. You'll have 8 minutes to complete the worksheet.

Activity Outcome

When you're done, you should have listed as many ideas as possible on the Optimal Arousal worksheet.

Optimal Arousal

You can help your athletes meet their need for fun by making the sport experience challenging and exciting, not boring or threatening. When athletes are bored, they don't have enough arousal. When they are threatened to the point of anxiety, they are experiencing too much arousal. As a coach, you can work to ensure that your athletes are neither bored nor fearful, because where you want them to be is between these two extremes—experiencing optimal arousal or flow. It's a tall order, but it can be done. Write your ideas below for how to accomplish this.

A. What can coaches do to keep athletes from getting bored in practices and competitions?

- Change up drills
- make conditioning competetive
- rotate athletes in drills

B. What can coaches do to limit athletes' anxiety or fear of failure?

- praise athletes
- don't be negative
- give confidence

C. What other ideas do you have for coaches to help athletes experience optimal arousal and, thus, flow?

- make the game enjoyable & fun
- don't give too much feedback
- limit pressure

C | What Athletes Need: To Feel Worthy (10 to 12 minutes)

On the DVD Segment, "Winners and Losers"

- Look for the athlete who exhibits success-oriented attributes.
- Look for the athlete who exhibits failure-oriented attributes.
- What characterizes athletes who are success-oriented?
- What typifies coaches who help athletes to be success-oriented?

Activity 7.3 Think Like a Winner

Introduction

We saw two athletes on the DVD—one was success-oriented and thought like a winner. Interestingly enough, her coach treated her positively. The other athlete was failure-oriented. Let's talk about what these two types of athletes are like and how their coaches can help both of them think like winners.

Resources

- The Think Like a Winner worksheet (provided after the following instructions and activity outcome)

Instructions

1. We'll work together as a class.
2. Use the Think Like a Winner worksheet to take notes during our discussion.
3. We'll list attributes of athletes who are failure-oriented and success-oriented, and we'll list attributes of coaches who help athletes think in these two different ways.
4. We'll have about 7 minutes to complete this activity.

Activity Outcome

When you're done, you should have completed the Think Like a Winner worksheet.

Think Like a Winner

A. Attributes of Athletes Who Are Failure-Oriented

excuses

luck

distractions

blame themselves

don't take credit for themselves

Set goals that are unreachable

B. Attributes of Coaches Who Help Athletes to Remain Failure-Oriented

agree w/athlete that they aren't as good

offered to move down to lower level

don't give as much time to this athlete

Submissive coach (no direction)

Command

C. Attributes of Athletes Who Are Success-Oriented

positive

eager to improve

Criticizes themselves (corrective)

Committed

blame selves on mistakes but not ability

D. Attributes of Coaches Who Help Athletes to Be Success-Oriented

provide positive feedback

push to be better

Cooperative style of coaching

help obtain goals (set goals)

D Unit Summary (2 minutes)

- Athletes need to have fun. If this need for fun isn't fulfilled, they'll lose motivation and perhaps quit.

- Too low a level of arousal leads to boredom. Too high a level of arousal leads to fear and anxiety. You can help athletes experience the optimal level of arousal.

- Some athletes think like winners and are motivated to achieve success. Some athletes think like losers and are motivated to avoid failure.

- You can help athletes think like winners by using the cooperative style of coaching and emphasizing realistic personal goals.

Unit 7 Activity Outcomes

▶ *Go With the Flow—Activity 7.2 Outcome* - - - - - - - - - - - - - - - - - -

Optimal Arousal

You can help your athletes meet their need for fun by making the sport experience challenging and exciting, not boring or threatening. When athletes are bored, they don't have enough arousal. When they are threatened to the point of anxiety, they are experiencing too much arousal. As a coach, you can work to ensure that your athletes are neither bored nor fearful, because where you want them to be is between these two extremes—experiencing optimal arousal or flow. It's a tall order, but it can be done. Write your ideas below for how to accomplish this.

A. What can coaches do to keep athletes from getting bored in practices and competitions?

Ideas may include, but are not limited to, the following:

- *Keep practices stimulating by using a wide variety of drills and activities to work on skills.*
- *Keep everyone active rather than standing around for long periods waiting their turns.*
- *Create a team environment that gives athletes the opportunity to enjoy social interaction with their teammates.*
- *Try not to overregiment practices and contests, which greatly reduces opportunities for players to socialize and to engage in spontaneous and frivolous activities, both of which are enjoyable aspects of sport participation.*
- *Try to create an environment that is not so competitive that players feel they are playing against each other rather than with each other.*

B. What can coaches do to limit athletes' anxiety or fear of failure?

Ideas may include, but are not limited to, the following:

- *Fit the difficulty of the skills to be learned or performed to the ability of the athletes.*
- *Help athletes set goals related to personal performance rather than to winning (coach to learn instead of coach to perform).*
- *Avoid putting the responsibility for winning a game on one athlete's shoulders.*
- *Use positive encouragement rather than negative or critical comments.*
- *Give feedback that is high in information rather than high in judgment (coach to learn instead of coach to perform).*

C. What other ideas do you have for coaches to help athletes experience optimal arousal and, thus, flow?

Ideas may include, but are not limited to, the following:

- *Avoid constant instruction during practices and games.*
- *Do not constantly evaluate your athletes, especially during competitions. The flow experience cannot occur when young athletes are being continuously evaluated or made to evaluate themselves—whether the evaluation is positive or negative. There is a time for evaluation, but it is not when a contest is in progress.*

Think Like a Winner

A. Attributes of Athletes Who Are Failure-Oriented

From the DVD:

- *Lorraine attributed her successful assist to luck.*
- *Lorraine used a hamstring strain as an excuse for poor performance.*
- *Lorraine gave only a token effort in an attempt to protect her sense of self-worth.*

Athletes who are failure-oriented:

- *Attribute their failures to a lack of ability, instead of seeing mistakes and errors as a natural part of the learning process.*
- *Blame themselves for failure, yet take little or no credit for their successes.*
- *Believe that no matter how hard they try, the outcome will always be the same: failure.*
- *Reject success because they fear they will be expected to succeed again. They may so fear impending success that they purposely perform to avoid winning.*
- *Play for extrinsic rewards rather than to attain personal goals.*

B. Attributes of Coaches Who Help Athletes to Remain Failure-Oriented

- *Use the command style of coaching.*
- *Allow athletes to set unrealistically high goals. When those goals aren't attained, some athletes conclude that they are failures.*
- *Focus on winning rather than on athletes' development or having fun.*
- *Respond to failure-oriented athletes by lowering their expectations of them.*
- *Spend less time with athletes for whom they have low expectations.*
- *Have closer relationships with their better players, giving the better players more input about what the team is doing.*

C. Attributes of Athletes Who Are Success-Oriented

From the DVD:

- *Even though she didn't make her first pass, Judy still showed a winning attitude by hustling.*
- *Judy thanked her coach for praising her effort.*
- *Judy recognized her need to stay focused.*

Athletes who are success-oriented:

- *Believe that winning is a consequence of their ability.*
- *Likely blame failures on insufficient effort rather than on insufficient ability. They believe they simply need to try harder. This increases motivation rather than reducing it.*
- *Believe that occasional failures are inevitable, and are willing to take reasonable risks to achieve success.*

- *Direct their energies to the challenges of sport rather than to worry and self-doubt.*
- *Take credit for their successes and accept responsibilities for their failures.*

D. Attributes of Coaches Who Help Athletes to Be Success-Oriented

From the DVD:

- *The coach praised Judy's effort.*
- *The coach involved Judy in decision making by asking her what she thought of the new motion offense.*

Coaches who help athletes to be success-oriented:

- *Use the cooperative style of coaching.*
- *Emphasize achieving personal goals over winning.*
- *Help athletes see success in terms of exceeding their own goals rather than surpassing the performances of others.*
- *Help athletes set realistic goals for things that they can control.*
- *Help athletes experience success by acknowledging effort and personal progress.*
- *Help athletes who have reached their personal limit of ability to face this limitation realistically so that they don't set unrealistic goals.*

Managing Your Athletes' Behavior

(25 minutes)

PURPOSE: To introduce you to positive discipline: what it is, why it's more effective than other forms of discipline, and how to implement it.

LEARNING OBJECTIVES

In this unit you will learn

- what positive discipline is and why it is more effective than negative discipline,
- the six building blocks of preventive discipline, especially what to reward and how to reward, and
- the positive discipline guidelines for corrective discipline.

Unit Overview

Topic	Activities	Time (minutes)
A. Unit Introduction	Hear about the unit's purpose, objectives, and agenda.	1
B. Positive Discipline	Watch DVD segment 8, "Positive Discipline."	6
C. Catch Them Doing Good	• As a class, complete Activity 8.1 Rewards, in which you brainstorm different types of rewards to give athletes. • In teams, complete Activity 8.2 Catch Them Doing Good, in which you decide how you would reward athletes in three scenarios.	15 to 17
D. Unit Summary	Review key unit points.	2

UNIT CONTENT

A Unit Introduction (1 minute)

- How to use positive discipline
- How to prevent discipline problems
- What, when, and how to reward

B Positive Discipline (6 minutes)

On the DVD Segment, "Positive Discipline"

- What is positive discipline?
- Why positive discipline is more effective than other forms of discipline
- Preventive discipline: Six steps to defend against disciplinary problems
- Corrective discipline: What to do when athletes misbehave

C Catch Them Doing Good (15 to 17 minutes)

Activity 8.1 Rewards

Introduction

Different rewards are reinforcing to different athletes. Athletes will reveal what rewards they like if you observe them or ask them.

In this activity we'll brainstorm different types of rewards that you might use with your athletes. Successful coaches use extrinsic rewards to motivate their athletes while encouraging them to recognize the intrinsic rewards of sport participation.

Resources

- The Rewards Table (provided after the following instructions and activity outcome)

Instructions

1. We'll work together as a class.
2. Together, we'll list rewards that can be given to your athletes. We'll try to think of tangible rewards, people rewards, and activity rewards.

3. You can take notes on the Rewards Table during our discussion.

4. We'll have about 5 minutes to complete this activity.

Activity Outcome

When we're done, we should have a comprehensive list of rewards that you can use in your coaching situation.

Rewards Table

Tangible rewards	People rewards	Activity rewards

Activity 8.2 Catch Them Doing Good

Introduction

One of the most powerful steps of positive discipline is catching your athletes doing good. But it's not always easy to know what to look for, when to reward, and what to use for the reward.

In this activity you'll read several scenarios and decide how you would reward each athlete.

Resources

- The Catch Them Doing Good worksheet (provided after the following instructions and activity outcome)

Instructions

1. Work in teams of two to four, preferably grouped by the sport you coach.
2. Read through each scenario in your group.
3. After reading each scenario, your team should decide
   - what behavior in the scenario you would reward,
   - what you would use as the reward, and
   - when you would give the reward.
4. Note your team's decisions on the Catch Them Doing Good worksheet, and be prepared to discuss your decisions with the class.
5. You'll have 8 minutes for this activity.

Activity Outcome

When you're done, you will have decided as a team how to respond to each scenario.

Catch Them Doing Good

Catch Them Doing Good Scenario 1: Mike

Mike easily pins a fellow wrestler during a practice session. The other wrestler, clearly embarrassed that he was so easily pinned, and mad at himself, starts to take out his frustration on Mike. He taunts Mike and pushes him in the chest. Mike backs away and says, "Hey, man, no hard feelings. You've pinned me before." The other wrestler keeps coming at him, but Mike backs away and doesn't engage in the fight.

1. What behavior in the scenario should you reward?

   Mike, for remaining calm

2. What should you use as the reward?

   positive praise, pat on back
   Call parents + praise him

3. When should you reward the athlete?

   after it happened

Catch Them Doing Good Scenario 2: Sherry

Sherry is one of your best sprinters, but she's often a negative influence on the team. She sometimes rolls her eyes at other runners' low times or poor form, and she often makes negative comments about the practice sessions under her breath. Today, when she and her teammate Teresa cross the finish line of a practice sprint neck-and-neck, Sherry turns to Teresa and says, "Great race! You pushed both of us to do our best." Teresa smiles and says, "Thanks." It's one of the few times Sherry's been nice to her.

1. What behavior in the scenario should you reward?

   Sherry congratulated her teammate for doing well
   Teresa ran well   Sportsmanship

2. What should you use as the reward?

   positive feed back, praise

3. When should you reward the athlete?

   when she is alone and in front of the team

Catch Them Doing Good Scenario 3: Brad

You've set up a basketball practice with small-sided teams on the half court and one team member acting as the official. The offense is fighting to keep control of the ball. The player serving as the official calls a foul on Brad, but it's clear to everyone that Tim was at fault.

The players start to argue with the player who's acting as the official. Brad speaks up in defense of the official and says, "It's just like a real game, guys. Whatever the official says, goes." The rest of the players quickly agree and go back to playing the game.

1. What behavior in the scenario should you reward?

    Brad for showing respect for his teammate

2. What should you use as the reward?

    praise
    award

3. When should you reward the athlete?

    immediately
    later to whole team

D Unit Summary (2 minutes)

- With positive discipline, coaches instruct, train, and correct athletes so that athletes develop self-control.

- Positive discipline breeds respect among players and coaches, encourages performance without fear of failure, and inspires excitement and enthusiasm for sport.

- Rewards can be tangible, people related, or activity related. Rewards should match the magnitude of the behavior exhibited—that is, small rewards for less significant behaviors, larger rewards for more significant behaviors—and they should be given in a timely manner.

- Catching athletes doing good reinforces athletes' appropriate behavior and creates a positive rapport between you and your players.

Unit 8 Activity Outcomes

▶ *Catch Them Doing Good—Activity 8.2 Outcome* - - - - - - - - - - - - -

Catch Them Doing Good

Catch Them Doing Good Scenario 1: Mike

Mike easily pins a fellow wrestler during a practice session. The other wrestler, clearly embarrassed that he was so easily pinned, and mad at himself, starts to take out his frustration on Mike. He taunts Mike and pushes him in the chest. Mike backs away and says, "Hey, man, no hard feelings. You've pinned me before." The other wrestler keeps coming at him, but Mike backs away and doesn't engage in the fight.

1. What behavior in the scenario should you reward?

   - *Mike chose not to enter a fight even though he was clearly provoked.*

2. What should you use as the reward?

   - *Sincere words of praise would be appropriate.*

   - *You could also mention the good behavior to Mike's parents. By telling Mike's parents of his wise choice and ability to control his anger in a tense situation, you're communicating volumes about this good behavior, and you give the parents a chance to reward (and feel good about) their son as well.*

3. When should you reward the athlete?

   - *The words of praise should be given immediately. Remember that the magnitude of the reward should match the magnitude of the behavior and should be given in a timely manner.*

Catch Them Doing Good Scenario 2: Sherry

Sherry is one of your best sprinters, but she's often a negative influence on the team. She sometimes rolls her eyes at other runners' low times or poor form, and she often makes negative comments about the practice sessions under her breath. Today, when she and her teammate Teresa cross the finish line of a practice sprint neck-and-neck, Sherry turns to Teresa and says, "Great race! You pushed both of us to do our best." Teresa smiles and says, "Thanks." It's one of the few times Sherry's been nice to her.

1. What behavior in the scenario should you reward?

   - *Sherry's good attitude and encouragement of another athlete may be worthy of reward.*

2. What should you use as the reward?

   - *A pat on the back or a word of praise would be appropriate.*

- *If you publicly reward good attitudes with certificates or points on a chart, this incident might put Sherry in the running for such a reward.*

- *You would have to be careful in this situation not to make too big of a deal over Sherry's positive attitude. Too big of a reward would draw too much attention to a behavior that should actually be a normal part of the team's culture, and it could lead to other athletes ridiculing Sherry. Given her tendency to feel negative, too big of a reward could also cause Sherry to feel patronized or defensive about her usual temperament.*

3. When should you reward the athlete?

- *Immediately, so that it's clear to Sherry which behavior you want to see more of.*

Catch Them Doing Good Scenario 3: Brad

You've set up a basketball practice with small-sided teams on the half court and one team member acting as the official. The offense is fighting to keep control of the ball. The player serving as the official calls a foul on Brad, but it's clear to everyone that Tim was at fault.

The players start to argue with the player who's acting as the official. Brad speaks up in defense of the official and says, "It's just like a real game, guys. Whatever the official says, goes." The rest of the players quickly agree and go back to playing the game.

1. What behavior in the scenario should you reward?

- *Brad showed respect for the player who was serving as the official.*
- *The rest of the players also eventually showed respect and went on with the game.*

2. What should you use as the reward?

- *You might use verbal praise.*
- *You might also mention the incident in the wrap-up at the end of the practice, and reward Brad and the rest of the players verbally in front of the entire team.*
- *If sportsmanship awards are given periodically, you might remember this incident as one that could lead to Brad receiving the sportsmanship award.*
- *You might reward the entire group that was playing on the half-court with an activity reward, such as the choice of what game to play in the next practice session or the option to change playing positions with fellow teammates for a day.*

3. When should you reward the athlete?

- *Verbal praise could be given immediately.*
- *Public praise could be given immediately or at the end of practice.*
- *The sportsmanship award may be given long after the incident, but hopefully would be a reflection of an accumulation of good sporting behaviors.*
- *Although the activity reward might be experienced a day or two later, you should let the players know about it the same day that the good behavior occurred.*

Coaching the Games Approach Way

(20 minutes)

PURPOSE: To introduce you to the games approach to coaching.

LEARNING OBJECTIVES

In this unit you will learn

- what the games approach is,
- how it differs from the traditional approach, and
- the advantages and disadvantages of both approaches.

Unit Overview

Topic	Activities	Time (minutes)
A. Unit Introduction	Hear about the unit's purpose, objectives, and agenda.	1
B. The Games Approach	• Watch DVD segment 9, "The Games Approach." • Individually, complete Activity 9.1 Traditional Approach Versus the Games Approach, in which you decide which approach each scenario illustrates and the advantages and disadvantages of the approaches.	15 to 18
C. Unit Summary	Review key unit points.	1

UNIT CONTENT

A Unit Introduction (1 minute)

- What the games approach is
- How it differs from the traditional approach
- What its advantages are
- How to incorporate it into your practices

B The Games Approach (15 to 18 minutes)

On the DVD Segment, "The Games Approach"

- Definitions: technical skills, tactical skills, game sense, strategy, tactics, skill
- The traditional approach
- The games approach
- Making the games approach work for you

Activity 9.1 Traditional Approach Versus the Games Approach

Introduction

Sometimes it's difficult to differentiate between the traditional and the games approach and to decide which is better to use. This activity will help you see the differences and the advantages and disadvantages of both approaches.

Resources

- Is It the Games Approach? worksheet, which includes four scenarios and two tables (provided after the following instructions and activity outcome)

Instructions

1. Work individually.
2. Read each pair of scenarios on the Is It the Games Approach? worksheet.
3. Decide which scenario in each pair describes the traditional approach and which describes the games approach. Note which is which in the tables.
4. List the advantages and disadvantages of each scenario in the tables.

5. You'll have 7 minutes to complete this activity.

Activity Outcome

When you're done, you should have identified which scenario in each pair illustrates the traditional approach and which illustrates the games approach, and you should have noted the advantages and disadvantages of each scenario.

Is It the Games Approach?

In scenarios 1 and 2, the coach is teaching wrestlers to use their hips in a lift.

Scenario 1

The coach has his wrestlers lift each other in fireman's carries back and forth across the wrestling room for a relay race.

Scenario 2

The coach has his wrestlers go to the weight room and perform the leg press and squat exercises.

In scenarios 3 and 4, the coach is teaching her soccer players to protect the ball from defenders while dribbling.

Scenario 3

The coach arranges for the players to participate in two activities during practice—one to teach keeping the ball close while dribbling and one to teach watching for defenders.

To teach keeping the ball close, the coach arranges for a cone-weaving session. Each player gets a ball and dribbles around cones that are arranged both in slalom style and staggered at great distances for 180-degree turns. The cones dictate changes in direction, causing players to keep the ball close. Players are encouraged to go as fast as they can through the cones.

To teach watching for defenders, the players dribble randomly within part of the field while the coach holds up a number of fingers. The coach changes the number of fingers every now and then, and players try to be the first one to shout out the new number, signifying that they're able to keep an eye on the coach and dribble at the same time.

At the end of practice, the coach puts together a scrimmage with a professional referee.

Scenario 4

The coach starts the practice with a game of Dribble Attack, a drill that helps encourage dribbling with both feet. She divides her team of 16 into three groups—two 3 v 3 groups and one 2 v 2 group. Each group gets a 30- by 20-yard area for play. The goal of the offense is to get from one side of the playing area to the other before the defense can break them up. The offense gets a point whenever a player is able to dribble past a defender. The offense can pass to advance the ball, but they don't receive any points for passing past a defender. Offense and defense switch roles when (1) the defense breaks up the offense or (2) all offensive players make it to the other side.

Soon into the games, the coach sees that the offensive players are having trouble keeping the ball close enough—the defenders are having an easy time getting at the ball. She lets the play go on for a bit, and then calls "freeze" at a point when most teams are suffering from interceptions. She asks the offense what they think the problem is. The players quickly identify that the defenders pick off the ball when it gets too far away from them, and most of them are losing control because they're not adept at dribbling in different directions because they have a "weaker" foot. The coach changes the game by adding a new twist to help players focus on keeping the ball close. Attackers still get a point if they dribble past a defender, but they also get an additional point for successfully dribbling past a defender while using their "weak" foot. At the end of the practice, the team plays a whole-group scrimmage, in which a similar point system prevails. Players score points by dribbling past a defender; they get an additional point for dribbling past a defender while using their "weak" foot, and of course this time they get to score by making goals as well.

Scenarios 1 and 2

Traditional Approach = Scenario # _2_		Games Approach = Scenario # _1_	
Advantages	**Disadvantages**	**Advantages**	**Disadvantages**
working on getting stronger	can be redundant (boring)	fun	Could be using the wrong technique
proper technique	not game-like	everyone involved	injury
		competition (race)	

Scenarios 3 and 4

Traditional Approach = Scenario # _3_		Games Approach = Scenario # _4_	
Advantages	**Disadvantages**	**Advantages**	**Disadvantages**
Working on keeping head up	they didn't actually play against defenders	break down skills then put them to use in a drill	no individual work
get to play a scrimmage	the coach didn't help the players individually	everyone was involved	
faster footwork	get bored	Stopped play to explain why offense wasn't scoring	
		rewarded for using weaker foot	

Traditional Approach Compared With the Games Approach

Traditional Approach	Games Approach
Uses drills primarily to practice technical skills.	Uses drills that are closely aligned with the game to teach technical and tactical skills.
Teaches the specific elements of the game and then combines them into the whole.	Teaches the whole game and then refines the parts.
Coach centered (The coach uses direct instructional methods that may or may not consider the players' needs.)	Player centered (The coach creates a learning environment that focuses on the players' needs using a variety of teaching methods.)
Practices are often boring and therefore unmotivating to the players.	Practices are fun, relevant, and challenging, and therefore increase intrinsic motivation.
Players become highly dependent on the coach.	Players develop increasing independence from the coach by being actively involved in the learning process.
Through extensive drilling coaches strive to develop automatic responses that promote mindlessness when playing.	Practices are designed to develop the thinking, understanding, and decision-making skills that are required in game performance.
Players provide little or no input to the coach, who makes most or all of the decisions.	Players have considerable input to the coach and help the coach make decisions.
Players are not encouraged to help each other master the skills of the sport.	Players are encouraged to help each other master the skills of the sport.
Preferred approach of command-style coaches.	Preferred approach of cooperative-style coaches.

C Unit Summary (1 minute)

- The traditional approach has several shortcomings, any of which can lead to athlete boredom or burnout.
- In the games approach, the emphasis is on learning the sport through gamelike practice activities that create realistic and enjoyable learning situations.
- The games approach can help your athletes learn to execute the techniques required at the right time and place.
- As you prepare for coaching, reflect on your practices and ask yourself whether adopting the games approach may improve your coaching.

Unit 9 Activity Outcomes

Scenarios 1 and 2

Traditional Approach = Scenario # _2_		Games Approach = Scenario # _1_	
Advantages	**Disadvantages**	**Advantages**	**Disadvantages**
No real planning needed.	Not very fun.	Focused.	Takes some thought to plan.
	Physical conditioning seems like a burden.	Competitive.	
		Accomplishes two goals at once: physical conditioning and having fun.	

(continued)

Scenarios 3 and 4

Traditional Approach = Scenario # _3_		**Games Approach** = Scenario # _4_	
Advantages	**Disadvantages**	**Advantages**	**Disadvantages**
Easy to plan.	The players might get bored with the drills, because they've probably done similar drills many times.	The players will have a good time.	
	Although all players get contact with the ball, they don't have to protect the ball from real defenders, and this limits their technical and tactical learning.	The coach lets the athletes find out for themselves what the problem is, so that they are interested in how to improve.	
	The athletes don't learn how to perform the skills in a game situation.	The players learn the technique and tactics at the same time. They'll know how to use the skills in a game situation.	
	There isn't any deliberate coaching of technique or correcting of errors.		

Teaching Technical Skills

(25 minutes)

PURPOSE: To help you learn how to teach technical skills in the sport you coach.

LEARNING OBJECTIVES

In this unit you will learn

- the three stages of learning technical skills,
- your teaching role when athletes are in each of the three stages, and
- the four steps to teaching technical skills effectively.

Unit Overview

Topic	Activities	Time (minutes)
A. Unit Introduction	Hear about the unit's purpose, objectives, and agenda.	1
B. Learning and Teaching Technical Skills	• Watch DVD segment 10, "Learning and Teaching Technical Skills." • In groups organized by the sport you coach, complete Activity 10.1 Teaching a Technical Skill, in which you decide how you'll teach one technical skill in the sport you coach.	20 to 23
C. Unit Summary	Review key unit points.	1

UNIT CONTENT

A Unit Introduction (I minute)

- The three stages of learning technical skills
- The coach's teaching role when athletes are in each of the three stages
- The four steps to teaching technical skills effectively
- How you would teach a technical skill in the sport you coach

B Learning and Teaching Technical Skills (20 to 23 minutes)

On the DVD Segment, "Learning and Teaching Technical Skills"

- Three stages of learning: mental, practice, and automatic
- Four steps of teaching technical skills

   - Step 1: Introduce the technical skill
   - Step 2: Demonstrate and explain the technical skill
   - Step 3: Have the athletes practice the technical skill
   - Step 4: Correct errors

Activity 10.1 Teaching a Technical Skill

Introduction

Teaching a technical skill effectively takes good planning. In this activity you'll get a chance to plan how to teach one technical skill in your sport.

Resources

- The Technical Skill Planning Sheet (provided after the following instructions and activity outcome)

Instructions

1. Work in teams of one to four, grouped by the sport you coach.
2. Answer each question on the Technical Skill Planning Sheet. It's OK to write only key words or short notes on this sheet today.
3. You'll want to quickly identify a technical skill from your sport to teach, and then spend most of your time on the other questions.

4. You'll have 10 minutes to complete this activity. Work to complete as much of the planning sheet as you can during that time.

Activity Outcome

When you're done, you should be ready to explain to the class how you would teach the technical skill you identified.

Technical Skill Planning Sheet

1. Identify a technical skill from your sport to teach.

   foul shot

2. Determine whether you will teach the whole skill, or break it into parts and teach the parts. If you decide to break it into parts, describe the parts here.

   ① how to stand
   ② how to place ball
   ③ how to shoot/follow through

3. Determine the overall approach you will use to teach the skills. Will you use the traditional approach, the games approach, or both? In either case, describe what those approaches will look like—what drills you will use or what games you might play.

   • both - first describe how to do it then demonstrate - then let the athletes do the skill
   • A game may be to see how many they can make out of 10

4. Determine teaching tips to use while teaching during the mental stage of learning the skill, and list those here. *• repitition*
   • go through steps
   • show skill

5. Identify the types of errors you expect to see during the mental stage, and explain the feedback approaches you'll use for those errors.
   • wrong positioning   *- To correct it, just reiterate how you did the*
   • improper follow through   *skill specifically pointing out mistakes*
   - maybe let them work through it

6. Determine teaching tips to use while teaching during the practice stage of learning the skill, and list those here.
   • point out specific errors + explain why its wrong
   • give motivation
   • point out good things + encourage them to challange themselves

7. Identify the types of errors you expect to see during the practice stage, and explain the feedback approaches you'll use for those errors.
   • improper form
   •

   • errors made will be minimal and coach could let athletes work out probs on own by practicing

Technical Skill Planning Evaluation

Criteria	Team 1	Team 2	Team 3
Traditional approach versus the games approach:			
If traditional approach: Is there a games approach that might work as well or better?			
For the mental stage:			
Was the number of teaching tips limited to avoid overload?			
Was a high number of errors expected?			
For the practice stage:			
Were more teaching tips identified than were identified for the mental stage?			
Was feedback withheld when the learner would already sense his or her errors?			
Was positive reinforcement included for correct skill performance?			

Team 4	Team 5	Team 6	Team 7

C Unit Summary (1 minute)

- Learners pass through a continuum of three stages as they learn technical skills—the mental stage, the practice stage, and the automatic stage.

- Each stage of learning requires different instructional strategies.

- During the mental stage, the coach needs to be careful not to teach too much because the learner is easily overloaded.

- During the practice stage, the coach can provide more feedback and should offer positive reinforcement when the learner's senses tell him or her that the skill was performed correctly.

- During the automatic stage, the learner takes on more responsibility for skill development, and the coach's role shifts to helping the learner perform the skills the learner knows how to do.

- The four basic steps of teaching technical skills are to
    - introduce the technical skill,
    - demonstrate and explain the technical skill,
    - have the athletes practice the technical skill, and
    - correct errors.

Teaching Tactical Skills

(30 minutes)

PURPOSE: To help you learn how to teach tactical skills in the sport you coach.

LEARNING OBJECTIVES

In this unit you will learn

- what tactics and tactical skills are,
- what's involved in "reading the situation" during play,
- what knowledge your athletes need to make good tactical decisions,
- factors that influence tactical decision making, and
- how to teach tactical skills.

Unit Overview

Topic	Activities	Time (minutes)
A. Unit Introduction	Hear about the unit's purpose, objectives, and agenda.	1
B. Tactics and Tactical Skills	• Watch DVD segment 11, "Tactical Triangle: Reading the Situation." • As a class, complete Activity 11.1 Improving Attention and Concentration, in which you watch DVD segments 12 through 15 and analyze how well a coach helps his athletes improve their concentration and attention. • Watch DVD segment 16, "Tactical Triangle: Tactical Knowledge and Decision-Making Skills." • In teams, complete Activity 11.2 Teaching a Tactical Skill, in which you decide how to teach one tactical skill in the sport you coach.	25 to 27
C. Unit Summary	Review key unit points.	2

UNIT CONTENT

A Unit Introduction (1 minute)

- What tactics are
- How to improve your athletes' attention and concentration
- How to improve tactical knowledge and decision making
- How you would teach a tactical skill in the sport you coach

B Tactics and Tactical Skills (25 to 27 minutes)

On the DVD Segment, "Tactical Triangle: Reading the Situation"

- Definition of *tactic*
- Tactical triangle: overview
- Tactical triangle: reading the situation
  - Cognitive skills
  - Improving your athletes' attention and concentration when they're playing sports

Activity 11.1 Improving Attention and Concentration

Introduction

As you saw on the DVD, you have an important role to play in improving your athletes' attention to, and concentration on, the tactical cues of your particular sport. In this activity we'll apply that knowledge to an actual competitive situation.

Resources

- The Attention and Concentration worksheet (provided after the following instructions and activity outcome)

Instructions

1. Work together as a class.
2. Watch four DVD segments of a basketball coach working with his team during a game.
3. After each segment discuss what the coach did well and not so well as he tried to help his athletes improve their attention and concentration.

4. Use the Attention and Concentration worksheet to take notes during the activity.

5. You'll have 8 minutes to complete this activity.

Activity Outcome

When you're done, you will have viewed four DVD segments and discussed the four questions on the Attention and Concentration worksheet.

Attention and Concentration

Coach Pierce's team is taking a beating from their crosstown rival. His offense has been in trouble tonight, mostly because the guards aren't making good decisions with the ball. When the guards receive passes, they aren't looking for cues while holding the "triple threat" position. In the triple threat position, the ball handler holds the ball and maintains a stance from which he can either shoot, dribble, or pass. This keeps the opponent guessing while the ball handler looks for cues as to what to do next.

Coach Pierce knows that it's not enough for him to simply explain moving from the triple threat position. His players need to receive the ball and make good decisions quickly. He wants them to develop their ability to read the cues of the game.

Watch DVD segment 12

1. What did Coach Pierce do wrong as he tried to improve his athletes' attention and concentration?

    Yelled onto the court & distracted his player

Watch DVD segment 13

2. What did Coach Pierce do right this time?

    · didn't yell
    · helped another player on the bench & explained what went wrong

Watch DVD segment 14

3. When Coach Pierce gave his guard feedback, what did Coach do right? What did he do wrong?

    · Singled player out (yelled)

Watch DVD segment 15

4. What did Coach Pierce do right when giving feedback this time around?

    · calm
    · positive
    · involved whole team
    · asked a lot of questions

On the DVD Segment, "Tactical Triangle: Tactical Knowledge and Decision-Making Skills"

- Tactical knowledge: overview and importance
- Tactical options
- Teaching tactical decision-making skills
- Five-step tactical skill development plan

Activity 11.2 Teaching a Tactical Skill

Introduction

Teaching a tactical skill effectively takes good planning. In this activity you'll get a chance to plan how to teach one tactical skill in your sport.

Activity Resources

- The Tactical Skill Planning Sheet (provided after the following instructions and activity outcome)

Instructions

1. Work in teams of one to four, grouped by the sport you coach.
2. Answer each question on the Tactical Skill Planning Sheet. It's OK to write only key words or short notes on this sheet today.
3. You'll want to quickly identify a tactical skill from your sport to teach, and then spend most of your time on the other questions.
4. You'll have 10 minutes to complete this activity.

Activity Outcome

When you're done, you should be ready to explain to the class how you would teach the tactical skill you identified.

Tactical Skill Planning Sheet

1. Identify one tactical skill from your sport to teach your athletes. This tactical skill should be an important decision that your athletes need to make as they play the sport.

2. *Tactical knowledge:* What knowledge do your athletes need in order to decide when to use the tactical skill? Consider rules of the sport, the game plan, playing conditions, strengths and weaknesses of opponents, and the athlete's own strengths and weaknesses.

3. *Reading the situation:* Given a situation in which your athletes might use this tactical skill, what cues should your athletes attend to? What cues should they not attend to? Describe the situation, and list both types of cues here.

4. What tactical options, guidelines, or rules should your players follow to use the tactical skill appropriately?

5. *Decision-making skills:* Design one practice game that would give your athletes the opportunity to work on reading the situation and selecting the appropriate tactic.

6. Identify the types of errors you expect to see, and explain the feedback approaches you'll use for those errors.

C Unit Summary (2 minutes)

- To improve their tactical skills, athletes need the ability to read the situation, tactical knowledge, and decision-making skills.

- Good coaching can help athletes improve in all of these tactical areas.

- You can teach athletes the skills needed to read the situation by helping them to improve their attention and concentration.

- Athletes make better tactical decisions when they have knowledge about certain elements of the game, and you can help them to learn these.

- The single best way to help your athletes learn to make good, timely decisions is to have them play practice games designed for this purpose.

Unit 11 Activity Outcomes

Attention and Concentration

1. What did Coach Pierce do wrong as he tried to improve his athletes' attention and concentration?

   Coach Pierce was distracting his guard with advice while the guard was playing.

   You should avoid distracting your athletes with your comments while they're playing. Of course you'll have words for your players while they're on the court. Sometimes the instructions can be a simple, welcome reminder of some earlier coaching point. But most coaches distract their players far too often, and for the wrong reasons.

   In this case, Coach Pierce is trying to accomplish way too much in one shouted set of instructions while his guard needs to be thinking about defense!

2. What did Coach Pierce do right this time?

   Coach Pierce used a teachable moment to give advice to a player.

   Instead of bombarding the guard who had made the mistake with shouted, distracting advice, Coach Pierce used the teachable moment to focus one of his other guards on the tactical decision point. Meanwhile, the other guard will be coming off the bench in a minute, but first he has a good chance to think over the advice his coach just gave.

3. When Coach Pierce gave his guard feedback, what did Coach do right? What did he do wrong?

   Coach Pierce was right to wait for the time-out to give advice to his guard.

   Coach Pierce was wrong to give such public, negative feedback to his guard.

   The coach wasn't distracting to the guard this time, but he wasn't practicing positive coaching, either. Younger players tend to be especially vulnerable to distraction when their self-esteem is at risk. If you really want your guard to learn the skill, you'll do more harm than good with this approach!

4. What did Coach Pierce do right when giving feedback this time around?

   Coach Pierce was positive.

   He helped to put players' focus in the right place.

   Coach Pierce made a few great moves as he talked to his players:

   • He helped them identify what to attend to (teammates, movement, guard spacing) and what to ignore (opposing forwards, crowd, scoreboard).

   • He delivered his comments to his guard in a "compliment sandwich."

   • He encouraged his players to focus on the situation and their performance, not on the outcome (scoreboard).

Planning for Teaching

(20 minutes)

PURPOSE: To help you learn how to develop instructional plans for the season and for individual practices.

LEARNING OBJECTIVES

In this unit you will learn

- how to develop instructional plans for the season and
- how to prepare instructional plans for each practice.

Unit Overview

Topic	Activities	Time (minutes)
A. Unit Introduction	Hear about the unit's purpose, objectives, and agenda.	1
B. Planning for Teaching	• Watch DVD segment 17, "Instructional Planning." • In teams, complete Activity 12.1 Practice Plan Evaluation, in which you evaluate sample practice plans.	15 to 17
C. Unit Summary	Review key unit points.	2

UNIT CONTENT

A Unit Introduction (1 minute)

- Preparing a seasonal practice plan
- Six steps of instructional planning
- Evaluating sample practice plans

B Planning for Teaching (15 to 17 minutes)

On the DVD Segment, "Instructional Planning"

- Benefits of planning
- Six steps of instructional planning
    - Step 1: Identify the skills your athletes need.
    - Step 2: Know your athletes.
    - Step 3: Analyze your situation.
    - Step 4: Establish priorities.
    - Step 5: Select the methods for teaching.
    - Step 6: Plan practices.

Activity 12.1 Practice Plan Evaluation

Introduction

Good planning is easier said than done. In this activity you'll evaluate an actual practice plan and decide what is good about the plan and what could be improved.

Resources

- The Practice Plan Evaluation form and either a practice plan that one of your fellow coaches brought or one of the practice plans in this study guide (provided after the following instructions and activity outcome)

Instructions

1. Work in teams of two to four, preferably grouped by the sport you coach.
2. Review the practice plan assigned to your team.
3. Rate the practice plan in each of the five areas listed on the Practice Plan Evaluation form.
4. Be sure to include additional comments or ideas that your team discusses.
5. You'll have 8 minutes to complete this activity.

Activity Outcome

When you're done, you should have evaluated one practice plan and rated it in each of the five areas listed on the Practice Plan Evaluation form.

Practice Plan Evaluation

Principle	Poor 1	2	Rating 3	4	Excellent 5	Comments
Athletes are given the opportunity to practice the technique in gamelike conditions.	1	2	③	4	5	
Practice time is used efficiently.	1	2	3	4	⑤	
Facilities and equipment are used in optimal ways.	1	2	3	④	5	
Athletes are given the opportunity to experience a reasonable amount of success.	1	2	3	④	5	
The practice incorporates fun.	1	2	③	4	5	

Additional notes:

Practice Plan 1: Basketball

DATE: December 12

LEVEL: Varsity

POINT IN SEASON: In-season

PRACTICE START TIME: 3:00 p.m.

LENGTH OF PRACTICE: 100 minutes

PRACTICE OBJECTIVES: (1) Reinforce technical skills: dribbling, passing, shooting; (2) Develop motion offense; (3) Work on transition defense.

EQUIPMENT: North Gym, six baskets

Practice Activities

Time	Name of activity	Description	Key teaching points
3:00-3:02	Pitino Dribble Drill	Jog, speed, cross, back	Keep eyes up. Push the ball ahead of you. Do not look at the ball.
3:02-3:08	Carolina Passing Game	Passing game	Run at game speed. Pass and catch while saying the name of the passer or receiver on every pass.
3:08-3:14	Texas Conversion	Push tempo game	Make the easy pass. Get the ball to the basket.
3:14-3:20	3 on 3 Full Court Games	3 consecutive stops	You must communicate on offense and defense. Offense: Pass and cut/screen; catch every pass ready to shoot (triple threat). Defense: Communicate screens; cut cutters; close out quickly with high hands; box out.
3:20-3:22	Free Throw Drill	Shoot four; two at a time; make 3/4	Elbow in front. Wide thumb. Ball on fingertips. Find the W on the front of the rim. No Stinkin' Thinkin'!
3:22-3:28	30-Second Shot Drill	Shooter: Catch with inside pivot foot, show target; do not drop ball below point where you catch Passer (rebounder): Pass to inside shoulder	No talking; elbow to elbow. Right wing to right baseline; left wing to left baseline.
3:28-3:30	Drink break	Everyone drinks 4-8 oz sport drink or water	
3:30-3:34	5 Man Weave	Pass and go behind two players. Middle players shoot at both.	Emphasize first opportunity attack; look for best attack in each rotation.

(continued) ☞

Practice Activities (continued)

Time	Name of activity	Description	Key teaching points
3:34-3:40	5 Man Weave Elimination	Rotate to your right one line. Last two to touch ball, back on D.	
3:40-3:56	Jarvis Secondary Break	4-1-5 lob pass; run down mid	Push the ball. 1 pass early to 5.
		4-1 make a move and penetrate	1 keep the ball. Make a move at the wing. Get to the basket.
		4-1-4 for a shot, 1 screen for 2, etc.	1 push to wing, pass to 4 for a shot, and screen for 2.
3:56-4:04	Conditioning drill	Conditioning, building aerobic endurance	Pace yourself. Finish strong.
4:04-4:06	Drink break	Everyone drinks 4-8 oz sport drink or water	
4:06-4:14	Basic 5 on 0	Man offense, 5 on 0, on the half court Practice entries: • Wing entry • High-post entry • Dribble entry	Add screen and roll when go to corner. Work on timing and spacing
4:14-4:25	Basic 5 on 5	Play 5 on 5 on the half court, working on the three entries. Defense has to get three stops to get on offense, and once they do, they run the secondary break 5 on 0 the other way. With a rebound or made basket, possession changes and players run the secondary break.	Proper spacing. "Head hunt" on screens. Curl off of screens. Be patient when setting screens. Take proper angles when setting screens.
4:25-4:30	Cool-down	Slow jogging, dribbling, easy play	
4:30-4:35	Cool-down and drink break	Main muscle group stretch Everyone drinks 4-8 oz sport drink or water	Emphasize slow and complete stretch.
4:35-4:40	Coach's comments	End-of-practice comments from the coach	General comments on how the whole team practiced; recognize any outstanding efforts or performances; point out what the team needs to improve; announcements.

The basketball plan and its outcome (evaluation) were developed in collaboration with John Woods, Champaign Central High School, Champaign, IL.

Practice Plan 2: Football

DATE: August 26

LEVEL: Varsity; offensive practice

POINT IN SEASON: Preseason; one week before first game

PRACTICE START TIME: 4:00 p.m.

LENGTH OF PRACTICE: 120 minutes

PRACTICE OBJECTIVES: Solidify the basics for the first game of the season: opposing team's coverages and blitz package, pass protection, passing game, running game

EQUIPMENT: Stand-up and hand-held dummies; pull-overs

Practice Activities

Time	Name of activity	Description	Key teaching points
4:00-4:05	Special Teams Practice—Punt Team	Team 1. Spread Punt 2. Tight Punt	• Interior Line splits and footwork. • Personal protector responsibilities. • Wide out's alignment and release techniques. • Punter post-punt responsibilities.
4:05-4:15	Inside 7 Run Game	QB, HB, FB, and O-Line 1. 32 Dive vs 50 Front 2. 32 Trap vs 40 Front 3. 28 Sweep vs 50 Front 4. 27 Sweep vs 40 Front	• O-Line alignment and responsibilities. • HB and FB footwork and timing. • QB footwork, timing, and carrying out run fakes.
4:05-4:15	Run Blocking	WR's 1. Perimeter run plays 2. Inside run plays	• Stance: Inside arm and leg back in sprinter's stance. • Start: Explode off the LOS and get in the DB's cushion. • If the DB turns his hips and runs, run him off. • If the DB squats, break down and attack his numbers. • Keep a wide base with both your feet and hands.
4:15-4:18	Fluid break	Everyone drinks 4-8 oz sport drink or water	
4:18-4:35	Eleven on Eleven Running Game	Team 1. 32 Dive vs 50 Front 2. 32 Trap vs 40 Front 3. 28 Sweep vs 50 Front 4. 27 Sweep vs 40 Front	• O-Line: Check Alignment-Stance-Start before each play. Maintain blocks to the echo of the whistle. • RB's: Check Alignment-Stance-Start before each play. Lower your pad level, read your block and run through arm tackles. • QB: Check stance and footwork on each play. Look the ball into the RB's hands and carry out all run fakes. • WR's: Check Alignment-Stance-Start before each play. Stalk block the man over or greatest threat.
4:35-4:40	Fluid break	Everyone drinks 8 oz sport drink or water	
4:40-4:50	Blitz Package Walk Through	QB, HB, FB, O-Line 1. 5-3 Mike Blitz 2. 5-3 Mike/Will Blitz 3. 4-4 Sam/Safety Blitz	• O-Line Slide Protection, Center & FB read Mike. • O-Line Slide Protection, QB responsible for Will. • O-Line Slide Protection, Tackles and HB responsible for Sam and Safety.

(continued)

Practice Activities *(continued)*

Time	Name of activity	Description	Key teaching points
4:50-5:00	Blitz/Hot/Read Segment	Team 1. 5-3 Mike Blitz 2. 5-3 Mike/Will Blitz 3. 4-4 Sam/Safety Blitz	• Slant route sight adjustment by HB's. • Slant route sight adjustment by WR's and stop route by HB's. • Stop route sight adjustment by FB and slant route sight adjustment by HB's. • QB recognition, audible, and adjustment.
5:00-5:05	Fluid break	Everyone drinks 8 oz sport drink or water	
5:05-5:15	5-step routes	QB, HB's, WR's 1. Michigan Right 2. 687 – S – 9 3. Dash Left 87	• Option route read #2 strong. • 6 route flat at 12 yards. • 7 route under 8 route.
5:05-5:15	Pass Protection	O-Line 1. Slide Protection 2. Gangster Protection	• Assignment. • Alignment. • Stance. • Footwork.
5:15-5:25	Eleven on Eleven Passing Game	Team 1. Michigan Right 2. 687 – S – 9 3. Dash Left 87	• O-Line: Slide protection rules don't get beat to the inside. • FB: Check pass-pro responsibility and check release. • QB: Presnap read then follow progression. Deliver the ball on time to the open receiver • HB's: Run designated route or check release if assigned. • WR's: Run the routes at the proper depth, look the ball into your hands, and then look for positive yards.
5:25-5:30	Fluid break	Everyone drinks 8 oz sport drink or water	
5:30-5:50	Pressure Practice	Team 1. 32 Dive vs 50 Front 2. 32 Trap vs 40 Front 3. 28 Sweep vs 50 Front 4. 27 Sweep vs 40 Front 5. Michigan Right 6. 687 – S – 9 7. Dash Left 87	Ball on the +10 yard line, 1st and Goal • Perfect huddle • Perfect alignment • Perfect stances • Perfect start • Perfect play • Score in the red zone
5:50-6:00	Cool-down and fluid break	Jogging and main muscle group stretch Everyone drinks 8 oz sport drink or water	Emphasize slow and complete stretch.
6:00	Coach's comments	End-of-practice comments from the coach	General comments on how the whole team practiced; recognize any outstanding efforts or performances; point out what the team needs to improve; announcements.

The football practice plan was written by Jerry Reeder, assistant football coach, Mahomet-Seymour High School.

Practice Plan 3: Volleyball

DATE: October 20

LEVEL: Junior varsity

POINT IN SEASON: In-season

PRACTICE START TIME: 4:00 p.m.

LENGTH OF PRACTICE: 90 minutes

PRACTICE OBJECTIVES: (1) Practice core ball-control skills of passing and setting: flat forearm platforms that redirect the ball to the target (minimize swinging) and setting "hands position" at forehead early with contact point on finger pads and thumbs closest to forehead; (2) Enhance player communication: calling first ball ("me" or "mine") and where to attack (line or angle); (3) Continue first opportunity attack emphasis; (4) Develop physical recovery skills with short, intense physical bursts and timed recovery.

EQUIPMENT: Bring stopwatches, balls, net, and cones; players need knee pads and court shoes.

Practice Activities

Time	Name of activity	Description	Key teaching points
4:00-4:10	Warm-up	Shuffle Passing Drill 10 to target and change direction	Emphasize posture and "quiet" passing platform
4:10-4:15	Warm-up	Wall sets—30 low/med/high, finish with jump sets	Emphasize hand shape and wrist position
4:15-4:25	Warm-up	Dynamic stretching	Emphasize full range of motion in stretches
4:25-4:26	Warm-up	Line jumps—forward, side, scissor	Quick-feet physical training
4:26-4:27	Drink break	Everyone drinks 4-8 oz sport drink or water	
4:27-4:57	Ball control	Weave Passing Drill in teams of 3, 15 to target (both sides)	Emphasize adjusting platform and movement to the ball
4:57-5:00	Drink break	Everyone drinks 4-8 oz sport drink or water	
5:00-5:03	Ball control	Line races (sprint, shuffle/back)	Physical training
5:03-5:18	Offensive system 6 on 6	4 before 2 game	Emphasize first opportunity attack; look for best attack in each rotation
5:18-5:23	Cool-down	Mat serving series	Emphasize serving routine and rhythm

(continued)

Practice Activities *(continued)*

Time	Name of activity	Description	Key teaching points
5:23-5:25	Cool-down and drink break	Main muscle group stretch Everyone drinks 4-8 oz sport drink or water	Emphasize slow and complete stretch
5:25-5:30	Coach's comments	End-of-practice comments from the coach	General comments on how the whole team practiced; recognize any outstanding efforts or performances; point out what the team needs to improve; announcements

Practice Plan 4: Soccer

DATE: August 25, hot and humid

LEVEL: Varsity (High School)

POINT IN SEASON: Fall preseason

PRACTICE START TIME: 3:00 p.m.

LENGTH OF PRACTICE: 130 minutes

PRACTICE OBJECTIVES: (1) Continue to improve conditioning and speed-endurance; (2) Work on passing with a purpose: maintaining possession of the ball and improving players' tactical awareness off the ball; (3) Improve individual defending (tackling).

EQUIPMENT: Ideally 1 ball per player, goals or flags, cones and disc cones, scrimmage vests (at least 2 colors)

Practice Activities

Time	Name of activity	Description	Key teaching points
3:00-3:05	Warm-up	Easy jogging	
3:05-3:15	Warm-up	Dynamic stretching	Emphasize full range of motion.
3:15-3:30	Slalom Drill	Stagger cones far apart for 180-degree turns; have players go as fast as can.	Keep ball close, emphasizing touch and moving faster through the cones.
3:30-3:45	Heads-Up Drill	Players dribble randomly in the penalty area and call out number of fingers coach is holding up.	Keep head up to look for passes or oncoming defenders.
3:45-4:00	Wind sprints	Players run full field sprints. Have players complete in 20 seconds or less. Players jog back to start in 60 seconds or less (a 3-to-1 ratio for their active recovery time).	Make sure recovery is active. Have individuals try to improve their time over the previous practice.
4:00-4:15	2 v 2 scrimmages: passing	Play 2 v 2: Set up multiple 15 × 20-yard grids. All players play at the same time in separate areas. Focus on passing, movement, and combination. Three consecutive passes earn 1 point. Once the ball goes across the line, the opposing team gets the ball and begins at own end line. Play 2 minutes and then have teams switch grids to compete against other pairs. Allow 1 minute of rest between scrimmages.	Make sure passes have a pace. Pass into space with accuracy. Work on timing the pass and the run. Freeze play when it's obvious players aren't providing passing options or reading each other.

(continued)

Practice Activities *(continued)*

Time	Name of activity	Description	Key teaching points
4:15-4:30	4 v 4 scrimmages: passing and tackling	Play 4 v 4: Set up multiple 25 × 30-yard or 35 × 40-yard grids. All players play at the same time in separate areas. Incorporate passing and tackling. Tackles in which the ball is taken directly from a player earn 2 points. Linking together three passes earns 1 point. Once the ball goes across the line, the opposing team gets the ball and begins at own end line.	Positioning for tackling: • Weight/stance • Looking at the ball • Knees slightly bent Decision making.
4:30-4:55	8 v 8 game	Play game in real-time, but still with modified scoring: Tackles in which possession is gained and combined with a pass earn 3 points. Combinations of five passes earn 1 point. Goals earn 2 points. *Variation:* To emphasize passing, combinations of five passes could earn 3 points and tackles in which possession is gained and combined with a pass could earn 1 point. If time, allow players to play without restrictions.	Offensive: Combination passing. Defensive: Positioning for tackling, decision making, and maintaining possession after the tackle.
4:55-5:05	Cool-down	Easy jogging while dribbling; stretching.	Stretch, ice, and massage any tight muscles.
5:05-5:10	Coach's comments	End-of-practice comments from the coach.	General comments; review what was learned; point out positives; announcements.

The soccer practice plan and its outcome (evaluation) were developed in collaboration with Bill Schranz, head women's soccer coach, Concordia University, Seward, NE.

Practice Plan 5: Track and Field: Middle-Distance Runners

DATE: March 12

LEVEL: Varsity

POINT IN SEASON: Preseason

PRACTICE START TIME: 3:00 p.m.

LENGTH OF PRACTICE: 100 minutes

PRACTICE OBJECTIVES: (1) Reinforce technique skills: lifting the knees high, raising the foot directly under the butt, "pawing" the track on foot strike, avoiding overstriding, and driving the arms powerfully; (2) Develop speed-endurance, or the ability to run fast when tired; (3) Practice concentrating on efficient running form when tired; and (4) Develop the tactical skills of accelerating in the middle of a race and kicking at the end.

EQUIPMENT: Workout takes place on a 400-meter track; coach must bring stopwatches and water; runners need their racing spikes.

Practice Activities

Time	Name of activity	Description	Key teaching points
3:00-3:10	Warm-up	Easy jogging	
3:10-3:20	Warm-up	Dynamic stretching	Emphasize full range of motion in dynamic stretches
3:20-3:30	Warm-up	5 × 100 meter strides @ 3/4 effort with 100-meter walk recovery	Emphasize technique skills during strides
3:30-3:35	Drink break	Everyone drinks 4–8 oz sport drink or water	
3:35-4:00	Technique drills	4 × 30 meters high-knee drill with 1-min recovery 4 × 30 meters butt-kick drill with 1-min recovery 4 × 30 meters fast-feet drill with 1-min recovery 4 × 1-min arm-pumping drill with 1-min recovery	Emphasize lifting the knees to be parallel to the track Emphasize keeping the foot close to the body and under the butt Emphasize "pawing" action, landing with the foot moving backward Emphasize "fast hands"
4:00-4:03	Drink break	Everyone drinks 4–8 oz sport drink or water	
4:03-4:23	Speed-endurance interval workout	3 sets of 1 × 300 meters and 1 × 200 meters with 1-min recovery between the 300 and 200, and 5-min recovery between sets	For the 300s, keep the runners on 1,600-meter race pace For the 200s, encourage a controlled, building sprint, adding a notch of speed every 50 meters Cue the runners to hold their form on the 200s

(continued) ☞

Practice Activities *(continued)*

Time	Name of activity	Description	Key teaching points
4:23-4:25	Drink break	Everyone drinks 4–8 oz sport drink or water	
4:25-4:35	Cool-down	10-min easy jogging	Stretch, ice, and massage any tight or sore muscles
4:35-4:40	Coach's comments	End-of-practice comments from the coach	General comments on how the whole team practiced; recognize any outstanding efforts or performances; announcements

C Unit Summary (2 minutes)

- Taking the time to plan pays off in big ways for your athletes and for you.
- Through planning you are far more likely to
  - keep your athletes actively involved;
  - teach skills in the appropriate progression to maximize learning and safety;
  - pace the learning and conditioning so that athletes are not overloaded or overtrained;
  - make the best use of available time, space, and equipment; and
  - minimize discipline problems.
- The six steps of instructional planning are these:
  - Step 1: Identify the skills your athletes need.
  - Step 2: Know your athletes.
  - Step 3: Analyze your situation.
  - Step 4: Establish priorities.
  - Step 5: Select the methods for teaching.
  - Step 6: Plan practices.

Unit 12 Activity Outcomes

▶ *Practice Plan Evaluation—Activity 12.1 Outcome* - - - - - - - - - - - -

Practice Plan 1: Basketball—Outcome

Principle	Rating Poor 1	2	3	Excellent 4	5	Comments
Athletes are given the opportunity to practice the technique in gamelike conditions.	1	2	3	**4**	5	There seems to be a good mix of games and drills in this plan. You could argue that games could be created to teach some of the techniques and tactics currently taught in drills. Still, the focus in this practice plan is on game play.
Practice time is used efficiently.	1	2	**3**	4	5	Athletes move from one activity to another fairly quickly in this plan, and many skills are covered. However, at this point in the season, a coach wouldn't be doing so many basic drills for skills that athletes would have mastered by now. Also, the plan seems to lack a warm-up time.
Facilities and equipment are used in optimal ways.	1	2	3	4	**5**	Using six baskets is a big plus, because all players can participate at one time in most of the activities.
Athletes are given the opportunity to experience a reasonable amount of success.	1	2	**3**	4	5	The opportunity for success is not evident in the brief drills—athletes will either execute well or not, and there's not much progression shown to indicate they'd get time and instruction to help them improve.
The practice incorporates fun.	1	2	3	**4**	5	This is difficult to interpret from a practice plan, but the students get a lot of variety in this practice and have several opportunities for gamelike play, and both of these factors typically help athletes to have fun.

Practice Plan 2: Football—Outcome

Principle	Rating Poor 1	2	3	4	Excellent 5	Comments
Athletes are given the opportunity to practice the technique in gamelike conditions.	1	2	3	4	**5**	This practice plan incorporates short-sided, modified, and actual games to teach techniques and tactics. Some drills are used, but these are followed by games that help athletes apply what they've learned in game situations.
Practice time is used efficiently.	1	2	3	4	**5**	All athletes are active at all times. Note the frequent drink breaks; the practice occurs during late August, and we can assume high heat and humidity.
Facilities and equipment are used in optimal ways.	1	2	3	4	**5**	All seems fine in this area.
Athletes are given the opportunity to experience a reasonable amount of success.	1	2	3	4	**5**	Progression is clearly built into this practice. Athletes often learn a skill in a drill or modified game, and then this is applied in a normal game situation. The eleven on eleven games allow adequate time for learning from mistakes.
The practice incorporates fun.	1	2	3	4	**5**	The practice incorporates variety and gamelike situations, making the practice fun for athletes.

Practice Plan 3: Volleyball—Outcome

Principle	Rating Poor 1	2	3	Excellent 4	5	Comments
Athletes are given the opportunity to practice the technique in gamelike conditions.	1	**2**	3	4	5	The Weave Passing Drill could be done in a shorter amount of time, and games could be added to the practice. Small court games (pass or set only) could be added to emphasize ball control. 3-on-3 and 3-on-3 backcourt battle drill (winner stays) could be used to emphasize ball control, reading skills, and communication.
Practice time is used efficiently.	**1**	2	3	4	5	Thirty minutes for the Weave Passing Drill is too long. This is an inefficient use of time.
Facilities and equipment are used in optimal ways.	1	2	3	**4**	5	
Athletes are given the opportunity to experience a reasonable amount of success.	1	2	**3**	4	5	They'll certainly get the Weave Passing Drill down, but adding more variety and progression would add more opportunity for success.
The practice incorporates fun.	1	2	**3**	4	5	Practicing in gamelike conditions would add more fun to the practice.

Practice Plan 4: Soccer—Outcome

Principle	Rating Poor 1	2	3	4	Excellent 5	Comments
Athletes are given the opportunity to practice the technique in gamelike conditions.	1	2	**3**	4	5	The first hour gets a 1. The second hour gets a 5. The first two drills are boring and don't meet the practice objectives. Players are not taught passing or tackling techniques, which would be better for the progression of this practice plan. Surprisingly, after an hour of drill-like activities, the practice becomes much more gamelike. Players move to match-related conditions and then to game situations.
Practice time is used efficiently.	1	**2**	3	4	5	The first two drills waste a lot of time. Shorter technique drills or games could be incorporated early in the practice and the wind sprints could be deleted so that the practice could be reduced to 120 minutes. An entire hour goes by before techniques and tactics are practiced in game situations. The wind sprint conditioning meets an objective, but players will be bored. Optimally, conditioning would be incorporated into all practice activities—with everyone working as hard as possible throughout the practice—so that a separate wind sprint segment might not be needed. It's August! Where are the drink breaks?
Facilities and equipment are used in optimal ways.	1	2	3	4	**5**	Enough equipment is brought for practice to be run effectively. Field layout and grid layout allow players to maximize training.
Athletes are given the opportunity to experience a reasonable amount of success.	1	2	3	**4**	5	This is not clear in the first hour of the practice, but in the second hour players get various opportunities to practice passing and tackling skills in a match condition environment. The second hour includes good progression, giving players a chance to practice passing and tackling skills in small-sided games before incorporating them in an actual game situation.
The practice incorporates fun.	1	2	**3**	4	5	The first hour gets a 1. The last hour, in which multiple games are included, is above average. Playing a game of 5 v 2 keep-away in a 25 $\times$ 30-yard grid at the outset of the practice would be a better way to warm up. It would help players learn how to maintain possession under pressure and allow their bodies to warm up for stretching.

Practice Plan 5: Track and Field: Middle-Distance Runners—Outcome

Principle	Rating Poor 1	2	3	Excellent 4	5	Comments
Athletes are given the opportunity to practice the technique in gamelike conditions.	1	**2**	3	4	5	This is difficult to evaluate in a track and field practice. However, in this practice session the runners aren't given any opportunity to practice in gamelike (competition-like) conditions. Runners can employ tactics—for example, taking the inside lane or deciding when to initiate the final kick—and these need to be practiced in competition-like conditions.
Practice time is used efficiently.	1	2	3	4	**5**	A lot of technique is packed into this practice. Good to see several water breaks.
Facilities and equipment are used in optimal ways.	1	2	3	**4**	5	Facilities and equipment are minimal but seem to be used well.
Athletes are given the opportunity to experience a reasonable amount of success.	1	2	3	**4**	5	Adequate time is given to practice each technique, which will give runners an opportunity to succeed.
The practice incorporates fun.	1	2	**3**	4	5	This drill-based practice incorporates minimal opportunity for fun.

Training Basics

(20 minutes)

PURPOSE: To help you assess the energy fitness and muscular fitness demands of the sport you coach.

LEARNING OBJECTIVES

In this unit you will learn about

- physical fitness,
- physical training, and
- the basics of energy fitness and muscular fitness.

Unit Overview

Topic	Activities	Time (minutes)
A. Unit Introduction	Hear about the unit's purpose, objectives, and agenda.	1
B. Fitness for Sport and Physical Training	• Watch DVD segment 18, "Fitness for Sport and Physical Training." • In teams, complete Activity 13.1 Energy and Muscular Fitness Demands, in which you evaluate the demands of the sport you coach.	15 to 17
C. Unit Summary	Review key unit points.	2

UNIT CONTENT

A Unit Introduction (1 minute)

- The benefits of training
- Energy fitness
- Muscular fitness
- Your role in helping athletes to train
- The physical demands for your sport

B Fitness for Sport and Physical Training (15 to 17 minutes)

On the DVD Segment, "Fitness for Sport and Physical Training"

- Definitions: *physical fitness, physical training*
- Benefits of training
- Components of physical fitness—energy fitness and muscular fitness
- Energy fitness: the anaerobic system and the aerobic system
- Muscular fitness: strength, muscular endurance, speed, power, flexibility, balance, agility
- Coach's role in physical training

Activity 13.1 Energy and Muscular Fitness Demands

Introduction

To plan your athletes' physical training program, you need to know the energy fitness and muscular fitness demands of your sport. In this activity you'll work with coaches of your same sport to determine the fitness demands of your sport.

Resources

- The Fitness Demands table (provided after the following instructions and activity outcome)

Instructions

1. Work in teams of two to four, grouped by the sport you coach.

2. Write your sport name in the first column of the Fitness Demands table. For now, consider your sport as a whole. In units 14 and 15, you'll get the opportunity to analyze various positions, events, and functions within your sport.

3. With your team, decide what the fitness demands of your sport are by writing "Low," "Medium," or "High" in each column. For instance, if you coach bowling, you would write "Low" in the "Aerobic" column because bowling does not require very much aerobic fitness.

4. You'll have 7 minutes to complete this activity.

Activity Outcome

When you're done, you should have completed the Fitness Demands table.

Fitness Demands

Sport or activity	Energy fitness		Muscular fitness				
	Aerobic	Anaerobic	Flexibility	Strength	Endurance	Speed	Power
basketball	H	M	M	M	H	M	H

Write "Low," "Medium," or "High" in each column, depending on the fitness demands of the sport you coach.

C Unit Summary (2 minutes)

- Physical fitness is not a permanent condition. Therefore, athletes must train to condition their bodies and improve performance.
- Training leads to significant benefits, including
  - better performance,
  - less fatigue,
  - quicker recovery, and
  - less susceptibility to injury.
- Physical fitness is made up of both energy fitness and muscular fitness.
- *Energy fitness* refers to cardiorespiratory fitness, or the ability of the body to supply the energy needed to meet the demands of the sport.

- The energy we need is supplied by the anaerobic system and the aerobic system.
    - The *anaerobic system* is for immediate movement and very intense exercise.
    - The *aerobic system* is for more enduring and less intense activity.

- *Muscular fitness* is the ability of muscles to meet the demands of the sport with optimal strength, endurance, power, speed, and flexibility.

- As a coach, one of your roles is to help prepare your athletes to meet the physical demands of your sport.

Unit 13 Activity Outcomes

▶ *Energy and Muscular Fitness Demands—Activity 13.1 Outcome* - - - - -

Refer to pages 276 to 278 in *Successful Coaching, Third Edition* for table 13.1, which lists the estimated energy and muscular fitness demands for various sports.

Training for Energy Fitness

(20 minutes)

PURPOSE: To help you learn the basic physiology of the body's energy systems and the anaerobic and aerobic demands of the sport you coach.

LEARNING OBJECTIVES

In this unit you will learn

- the basic physiology of the body's energy systems and
- how to determine the energy demands of the sport you coach.

Unit Overview

Topic	Activities	Time (minutes)
A. Unit Introduction	Hear about the unit's purpose, objectives, and agenda.	1
B. Energy Fitness	• Watch DVD segment 19, "Energy Fitness." • In teams, complete Activity 14.1 Energy Demands of Your Sport, in which you evaluate the anaerobic and aerobic demands of the sport you coach.	15 to 17
C. Unit Summary	Review key unit points.	2

UNIT CONTENT

A Unit Introduction (1 minute)

- The body's energy systems and how to determine the energy demands of the sport you coach

- Muscle fiber types and energy systems
- The anaerobic and aerobic demands of the sport you coach

B Energy Fitness (15 to 17 minutes)

On the DVD Segment "Energy Fitness"

- Energy fitness defined
- Muscle fiber types, energy systems, and training design
- Energy demands of your sport

Activity 14.1 Energy Demands of Your Sport

Introduction

To plan your athletes' physical training program, you need to know the anaerobic and aerobic energy demands of your sport. In this activity you'll work with coaches of your same sport to determine the energy demands of your sport.

Resources

- Table 14.2 on page 296 of *Successful Coaching*
- Figure 14.3 on page 297 of *Successful Coaching*
- The Energy Demands of Your Sport table that follows the activity instructions and activity outcome in the study guide

Instructions

1. Work in teams of two to four, grouped by the sport you coach.
2. Begin by writing the
   a. various positions (e.g., goalie and forwards),
   b. various events (e.g., sprints and pole vaulting), or
   c. different functions (e.g., fielding and hitting)

   of the sport you coach in the first column of the Energy Demands of Your Sport table.
3. With your team, rate the importance of anaerobic and aerobic fitness by circling the letter you think is appropriate for each position, event, or function.
   a. "L" means low importance, "M" is medium importance, and "H" is high importance.
   b. You may circle more than one letter. For instance, if the aerobic demands for a certain position are low to medium, you would circle "L" and "M."

c. As an example, if you are evaluating the energy demands for a soccer goalie, you might circle "L" in the "Aerobic" column and "M" and "H" in the "Anaerobic" column because the anaerobic demands for a soccer goalkeeper are medium to high.

d. Remember that in table 14.2 of *Successful Coaching,* both the ATP-PCr and the anaerobic glycolysis systems are *anaerobic* in nature.

e. Figure 14.3 in *Successful Coaching* shows energy sources for various overall sports, with the percent of aerobic demand on the left and the percent of anaerobic demand on the right. Remember, though, that some positions or functions within a sport may vary in their energy demands from what is shown in this figure.

4. You'll have 10 minutes to complete this activity.

Activity Outcome

When you're done, you should have completed as much of the Energy Demands of Your Sport table as you can in the time allotted.

C Unit Summary (2 minutes)

- Energy fitness is the ability of the anaerobic and aerobic energy systems to use the energy the body has stored. As fitness improves, the body is better able to convert stored carbohydrates and fat to more efficiently generate energy.

- The energy we need is supplied by anaerobic and aerobic systems.

  - The ATP-PCr system provides immediate energy from ATP stored in the muscle cells and does so anaerobically (without oxygen).

  - The anaerobic glycolysis system is also anaerobic in nature and provides enough energy for another one to three minutes from carbohydrates stored as glycogen in the muscles and from blood glucose, which is converted to ATP.

  - The aerobic energy system uses fat and carbohydrates for fuel, which, combined with oxygen, provides more enduring and more efficient fuel for the body.

- Slow-twitch fibers are used for endurance work and obtain their energy primarily from the aerobic energy system, whereas fast-twitch fibers are used for power and speed work and obtain their energy from the anaerobic energy systems.

- By analyzing the energy demands of each position of the sport you coach, you can design a training program that will improve your athletes' performance.

Energy Demands of Your Sport

Position, event, or function	Anaerobic fitness			Aerobic fitness		
	L	M	H	L	M	H
	L	M	H	L	M	H
	L	M	H	L	M	H
	L	M	H	L	M	H
	L	M	H	L	M	H
	L	M	H	L	M	H
	L	M	H	L	M	H
	L	M	H	L	M	H
	L	M	H	L	M	H
	L	M	H	L	M	H

L = low importance; M = medium importance; H = high importance.

Unit 14 Activity Outcomes

▶ *Energy Demands of Your Sport—Activity 14.1 Outcome* - - - - - - - - -

Refer to pages 276 to 278 in *Successful Coaching, Third Edition* for table 13.1, which lists the estimated energy fitness demands for various sports.

Training for Muscular Fitness

(15 minutes)

PURPOSE: To help you learn how muscles work and how to determine the muscular demands of the sport you coach.

LEARNING OBJECTIVES

In this unit you will learn

- what muscular fitness is,
- how muscles work and the effect training has on muscles, and
- how to determine the muscular demands of the sport you coach.

Unit Overview

Topic	Activities	Time (minutes)
A. Unit Introduction	Hear about the unit's purpose, objectives, and agenda.	1
B. Muscular Fitness	• Watch DVD segment 20, "Muscular Fitness." • In teams, complete Activity 15.1 Muscular Demands of Your Sport, in which you evaluate the muscular demands of the sport you coach.	13
C. Unit Summary	Review key unit points.	1

UNIT CONTENT

A Unit Introduction (1 minute)

- Muscle physiology
- Training for muscular fitness
- Evaluating the muscular demands of the sport you coach

B Muscular Fitness (13 minutes)

On the DVD Segment, "Muscular Fitness"

- How muscles work: mechanics and physiology
- Training for muscular fitness

  - Flexibility training
  - Resistance training

- Muscular demands of your sport

Activity 15.1 Muscular Demands of Your Sport

Introduction

To plan your athletes' physical training program, you need to know the muscular demands of your sport. In this activity you'll work with coaches of your same sport to determine the muscular demands of your sport.

Resources

- The table, Muscular Demands of Your Sport (provided after the following instructions and activity outcome)

Instructions

1. Work in teams of two to four, grouped by the sport you coach.
2. Begin by writing two

   a. positions (e.g., goalie and forwards),
   b. events (e.g., sprints and pole vaulting), or
   c. functions (e.g., fielding and hitting)

   of the sport you coach in the first column of the Muscular Demands of Your Sport table. Although your sport likely has more than two positions, events, or functions, focus on only two of them for now. You will be able to analyze others during the self-study phase of the course.

3. With your team, rate the demand for flexibility, strength, muscular endurance, speed, and power by circling the letter you think is appropriate for each position, event, or function.

   a. "L" means low demand, "M" is medium demand, and "H" is high demand.

   b. You may circle more than one letter. For instance, if the power demands for a certain function are medium to high, you would circle "M" and "H."

   c. As an example, if you are evaluating the power requirements for base running in baseball or softball, you might circle "M" and "H" in the "Power" column because base running requires a medium to high amount of power.

4. You'll have 7 minutes to complete this activity.

Activity Outcome

When you're done, you should have completed two rows of the Muscular Demands of Your Sport table.

Muscular Demands of Your Sport

Position, event, or function	Flexibility	Strength	Endurance	Speed	Power
	L M H	L M H	L M H	L M H	L M H
	L M H	L M H	L M H	L M H	L M H
	L M H	L M H	L M H	L M H	L M H
	L M H	L M H	L M H	L M H	L M H
	L M H	L M H	L M H	L M H	L M H
	L M H	L M H	L M H	L M H	L M H
	L M H	L M H	L M H	L M H	L M H
	L M H	L M H	L M H	L M H	L M H
	L M H	L M H	L M H	L M H	L M H
	L M H	L M H	L M H	L M H	L M H

L = low demand; M = medium demand; H = high demand.

c Unit Summary (I minute)

- When a muscle shortens, or contracts, it moves the bone that is connected to it.
- Muscles produce concentric, eccentric, and isometric actions.
- Flexibility training increases range of motion, improves performance, and reduces the chances of injury.
- Resistance training can be used to increase strength, muscular endurance, power, and speed.
- By analyzing the muscular demands of each position of your sport, you can design a training program that will improve your athletes' performance.

Unit 15 Activity Outcomes

▶ *Muscular Demands of Your Sport—Activity 15.1 Outcome* - - - - - - - -

Refer to pages 276 to 278 in *Successful Coaching, Third Edition* for table 13.1, which lists the estimated muscular fitness demands for various sports.

Fueling Your Athletes

(15 minutes)

LEARNING OBJECTIVES

In this unit you will learn

- your role in athletes' nutrition,
- the six basic nutrients,
- what athletes should eat, and
- the role of nutritional supplements for athletes.

Unit Overview

Topic	Activities	Time (minutes)
A. Unit Introduction	Hear about the unit's purpose, objectives, and agenda.	1
B. Fueling Your Athletes	In teams, complete Activity 16.1 Nutrition Quiz, in which you answer nutrition questions in a team competition.	10 to 12
C. Unit Summary	Review key unit points.	2

UNIT CONTENT

A Unit Introduction (1 minute)

- Your role in athletes' nutrition
- The six basic nutrients

- The athlete's diet
- Nutritional supplements used in sports

B Fueling Your Athletes (10 to 12 minutes)

Activity 16.1 Nutrition Quiz

Introduction

As a coach, you want to help your athletes fuel their bodies so that they have the energy to compete at their best. In doing so, you also teach them healthy eating habits for a lifetime. Teaching athletes how to "eat to win" is no easy task, but knowing the basics of sport nutrition can help.

In this activity you'll compete against each other in teams to see how much you know about sport nutrition.

Resources

- Chapter 16 in *Successful Coaching*
- The Nutrition Quiz (provided after the following instructions and activity outcome)

Instructions

1. Work in teams of six to eight, with the same number of coaches on each team.
2. Your team's goal is to answer all 20 questions on the Nutrition Quiz.
3. To do so in the time allotted, divide your team into subgroups to answer certain questions. For example, if you have a team of six people, you might decide to divide into three subgroups of two coaches each, with one subgroup answering questions 1 to 7, another subgroup answering questions 8 to 14, and the third subgroup answering questions 15 to 20.
4. You'll want to decide on your subgroups and the question assignments within the first minute of the activity so that you can spend the remaining time answering the questions.
5. You can use chapter 16 of *Successful Coaching* to help answer the quiz questions.
6. You'll have 8 minutes to take the quiz, after which we'll score the quiz and points will be awarded.

Activity Outcome

When you're done, your team should have answered all of the questions on the Nutrition Quiz.

▶ Nutrition Quiz -

1. As a coach, you should
   a. educate athletes about healthy eating.
   b. model healthy eating habits.
   c. psychologically counsel athletes with eating disorders.
   d. provide your athletes with nutritional supplements.
   e. a and b
   f. a, b, and d

2. It's found in potatoes, pasta, bread, cereal, and beans.
   a. carbohydrates
   b. protein
   c. fat
   d. vitamins
   e. minerals
   f. water

3. This nutrient is responsible for carrying other nutrients to the body's cells.
   a. carbohydrates
   b. protein
   c. fat
   d. vitamins
   e. minerals
   f. water

4. Calcium, which keeps bones strong, is an example of this nutrient.
   a. carbohydrates
   b. protein
   c. fat
   d. vitamins
   e. minerals
   f. water

5. This nutrient can't be stored in the body, so it should be consumed daily.
   a. carbohydrates
   b. protein
   c. fat
   d. vitamins
   e. minerals
   f. water

6. A diet too high in protein usually means a diet too low in this nutrient.

    a. carbohydrates

    b. protein

    c. fat

    d. vitamins

    e. minerals

    f. water

7. This nutrient, which can be stored, provides energy for long-term aerobic activity.

    a. protein

    b. fat

    c. vitamins

    d. minerals

    e. water

8. In one day, an athlete should eat

    a. eight eggs.

    b. 7 ounces (196 grams) of meat, chicken, turkey, or fish.

    c. three 7-ounce (196-gram) cuts of meat, chicken, turkey, or fish.

9. One of your athletes has about a 1-cup salad and a half-cup serving of cooked broccoli for lunch. How close is this athlete to a healthy daily dose of veggies?

    a. One serving down, six to go

    b. Not even halfway

    c. Almost there

10. A basketball player has two bananas and 2 cups of fruit juice for lunch. The player has

    a. met the minimum recommended daily amount of fruits

    b. exceeded the maximum recommended daily amount of fruits

    c. a long way to go

11. One of your runners has two cheese sandwiches on wheat bread and two cookies for lunch. How many servings of "bread, cereal, rice, and pasta" has the runner consumed?

    a. two

    b. three

    c. five

12. This beverage contains water, sugar, and sometimes sodium, but no other nutrients.

    a. nondiet soft drink

    b. coffee

    c. water

    d. sport drink

    e. fruit juice

13. This beverage has no caffeine, no sugar, and only one important nutrient.

    a. nondiet soft drink

    b. coffee

    c. water

    d. sport drink

    e. fruit juice

14. This drink can speed up rehydration in your athletes. It also replaces vital nutrients that are lost through sweat.

    a. nondiet soft drink

    b. coffee

    c. water

    d. sport drink

    e. fruit juice

15. This drink provides water as well as other nutrients, but it doesn't replace nutrients lost through sweat, and it takes a while to absorb into the bloodstream.

    a. nondiet soft drink

    b. coffee

    c. water

    d. sport drink

    e. fruit juice

16. For every pound of weight lost after exercise, an athlete should drink this much fluid:

    a. 4 ounces

    b. 8 ounces

    c. 12 ounces

    d. 16 ounces

17. During exercise, athletes should drink

    a. once they feel thirsty.

    b. 4 to 8 ounces every 20 minutes.

    c. 16 ounces every 20 minutes.

    d. 4 to 8 ounces every 30 minutes.

18. Vitamins

    a. regulate metabolic reactions.

    b. are in more demand when an athlete trains extensively.

    c. can be obtained through eating balanced meals.

    d. All of the above.

    e. a and c

19. The nutritional supplement creatine

    a. should not be provided to athletes by coaches.

    b. increases speed and power in short-duration, high-intensity sport events.

    c. appears safe in the short term but has unknown long-term effects.

    d. increases muscle mass when combined with resistance training.

    e. all of the above

20. This substance can stimulate the nervous system and increase performance, but it can also make some athletes jittery; cause gastrointestinal distress; and cause increased urination, leading to dehydration.

    a. electrolytes

    b. caffeine

    c. water

    d. folic acid

C Unit Summary (2 minutes)

- Athletes get energy from foods that contain carbohydrates, protein, and fat.

- Vitamins and minerals are not direct sources of energy, but are needed to derive energy from carbohydrates, proteins, and fat.

- An overly high protein diet usually means the body is low in carbohydrates and fats, which are needed to produce energy. The body, in turn, burns off crucial tissue-building protein to compensate!

- Water is crucial in muscle development and temperature control. Athletes should drink 4 to 8 ounces of fluid every 20 minutes while exercising.

- Although some nutritional supplements, such as creatine, have proven beneficial effects, they also carry risks. Other than supplying sport drinks, coaches should not provide nutritional supplements to athletes.

- Your role as a coach is to educate your athletes about healthy eating and to model healthy eating habits.

Unit 16 Activity Outcomes

1. As a coach, you should
   a. educate athletes about healthy eating.
   b. model healthy eating habits.
   c. psychologically counsel athletes with eating disorders.
   d. provide your athletes with nutritional supplements.
   E. A and B
   f. a, b, and d

Correct answer: e, a and b. *Your role as a coach is to educate your athletes about healthy eating and to model healthy eating habits. If you suspect that an athlete has an eating disorder, you'll need professional help to address the problem. You should consult a physician, clinical psychologist or psychiatrist, or nutrition therapist who specializes in eating disorders. Pages 382 to 384 in Successful Coaching provide more information about eating disorders.*

You may share facts with athletes about nutritional supplements, but you should not actually supply nutritional supplements to athletes. The one exception is sport drinks, which you should supply, and which are considered by some to be a nutritional supplement.

2. It's found in potatoes, pasta, bread, cereal, and beans.
   A. CARBOHYDRATES
   b. protein
   c. fat
   d. vitamins
   e. minerals
   f. water

Correct answer: a, carbohydrates. *All of the foods mentioned are a source of digestible complex carbohydrates.*

3. This nutrient is responsible for carrying other nutrients to the body's cells.
   a. carbohydrates
   b. protein
   c. fat
   d. vitamins
   e. minerals
   F. WATER

Correct answer: f, water. *Water is also crucial in muscle development and temperature control.*

4. Calcium, which keeps bones strong, is an example of this nutrient.

    a. carbohydrates

    b. protein

    c. fat

    d. vitamins

    E. MINERALS

    f. water

Correct answer: e, minerals. *Calcium, phosphorus, and magnesium all make for strong bones. Other minerals play important roles in oxygen and energy functions.*

5. This nutrient can't be stored in the body, so it should be consumed daily.

    a. carbohydrates

    B. PROTEIN

    c. fat

    d. vitamins

    e. minerals

    f. water

Correct answer: b, protein. *Meats, poultry, fish, dry beans, eggs, and nuts are all great sources of protein. Protein helps control the water level inside and outside the cells. Protein is also responsible for the development of new tissue including muscles, red blood cells, and hair.*

6. A diet too high in protein usually means a diet too low in this nutrient.

    A. CARBOHYDRATES

    b. protein

    c. fat

    d. vitamins

    e. minerals

    f. water

Correct answer: a, carbohydrates. *Oddly enough, an overly high protein diet usually means the body is low in carbohydrates and fats. The body, in turn, burns off crucial tissue-building protein to compensate!*

7. This nutrient, which can be stored, provides energy for long-term aerobic activity.

   a. protein

   B. FAT

   c. vitamins

   d. minerals

   e. water

Correct answer: b, fat. *Fats play a vital role in the production of energy, but they are usually overconsumed, even by athletes. When athletes reduce the fat intake in their diets, they need to replace it by consuming twice the caloric amount from complex carbohydrates, or by combining complex carbohydrates with unsaturated fats to meet their daily energy needs. Otherwise, the body will deplete important proteins to make up the energy difference!*

8. In one day, an athlete should eat

   a. eight eggs.

   B. 7 OUNCES (196 GRAMS) OF MEAT, CHICKEN, TURKEY, OR FISH.

   c. three 7-ounce (196-gram) cuts of meat, chicken, turkey, or fish.

Correct answer: b, 7 ounces of meat, chicken, turkey, or fish. *Variations of eggs, beans, nuts, or peanut butter can be worked into this daily intake as well. Because many protein foods are fatty as well, athletes should not take in more protein than what the Food Guide Pyramid recommends. Athletes who follow these guidelines will build more amino acids, which are used to build and repair muscles, bones, tendons, and ligaments. Because eggs are packed with artery-clogging cholesterol, they need to be eaten in moderation.*

9. One of your athletes has about a 1-cup salad and a half-cup serving of cooked broccoli for lunch. How close is this athlete to a healthy daily dose of veggies?

   a. One serving down, six to go

   B. NOT EVEN HALFWAY

   c. Almost there

Correct answer: b, not even halfway. *This athlete has managed two servings out of six. The 1-cup leafy salad counts for one serving, and the broccoli is another. Try to encourage carrot or celery sticks as a midday snack, and hopefully dinner will round out the day. And it might be a good idea to mention that most salad dressings are ridiculously high in saturated fats!*

10. A basketball player has two bananas and 2 cups of fruit juice for lunch. The player has

A. MET THE MINIMUM RECOMMENDED DAILY AMOUNT OF FRUITS

b. exceeded the maximum recommended daily amount of fruits

c. a long way to go

Correct answer: a, met the minimum recommended daily amount of fruits. *Compared to vegetables, fruits are usually an easier category for your athletes to succeed in. This player has more than four servings down the hatch; the recommended range for an athlete is 4 to 10 servings.*

11. One of your runners has two cheese sandwiches on wheat bread and two cookies for lunch. How many servings of "bread, cereal, rice, and pasta" has the runner consumed?

   a. two

   b. three

C. FIVE

Correct answer: c, five. *Even though athletes should try for 11 to 20 servings from this group, it's not as daunting as it sounds! Each piece of bread is a serving, which means that a sandwich counts for two servings. The two cookies count for one more serving. Three or four small crackers even count as one full serving. This category is where most of the carbohydrates come from, so it's especially important to athletes.*

12. This beverage contains water, sugar, and sometimes sodium, but no other nutrients.

A. NONDIET SOFT DRINK

   b. coffee

   c. water

   d. sport drink

   e. fruit juice

Correct answer: a, nondiet soft drink. *Soft drinks contain sugar, which can help fuel muscles, but they don't absorb into the bloodstream very quickly. Additionally, carbonated soft drinks may cause gastrointestinal distress during and after athletic performance. Caffeinated soft drinks also cause increased urination in many athletes, leading to increased dehydration.*

13. This beverage has no caffeine, no sugar, and only one important nutrient.

   a. nondiet soft drink

   b. coffee

C. WATER

   d. sport drink

   e. fruit juice

Correct answer: c, water. *Water is usually the most convenient and practical hydration beverage available. It contains that most important of nutrients—water! However, athletes training for long periods or in hot conditions are losing much more than water. Sodium, carbohydrates, and other electrolytes can't be replaced by water breaks.*

14. This drink can speed up rehydration in your athletes. It also replaces vital nutrients that are lost through sweat.

    a. nondiet soft drink

    b. coffee

    c. water

    D. SPORT DRINK

    e. fruit juice

Correct answer: d, sport drink. *A sport drink with the right blend of sugars can actually speed up the hydration of the bloodstream. The right amount of carbohydrates, sodium, and other electrolytes can replenish an athlete in training without causing any gastrointestinal distress or increased urination. Sport drinks contain around 14 grams, or 50 to 80 calories, of carbohydrates per 8 fluid ounces (240 milliliters).*

15. This drink provides water as well as other nutrients, but it doesn't replace nutrients lost through sweat, and it takes a while to absorb into the bloodstream.

    a. nondiet soft drink

    b. coffee

    c. water

    d. sport drink

    E. FRUIT JUICE

Correct answer: e, fruit juice. *Fruit juice can help your athletes get some valuable vitamins, fiber, and other nutrients. However, fruit juice is not the drink of choice for hydration under hot or intense exercise conditions.*

16. For every pound of weight lost after exercise, an athlete should drink this much fluid:

    a. 4 ounces

    b. 8 ounces

    c. 12 ounces

    D. 16 OUNCES

Correct answer: d, 16 ounces. *One of the best ways for athletes to prevent dehydration is to weigh themselves before and after practices and competitive events to monitor their water loss. The American College of Sports Medicine recommends that athletes drink 16 ounces of fluid for every pound of weight lost after exercise. When athletes return for their next practice, they should be back to their usual preexercise weight.*

17. During exercise, athletes should drink

    a. once they feel thirsty.

    B. 4 TO 8 OUNCES EVERY 20 MINUTES.

    c. 16 ounces every 20 minutes.

    d. 4 to 8 ounces every 30 minutes.

Correct answer: b, 4 to 8 ounces every 20 minutes. *By the time an athlete feels thirsty, the athlete could have lost 1.5 liters of water and may find it difficult to drink enough fluid to avoid becoming dehydrated. Athletes should begin drinking before they feel thirsty and drink on a schedule rather than relying on their thirst mechanism. Sport nutritionists recommend that athletes drink before exercising and then also 4 to 8 ounces every 20 minutes while exercising.*

18. Vitamins

    a. regulate metabolic reactions.

    b. are in more demand when an athlete trains extensively.

    c. can be obtained through eating balanced meals.

    d. All of the above.

    E. A and C

Correct answer: e, a and c. *Vitamins regulate metabolic reactions—helping chemical reactions take place that protect and maintain the body. For example, vitamins help the immune system and the nervous system to work effectively. Both vitamins and minerals are needed to derive energy from carbohydrates, proteins, and fat. Athletes don't need more vitamins the more they exercise. Athletes can get all the vitamins they need by eating a balanced diet, including adequate fruits and vegetables. There's no strong scientific evidence that extra vitamins improve performance.*

19. The nutritional supplement creatine

    a. should not be provided to athletes by coaches.

    b. increases speed and power in short-duration, high-intensity sport events.

    c. appears safe in the short term but has unknown long-term effects.

    d. increases muscle mass when combined with resistance training.

    E. ALL OF THE ABOVE

Correct answer: e, all of the above. *In addition, creatine appears to be far less effective for females than it is for males. There are some anecdotal reports of cramping, dehydration, and muscle strain associated with its use. The National Federation of State High School Associations (NFHS) advises coaches not to recommend supplements to athletes, but they exclude vitamins and sport drinks from this directive.*

20. This substance can stimulate the nervous system and increase performance, but it can also make some athletes jittery; cause gastrointestinal distress; and cause increased urination, leading to dehydration.

    a. electrolytes

    B. CAFFEINE

    c. water

    d. folic acid

Correct answer: b, caffeine. *The caffeine in coffee and soft drinks can boost performance and endurance for some, but it is also a diuretic, meaning that it can overactivate the kidneys, causing them to take too much water away from the blood. High doses can exceed the limit allowed by the International Olympic Committee (IOC).*

Battling Drugs

(15 minutes)

PURPOSE: To help you learn what you can do to prevent substance abuse among athletes.

LEARNING OBJECTIVES

In this unit you will learn

- some of the things you can do to prevent substance abuse among athletes, and
- rules, and consequences for breaking the rules, that can help prevent substance abuse.

Unit Overview

Topic	Activities	Time (minutes)
A. Unit Introduction	Hear about the unit's purpose, objectives, and agenda.	1
B. Drugs, You, and Your Team	In teams, complete Activity 17.1 Team Policy for Drug Use, in which you determine consequences for first, second, and third offenses.	13
C. Unit Summary	Review key unit points.	1

UNIT CONTENT

A Unit Introduction (1 minute)

- What you can do to help prevent substance abuse among athletes.
- Determine consequences for athletes when they violate your policy for drug use.

B Drugs, You, and Your Team (13 minutes)

Activity 17.1 Team Policy for Drug Use

Introduction

One of the steps you can take to help prevent drug use is to establish and enforce rules. Often you will be charged with enforcing your school district's code of conduct. The rules you set for your team will have to be consistent with the school district's policy. A drug policy should include consequences that are administered fairly and consistently. In this activity you'll work in teams to determine consequences for first, second, and third offenses of a team drug policy.

Resources

- The Team Policy for Drug Use (provided after the following instructions and activity outcome)

Instructions

1. Work in teams of two to four, grouped by the sport you coach.
2. Read the sample Team Policy for Drug Use on pages 151 to 152 in this study guide.
3. With your team, complete number 7 on the policy by determining the consequences you would administer for athletes who violate the team rules.
4. Write in the consequences for the first, second, and third offenses. Consider

    a. whether the athlete will be allowed to participate in practices;

    b. whether the athlete will be prohibited from participating in contests, and for how long;

    c. whether you would contact the athlete's parents, and how that would occur; and

    d. anything else you think is important in determining the consequences.

  5. You'll have 9 minutes to complete this activity.

Activity Outcome

When you're done, you should have written the consequences for the first, second, and third offenses in the Team Policy for Drug Use.

▶ Team Policy for Drug Use -

To make participation on [your team name] a safe, positive, and healthy experience, your coaches will enforce the following team policy with regard to the use of alcohol, tobacco, illicit drugs, and performance-enhancing drugs.

  1. All members of the team are prohibited from using, purchasing, possessing, manufacturing, or selling any

    a. illicit drugs;

    b. performance-enhancing drugs banned by the International Olympic Committee, United States Olympic Committee, or National Collegiate Athletic Association; or

    c. any drugs banned by [insert the name of any sport governing body regulating competition in your sport].

  2. All members of the team are prohibited from using alcohol and tobacco at any team facility or function. This includes locker rooms, practice and contest facilities, meeting rooms, eating facilities, and transportation vehicles. It also includes not only competitive events, but also team meetings, awards banquets, and official team events.

  3. Athletes of minority age are not permitted to use alcohol and tobacco products at any time because they are illegal.

  4. Athletes of majority age are not denied the right to smoke when not participating in a team event because it is legal to do so, but they are highly encouraged not to smoke because of the negative consequences to their health.

  5. Athletes of majority age are not denied the right to use alcohol when not participating in a team event because it is legal to do so, but they are highly encouraged to use alcohol responsibly and in moderation. Athletes who use alcohol irresponsibly are subject to the same penalties as for illegal and banned substance use.

6. All members of the team are required to attend the annual Drug-Free Sport seminar prior to the beginning of the season and to carefully review and sign the Athlete Code of Conduct (see chapter 8 in *Successful Coaching*) and to abide by the code throughout the season.

7. If an athlete violates any of these team rules, the following actions will be taken:

   a. First offense:

   b. Second offense:

   c. Third offense:

8. Any athlete who is subject to the corrective action of the team policy by the coach has the right to appeal to [title of position overseeing the sports program].

9. Athletes will continue to participate in practices while disciplinary action and rehabilitation are occurring.

Recommended Coach's Position on Athlete Drug Use

If you are unsure about your position on athletes' use of drugs, consider ASEP's position:

- Athletes should not use illicit drugs. Not only are they illegal, but they are also dangerous to your athletes' health. Moreover, illicit drugs don't solve problems. They create problems.

- Athletes should not use tobacco. It's very harmful to their health, is highly addictive, and is a gateway to using illicit drugs.

- Athletes should not use alcohol when under age, and when of legal age, they should use alcohol in moderation and responsibly.

- Athletes should not use performance-enhancing drugs that are banned by the IOC, NCAA, or USOC because it is cheating and is likely to be harmful to your athletes' health. Even if these drugs are not banned by your sport governing body, athletes should not use them. Help your athletes improve their performance through safe and fair training methods.

Additional Points About Battling Drug Use

- Discuss your policies and expectations with your team in advance.

- When the policies are violated, administer the consequences fairly and consistently.

- Praise your athletes when they follow the policies, especially when you know they have made a deliberate choice to do so.

- Consider using a drug testing program that checks for all illegal and banned substances.

- If you automatically cut an athlete from the team for using alcohol or drugs, you will not be able to help the young person become a responsible adult. By allowing the athlete to continue to practice with the team but not play in contests, you at least keep some connection to the athlete and can be a positive influence.

C Unit Summary (1 minute)

The bricks in the Wall of Drug Prevention, which can also be found on page 398 of *Successful Coaching*, nicely sum up the coach's role in battling drug use:

- Take an antidrug stance.
- Be a positive role model against the use of drugs.
- Establish and enforce an antidrug policy on your team.
- Provide your athletes with education about performance-enhancing and illicit drugs.

Unit 17 Activity Outcome

Suggested consequences for first, second, and third offenses follow. Your team's ideas may be equally valid.

7. If an athlete violates any of these team rules, the following actions will be taken:

   a. First offense: *The athlete is not permitted to participate in the next two consecutive contests or two weeks of the competitive season, whichever is greater. The athlete's parents or guardian will meet with the coach to receive notification of the violation and to agree to the athlete's participation in [describe available counseling or educational session]. The athlete must also comply with any legal or other disciplinary action mandated by the law or applicable authority.*

   b. Second offense: *The athlete is not permitted to participate in any contests for six weeks. The athlete's parents or guardian will meet with the coach to receive notification of the violation. If the athlete wishes to return to the team, the athlete must agree to participate in [describe available counseling or educational session]. The athlete must also comply with any legal or other disciplinary action mandated by the law or applicable authority.*

   c. Third offense: *The athlete is not permitted to participate in any contests for the remainder of the competitive season, including postseason tournaments. The athlete's parents or guardian will meet with the coach to receive notification of the violation. If the athlete wishes to return to the team the next season, the athlete must agree to participate in [describe more intensive counseling available or educational session]. The athlete must also comply with any legal or other disciplinary action mandated by the law or applicable authority.*

Managing Relationships

(25 minutes)

PURPOSE: To help you learn how to work more effectively with the people around you.

LEARNING OBJECTIVES

In this unit you will learn

- the four interpersonal skills that are vital to your coaching success;
- how to work more effectively with fellow coaches, administrators, medical personnel, officials, parents, and the media; and
- how to prevent and deal with parent problems.

Unit Overview

Topic	Activities	Time (minutes)
A. Unit Introduction	Hear about the unit's purpose, objectives, and agenda.	1
B. Managing Relationships	Watch DVD segment 21, "Managing Relationships."	8
C. Start With the Parents	Complete Activity 18.1 Parent Problems, in which you list typical problems with parents and then in teams brainstorm how to deal with the problems.	15
D. Unit Summary	Review key unit points.	1

UNIT CONTENT

A Unit Introduction (1 minute)

- Four interpersonal skills that are especially important for coaches
- How to build and maintain positive relationships with fellow coaches, administrators, medical personnel, officials, parents, and the media
- How to deal with problems coaches commonly face with parents

B Managing Relationships (8 minutes)

On the DVD Segment, "Managing Relationships"

- Four interpersonal skills
  - Knowing and trusting yourself and others
  - Communicating effectively
  - Accepting and supporting others
  - Resolving conflict

- Working with others
  - Assistant coaches
  - Other coaches
  - Administrators
  - Medical personnel
  - Officials
  - Parents
  - Media

C Start With the Parents (15 minutes)

Activity 18.1 Parent Problems

Introduction

Many coaches find that the most challenging relationship to manage is their relationship with the parents of their athletes. If you've been coaching for a while, you might find this an understatement.

- You need to give parents clear guidelines about their roles and your expectations of them.
- In turn, you need to remember that parents are ultimately responsible for their children and desire only the best for them.

In this activity we'll brainstorm typical problems coaches have with parents and discuss possible solutions.

Resources

- The Parent Problems worksheet (provided after the following instructions and activity outcome)

Instructions

1. First we'll work together as a class.
2. We'll brainstorm a list of problems that coaches commonly encounter with parents.
3. Record these on your Parent Problems worksheet.
4. Then we'll break into teams grouped by the sport you coach.
5. Each team will be assigned two or three of the parent problems.
6. With your team, determine
   a. the steps you could take to prevent the problem and
   b. how you can deal with the problem if it still occurs.
7. We'll have 3 to 5 minutes to brainstorm our list of problems, and then you'll have 7 minutes to discuss the problems with your team.

Activity Outcome

When you're done, you should have listed all of the problems on the Parent Problems worksheet. For the problems assigned to your team, you should have determined prevention steps and how to deal with the problem.

Parent Problems

1. _____

Prevention steps

How to deal with the problem if it occurs

2. _____

Prevention steps

How to deal with the problem if it occurs

3. _____

Prevention steps

How to deal with the problem if it occurs

4. _____

Prevention steps

How to deal with the problem if it occurs

5. _____

Prevention steps

How to deal with the problem if it occurs

6. _____

Prevention steps

How to deal with the problem if it occurs

7. _____

Prevention steps

How to deal with the problem if it occurs

8. _____

Prevention steps

How to deal with the problem if it occurs

9. _____

Prevention steps

How to deal with the problem if it occurs

10. _____

Prevention steps

How to deal with the problem if it occurs

Principles of Dealing With Parent Problems

- Many parent problems can be avoided when coaches hold a preseason parent orientation program. You can find guidelines for a parent orientation program on pages 455 to 458 of *Successful Coaching.*
- Let parents know what is expected of the athletes and of them.
- Provide parents with guidelines for their behavior during practices and contests.
- Listen carefully to parents' concerns.
- Establish clear lines of communication between you and the parents.

D Unit Summary (1 minute)

- Developing positive relationships with the people around you can help you to be productive and successful.
- To build and maintain effective relationships with fellow coaches, administrators, medical personnel, officials, parents, and the media, you must

  - know and trust yourself and others,
  - communicate effectively,
  - accept and support others, and
  - resolve conflict.

- Many parent problems can be avoided by holding a preseason parent orientation program.
- You need to give parents clear guidelines about their roles and your expectations of them.
- In turn, you need to remember that parents are ultimately responsible for their children and desire only the best for them.

Managing Risk

(15 minutes)

PURPOSE: To help you learn how to reduce your legal risk.

LEARNING OBJECTIVES

In this unit you will learn

- what risk management means for coaches,
- steps you can take to manage your risk, and
- the nine legal duties of coaches.

Unit Overview

Topic	Activities	Time (minutes)
A. Unit Introduction	Hear about the unit's purpose, objectives, and agenda.	1
B. Risk Management	Watch DVD segment 22, "Risk Management."	10 to 12
C. Unit Summary	Review key unit points.	2

UNIT CONTENT

A Unit Introduction (1 minute)

- The objective of risk management
- Steps to take to manage your risk
- How to fulfill your nine legal duties

B Risk Management (10 to 12 minutes)

On the DVD Segment, "Risk Management"

- The risk management process
- Immunity
- The nine legal duties of coaches
- Waivers and participation agreements
- Insurance for coaches

C Unit Summary (2 minutes)

- The objective of risk management is to produce the safest environment possible for your athletes and others and to avoid litigation.
- The legal duties of coaches encourage coaches to be responsible and professional in order to protect athletes and others.
- To manage risk, take these four steps:

    1. Identify the risks.
    2. Evaluate the risks.
    3. Select an approach to manage the risk.
    4. Implement the approach.

- Participation agreements cannot prevent lawsuits or absolve you from negligence, but they clearly establish that you fulfilled your duty to warn.
- You should not coach without liability insurance, and sponsoring agencies should not permit anyone to coach without it.

Coaching Principles
Wrap-Up

(20 minutes)

PURPOSE: To help you review what you have learned in the class and to help you understand the process and procedures for completing the rest of the Coaching Principles course.

LEARNING OBJECTIVES

In this unit you will learn

- answers to any of your remaining questions and
- the process and procedures for completing the rest of the Coaching Principles course.

Unit Overview

Topic	Activities	Time (minutes)
A. Unit Introduction	Hear about the unit's purpose, objectives, and agenda.	1
B. Coaching Principles Classroom Course Summary	Participate in Activity 20.1 Course Summary, in which you hear a summary of the course, see if you learned what you said you hoped to learn in unit 1, and get answers to any remaining questions about the coaching principles you've learned today.	4
C. Coaching Principles Classroom Course Evaluation	Complete Activity 20.2 Course Evaluation, in which you fill out the course evaluation.	5
D. Completing the Coaching Principles Self-Study and Test	• Participate in Activity 20.3 Self-Study Procedures, in which you learn about procedures for completing the self-study portion of the course. • Participate in Activity 20.4 Testing Procedures, in which you learn about procedures for completing the Coaching Principles Test.	8
E. Goodbye and Thanks	Final questions and goodbyes.	2

UNIT CONTENT

A Unit Introduction (1 minute)

- Review what was covered in the course
- See if you learned what you hoped to learn today
- Ask any remaining questions
- Fill out a course evaluation
- Learn the procedures for completing the self-study and the course test

B Coaching Principles Classroom Course Summary (4 minutes)

Activity 20.1 Course Summary

Today we have discussed many topics, which can be summarized by the five part titles in *Successful Coaching:*

- Principles of Coaching—including developing your coaching philosophy, objectives, and style; coaching for character; and coaching diverse athletes.
- Principles of Behavior—including motivating your athletes and managing their behavior.

- Principles of Teaching—including using the games approach, and teaching technical and tactical skills.
- Principles of Physical Training—including training for energy fitness and muscular fitness, fueling your athletes, and battling drugs.
- Principles of Management—including managing relationships and managing risk.

C Coaching Principles Classroom Course Evaluation (5 minutes)

Activity 20.2 Course Evaluation

Introduction

We are interested in knowing your reactions to this course, so we'd like you to complete a course evaluation. Your evaluation will be used to make improvements in future courses.

Resources

Take out the Coaching Principles Classroom Test Package, including

- an ASEP Bronze Level Evaluation Form to evaluate the course,
- a Coaching Principles Classroom Test,
- an ASEP Test Answer Form A to record test answers,
- the Coaching Principles Test Instructions,
- a preaddressed ASEP mailing envelope in which to mail the completed ASEP Test Answer Form A, and
- a cardboard insert to ensure that the test form is not damaged in the mail.

To complete the course evaluation, you'll use

- the ASEP Bronze Level Evaluation Form,
- a pencil or black or blue ballpoint pen,
- the course code on the last page of your Coaching Principles Classroom Test,
- your instructor's identification number,
- your instructor's last name, and
- today's date.

Instructions

1. Review the marking instructions for completing the ASEP Bronze Level Evaluation Form.

2. At the top of the evaluation, enter the instructor's identification number, the instructor's last name, and today's date under "Last Date of Course."

3. Find the course code on the last page of the Coaching Principles Classroom Test, and enter it on the evaluation. The course code is four characters long and begins with AA, followed by a two-digit number.

4. Complete the rest of the evaluation. You'll have about 3 minutes to complete the evaluation.

5. Hand in your completed evaluation to your instructor.

Activity Outcome

When you're done, you should have completed and handed in the evaluation.

D Completing the Coaching Principles Self-Study and Test (8 minutes)

Activity 20.3 Self-Study Procedures

Introduction

Over the next several weeks, you need to complete the self-study portion of the course and the Coaching Principles Test.

• You should plan to complete these activities by _____ _____.

• If you do not successfully pass your Coaching Principles Test within six months of the last date of your course (today), you will have to take the entire course over again and pay all of the course fees again.

Contents for the Self-Study

• An introductory unit (unit 1)
• A wrap-up unit that discusses taking the course test (unit 22)
• 20 other units, one unit for each chapter in *Successful Coaching*

Example: Unit 2 Developing Your Coaching Philosophy

• Lists the learning objectives for the unit
• Indicates which chapter to read in *Successful Coaching*
• Includes activities to help you learn and apply the concepts and skills covered in the chapter

Activity 20.4 Testing Procedures

Introduction

The last thing you'll do to complete the course is to complete the course test.

Resources

To complete the test, you'll need

- the Coaching Principles Test Instructions,
- the Coaching Principles Classroom Test,
- the ASEP Test Answer Form A,
- a pencil or black or blue ballpoint pen, and
- the text *Successful Coaching.*

Test Procedures

- Three things to do:

  1. Decide whether you'll complete the test paper-pencil or online.
  2. Complete the test.
  3. Get your test scored.

- The course test can be completed paper-pencil, using the Coaching Principles Classroom Test and ASEP Test Answer Form A, or it can be completed online using the Coaching Principles Online Test.

- The course test is open book. You can refer to *Successful Coaching* and any other course materials while you complete the test. However, you should complete the test individually—*it is not a team activity.*

- If you do not pass the test the first time, you can take it again. The procedures for taking a retest are described in the test instructions.

Important Points About the Test

- Both the paper-pencil and online tests test the same content and include 50 multiple choice and 50 true/false questions. Each test includes questions for each chapter in *Successful Coaching.*

- The passing score for the test—whether paper-pencil or online—is 80 percent.

- There are several forms (or versions) of the classroom test. Which form you get is determined by chance.

- The questions for the online test are randomly generated from a pool of 300 questions—the same questions used to create the three forms of the classroom test. Consequently, there are virtually thousands of forms (or versions) of the online test. Which form you get is determined by chance.

- No two forms of the test—whether paper-pencil or online—include all of the same questions. **THE ONLINE TEST WILL NOT INCLUDE THE SAME QUESTIONS THAT ARE ON THE PAPER-PENCIL TEST INCLUDED IN YOUR COACHING PRINCIPLES TEST PACKAGE.**

- The online test is scored immediately, so you get your score within seconds of completing the test. The paper-pencil test must be sent into ASEP for scoring, and you will get your score in about three weeks.

- Once you begin taking the test online, you can't change your mind and take the paper-pencil test because the code that you enter online will deactivate the code on your scan form.

- If you need to take a retest, you must complete the retest in the same way—paper-pencil or online—that you completed the original test. If you took the original test paper-pencil, you must take the retest paper-pencil. And if you took the original test online, you must take the retest online.

- The test form you use for the retest will have different questions than the form you used the first time.

- The retest fee for the paper-pencil test is $20. The retest fee for the online test is $10.

Coaching Principles Test Instructions

- These instructions include specific steps for completing the test online—step 2 in the instructions—and for completing the test paper-pencil—step 3 in the instructions.

- If you take the paper-pencil test, instructions for mailing your test to ASEP are included in the test instructions.

- Information to enter:

  - Your key code. The key code is the 10-digit number printed on the instructions.
  - The instructor's identification number.
  - The instructor's last name.
  - The organization code.
  - The last date of the course.
  - Current CPR certification: This information is required for ASEP's Bronze Level certification.
  - For the paper-pencil test **ONLY,** you'll need to enter the course code. This is the same code you entered on the course evaluation. It is four characters long and begins with AA followed by two numbers.

Final Points About the Test

- Please do not throw away any of the pieces of your test package (other than the plastic shrink-wrap).
- Make sure you keep the cardboard too.
- Put this package in a safe place until you have read *Successful Coaching,* completed the self-study activities, and are ready to take the test.
- If you lose your scan form or test instructions (containing your test key code), you will be charged a $10 replacement fee.

Instructor Contact Information

- Instructor's phone number: _____

- Instructor's e-mail address: _____

- Instructor's best days and times to be contacted: _____

_____

E   Goodbye and Thanks (2 minutes)

- Questions?
- Goodbyes.

COACHING PRINCIPLES
SELF-STUDY UNITS

Unit 1   Introduction to Coaching Principles Self-Study 171

Unit 2   Developing Your Coaching Philosophy 174

Unit 3   Determining Your Coaching Objectives 176

Unit 4   Selecting Your Coaching Style 179

Unit 5   Coaching for Character 184

Unit 6   Coaching Diverse Athletes 188

Unit 7   Communicating With Your Athletes 193

Unit 8   Motivating Your Athletes 199

Unit 9   Managing Your Athletes' Behavior 205

Unit 10   Coaching the Games Approach Way 214

Unit 11   Teaching Technical Skills 219

Unit 12   Teaching Tactical Skills 224

Unit 13   Planning for Teaching 229

Unit 14   Training Basics 236

Unit 15   Training for Energy Fitness 244

Unit 16   Training for Muscular Fitness 252

Unit 17   Fueling Your Athletes 260

Unit 18   Battling Drugs 266

Unit 19   Managing Your Team 274

Unit 20   Managing Relationships 277

Unit 21   Managing Risk 287

Unit 22   Coaching Principles Self-Study Wrap-Up 302

Introduction to Coaching Principles Self-Study

LEARNING OBJECTIVES

In this unit you will learn

- the purpose,
- process, and
- benefits

of completing the Coaching Principles self-study units.

WHAT TO READ

Read the following sections, which describe the purpose and objectives of the Coaching Principles self-study units and provide tips for getting the most out of the self-study process.

Purpose of the Self-Study Units

In the self-study portion of the course, you'll learn coaching principles material that was not presented in the classroom sessions. You'll need to know this material to pass the Coaching Principles Test. In the classroom portion of the course, you learned coaching principles that were best presented in person, on the DVD, or through practice in the classroom. But that's only part of what you need to know to be a prepared coach. Now you need to get into the *Successful Coaching* text and learn other details about coaching athletes.

This self-study guide will serve as an invaluable learning tool after you have read the *Successful Coaching* text. In this self-study portion of the course, you'll be able to gauge your understanding of the material, brush up on weak areas, and prepare for the Coaching Principles Test.

Objectives of the Self-Study Units

The objectives of the Coaching Principles self-study units are to

- encourage you to read *Successful Coaching,*
- provide activities that will help you test your understanding of the material,
- challenge you to refer back to the book to refresh your memory if your answers are not correct,
- help you apply the general concepts you learn to a wide variety of coaching situations, and
- develop your ability to use *Successful Coaching* as a resource when coaching your athletes.

Getting the Most Out of the Coaching Principles Self-Study Process

How can you get the most out of the self-study process?

1. Read the related *Successful Coaching* chapter before beginning each self-study unit.

2. As you read *Successful Coaching,* write notes in the book, flag pages that include important points, and etch in your mind particularly important or useful passages, forms, and so on.

3. Do one unit at a time—first reading the chapter in the book and then completing the unit—and complete the units in order. The units are ordered in the same way as the topics in the book. This will help you learn where to find information in the book.

4. Try to complete each activity without looking in *Successful Coaching* or at the unit solutions, which are found at the end of each unit. This will give you the most accurate assessment of your level of understanding.

5. Don't fret if you don't get all the answers correct. No one besides you will see your work for this self-study portion of the course. Learn from your errors and build on your successes. Use the self-study units as a learning tool to help you prepare for the Coaching Principles Test.

COACHING PRINCIPLES SELF-STUDY RESOURCES

You'll need two resources to complete the Coaching Principles self-study process:

- *Successful Coaching, Third Edition*
- *Coaching Principles Classroom Study Guide* (the book you are currently reading)

Successful Coaching, Third Edition

Eventually, you'll want to read *Successful Coaching* in its entirety. We recommend that you read each chapter before completing its related self-study unit. Everything you need to know to pass the Coaching Principles Test is in that book. Remember that the Coaching Principles Test is an open-book test. You'll want to be very familiar with *Successful Coaching* before taking the test.

Coaching Principles Classroom Study Guide

Completing self-study units 2 to 22 in this study guide will help you pass the Coaching Principles Test. Complete the units in order, and check your answers against the solutions given at the end of each unit. If you find that you did not answer correctly, go back to *Successful Coaching* to refresh your memory and to gain a better understanding of the subject matter. In unit 22 you'll learn the process and procedures for taking the Coaching Principles Test.

Good luck, and have fun learning!

Developing Your Coaching Philosophy

LEARNING OBJECTIVES

In this unit you will learn

- the value of a coaching philosophy and
- the importance of knowing who you are and what kind of coach you want to be.

WHAT TO READ

Read chapter 1, Developing Your Coaching Philosophy, in *Successful Coaching*.

ACTIVITY 2.1

Coach Self-Assessment Inventory

In the first unit of the classroom course—Introduction to Coaching Principles—you should have completed the Coach Self-Assessment Inventory. Now that you've finished the classroom portion of Coaching Principles, revisit the inventory and see what you've learned.

Instructions

1. Turn back to Activity 1.1, Coach Self-Assessment on page 5 in the *Coaching Principles Classroom Study Guide,* and rate yourself again on each item on the inventory.

2. Total your points for your new ratings, and compare them to your old ratings. Have you gotten stronger?

3. After you've completed the self-study and taken the course test, rate yourself a third time. And after you've completed the upcoming season, rate yourself again. Are you getting stronger?

ACTIVITY 2.2

What Is Character?

Russell Gough, in his 1998 book *Character Is Destiny,* suggested that, to assess our character, we think about what good or bad characteristics we would be likely to exhibit if we thought no one was watching.

How do you act when you think no one is watching? How do you act when only your athletes are watching?

Instructions

1. In the table that follows, rate yourself on a continuum for each of the pairs of characteristics. How do you think you rate on these when you are coaching?

2. Ask someone who has watched you coach to rate you on the same characteristics, someone you know will be fair but honest with you. If you disagree with some of the ratings, ask the person who rated you why he or she thinks that about you.

Characteristic	1	2	3	4	5	6	7	8	9	10	Characteristic
Kind											Unkind
Honest											Dishonest
Trustworthy											Untrustworthy
Respectful											Disrespectful
Loyal											Not loyal
Self-controlled											Not self-controlled
Responsible											Irresponsible

Determining Your Coaching Objectives

LEARNING OBJECTIVES

In this unit you will learn

- the three major objectives of sport,
- society's objectives for sport programs and the compatibility of your objectives with society's,
- the *Successful Coaching* perspective on winning as an objective in sport, and
- your personal objectives for coaching.

WHAT TO READ

Read chapter 2, Determining Your Coaching Objectives, in *Successful Coaching.*

ACTIVITY 3.1

Your Objectives for Coaching

In chapter 2 of *Successful Coaching,* Rainer Martens notes that developing your coaching philosophy requires that you consider two types of objectives for coaching: professional and personal. Your professional objectives are guided by the importance you place on helping your athletes develop, on helping them have fun, and on winning. Your personal objectives are guided by your personal reasons for coaching—for example, to be involved in a sport you like, to earn a living, or to help secure another job.

Chapter 2 invited you to assess Your Coaching Objectives (page 19 in *Successful Coaching*) and Personal Reasons for Coaching (page 27 in *Successful Coaching*). If you didn't complete these assessments, do so now.

Instructions

1. Complete Your Coaching Objectives and Personal Reasons for Coaching in chapter 2 of *Successful Coaching*.

ACTIVITY 3.2

Win-Centered Versus Athlete-Centered

No other decision you make about your role as coach will be as important as the one you make about the emphasis you give to winning. It will be a core component of your coaching philosophy.

Winning is an important objective to pursue. Athletes and coaches should try their best when they agree to compete in sport. But at what costs are you willing to pursue the goal of winning? Are you willing to risk your own health or the health of your athletes? Do you put winning ahead of your athletes' personal development, ahead of your family?

Consider this example: A former university swim coach observed that when he first started his career, he coached to enhance his own ego. He relished the power the position gave him, and when his authority was questioned, he took it as a personal affront. Coaching permitted him to continue to compete vicariously through his swimmers. The purpose of a meet was not to see who were the best swimmers; the purpose of a meet was to see who was the best coach.

Later in his career the coach changed. His coaching philosophy gradually shifted as he changed from being a win-centered coach to being an athlete-centered coach. No longer did his swimmers have to win races to be successful in his eyes, or for him to feel successful. The development of the athletes as swimmers and as people became the coach's new measurement of success. Helping his athletes develop self-discipline and autonomy, to be responsible for themselves, became more important to him than winning races.

As you know from reading *Successful Coaching,* the ASEP philosophy of Athletes First, Winning Second is an athlete-centered philosophy that places the highest regard on the people being coached, whereas a win-centered philosophy places the highest regard on the outcome of competition. These two objectives, although they may appear as dichotomies, actually fall on a continuum. The extreme athlete-centered coach would always consider what's best for the athletes first; winning is never given preference. On the other extreme of the continuum, winning is the ultimate objective; it's the reason for sport, and the win-centered coach will do what's best for the athletes only as long as doing so does not jeopardize winning. Athlete-centered coaches see the sport as existing for the athletes; win-centered coaches see the athletes as resources to achieve their objective of winning.

Where do you fall on this continuum?

Instructions

1. Think of some famous coaches and of some coaches you know personally (whether famous or not). Identify one coach you think falls on each point of the following athlete-centered/win-centered continuum, and write his or her name on the appropriate blank line.

2. Ask yourself where you are on this continuum, and mark that spot with an *N*—for *now*.

3. Ask yourself where you think you should be on this continuum, and mark that spot with an *F*—for *future*.

4. As you read the rest of *Successful Coaching* and complete the self-study, highlight (with a highlighter pen, a check mark, or an *F*) the key areas you need to learn more about so that you can move from where you are now to where you want to be in the future.

Athlete-Centered	1----------------2----------------3----------------4----------------5	**Win-Centered**

1. _____

2. _____

3. _____

4. _____

5. _____

Selecting Your Coaching Style

LEARNING OBJECTIVES

In this unit you will learn

- about three coaching styles and how those styles affect your athletes;
- what leadership is when coaching;
- how to develop your team culture;
- three other qualities of successful coaches—knowledge of the sport, motivation, and empathy; and
- a code of ethics to follow.

WHAT TO READ

Read chapter 3, Selecting Your Coaching Style, in *Successful Coaching*.

ACTIVITY 4.1

The Cooperative-Style Coach

Command-style coaches and submissive-style coaches not only create problems for themselves in practices, but also do little to promote their athletes' development. Good coaching calls for the appropriate use of a variety of approaches. Some situations require a coach to be more directive, and others demand that a coach be less directive. The cooperative-style coach seeks to involve athletes when it is appropriate, but also knows when to be more directive. By contrast, command-style coaches choose to use directive approaches much, if not all, of the time, and submissive-style coaches seldom provide leadership of any type.

Let's see how you could improve the coaching style of both a command-style coach and a submissive-style coach.

Instructions

1. Read the following scenarios.

2. For each scenario, identify suggestions you would make to help the coach improve the situation. One suggestion is provided to get you going. Base your suggestions on what you learned about cooperative-style coaches in chapter 3 of *Successful Coaching*.

3. Review your list of suggestions for both scenarios, and check the ones you've used in the past or would consider using in the future.

▶ *Scenario 1—Coach Neumann* -

Coach Neumann is ending her basketball practice with a bit of a rant: "We'll run this drill every day for the rest of the season if we have to. If you can't break down the defense, you can't win. Now hit the showers and come back tomorrow ready to make it work!"

Sarah and Lisa are on their way to the locker room. Sarah says, "She just has no clue. I mean, we aren't getting any better, but it's not like we're stupid or anything."

Lisa responds, "I know. If she'd just listen for a change. We want to get better. We're just so tired of that drill that nobody even cares anymore."

"No joke, Lisa," Sarah say. "I can't wait for this season to be over!"

COACH NEUMANN, I CAN HELP. WHY DON'T YOU . . .

1. *Ask the team captains (or the entire team) why they are having so much difficulty performing the drill.*

2. _____

_____

_____

3. _____

_____

_____

4. _____

_____

_____

▶ *Scenario 2—Coach Linn* -

Coach Linn sits on the bleachers, reading the newspaper. He looks at his watch and says, "All right. Let's call it a day. Same time tomorrow!"

Matt shakes his head as he turns to his doubles partner. "You know, I'm getting tired of getting killed every week. If Coach isn't going to teach us anything, why does he even bother?"

"I know it," replies Marcus. "And if those idiots don't stop hitting tennis balls into our court on purpose, I'm going to find a new use for my racket."

COACH LINN, I CAN HELP. WHY DON'T YOU . . .

1. *Identify specific reasons why your team "is getting killed" each week, and address these reasons during practice.*

2. _____

_____

_____

3. _____

_____

_____

4. _____

_____

_____

ACTIVITY 4.2

Evaluating Your Coaching Style

Which style best describes you: command, submissive, or cooperative? Although some coaches neatly fit into one of these three styles, many coaches tend to be dominant in one but possess some of the attributes of the other styles too.

Look at the following Coaching Style Evaluation figure. It depicts a somewhat simplistic view of the dynamics that occur between the athletes and their coach. The athletes can decide what they should do always, sometimes, or never. By the same token, the coach can direct what the athletes should do never, sometimes, or always. Consider how often you give your athletes opportunities to make decisions, as shown on the vertical axis. Then consider how directive you are, as shown on the horizontal axis.

Instructions

1. Place an *A* on the vertical axis that represents how often you give your athletes opportunities to make decisions, and draw a horizontal line from the *A* to the right, across the figure.

2. Place a *C* on the horizontal axis that represents how directive you are, and draw a vertical line from the *C* upward, across the figure.

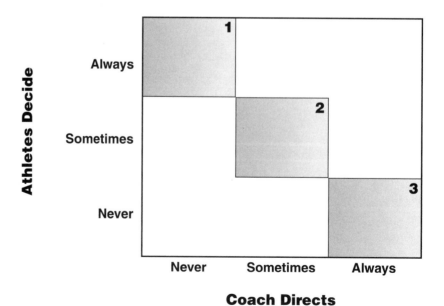

Coaching Style Evaluation

Your current coaching style is represented by the intersection of the two lines you drew.

- If the lines intersect in box 1, your primary coaching style is submissive.
- If the lines intersect in box 2, your primary coaching style is cooperative.
- If the lines intersect in box 3, your primary coaching style is command.
- If the lines intersect outside of the shaded boxes in the lower left portion of the figure, this indicates that you're seldom directing your athletes, and they're seldom making decisions. You need to consider who's leading your team.
- If the lines intersect outside of the shaded boxes in the upper right portion of the figure, this indicates that you're usually directing your athletes, and they're usually making decisions. You need to consider who's leading your team.

3. Now put an *X* on the figure that represents what you would like your coaching style to be in the future.
4. If the *X* is not at the intersection of the two lines you drew previously, list three things you think you need to do to move your style from what it is to what you would like it to be.

▶ *Things to Do to Move My Coaching Style* - - - - - - - - - - - - - - - -

1. _____

   _____

2. _____

   _____

3. _____

   _____

   _____

Coaching for Character

LEARNING OBJECTIVES

In this unit you will learn

- why character education is an essential duty of coaches,
- the definitions of character and sportsmanship, and
- how to coach to help your players develop good character.

WHAT TO READ

Read chapter 4, Coaching for Character, in *Successful Coaching*.

ACTIVITY 5.1

Athletes Character Code

By now—having completed the classroom course and read chapter 4—you've spent some important time thinking about character and how to help develop it in your athletes. One good place to start is to consider how your athletes rate on the six moral values that comprise the Athletes Character Code.

Instructions

1. There are two identical tables on the next page. The first one is for you to use to complete step 1 of this activity. Specifically, use this table to rate yourself on the six moral values that comprise the Athletes Character Code.

2. Make copies of the second table, one copy for every athlete you coach. Use these copies to rate your athletes on the six moral values that comprise the Athletes Character Code. Refer to these ratings throughout the season to help determine the character education you should provide for your athletes.

Athletes Character Code Rating

Your name: _____

Moral value	Very weak	Somewhat weak	Moderate	Somewhat strong	Very strong
Be Respectful					
Be Responsible					
Be Caring					
Be Honest					
Be Fair					
Be a Good Citizen					

Athletes Character Code Rating

Athlete name: _____

Moral value	Very weak	Somewhat weak	Moderate	Somewhat strong	Very strong
Be Respectful					
Be Responsible					
Be Caring					
Be Honest					
Be Fair					
Be a Good Citizen					

Additional comments or suggestions for this athlete (what would you like to see the athlete start doing, or do more of):

_____

_____

_____

ACTIVITY 5.2

Building a Team Culture

Chapter 4 discussed six strategies for teaching the principles embodied in the Athletes Character Code. The first strategy was creating a moral team environment, and one of the keys to accomplish this was building a team culture.

As the coach, you play a critical role in building a team culture that encourages character development. Chapter 4 included some characteristics of team culture that may reflect the role you're playing—whether that role is negative or positive. How you see yourself in terms of these characteristics is important information for you to consider.

Instructions

1. In the following table, rate how you influence your team's culture. For each pair of negative and positive influences, place an *X* in the cell that best represents what you do now, or, if you're not coaching now, where you expect to be when you start coaching.

Team Culture and Character Development

Negative influence	1	2	3	4	5	Positive influence
Overemphasis on winning						Athletes First, Winning Second emphasis
Ignoring or even rewarding unsportsmanlike behavior						Recognizing and rewarding sportsmanship
Demanding a period of "mourning" after losing						Helping athletes put losing into proper perspective
Dictating all team actions and discouraging questions and input from team members						Encouraging questions and sharing the decision making with the team
Being distant from players, their parents, and others involved with the team						Being appropriately warm, involved, and caring with all who are involved with the team
Showing favoritism toward the better players and picking on the weaker ones						Respecting all players and helping each to become a better player and person
Encouraging cutthroat competition within the team						Encouraging cooperation among teammates and respect for opponents within the competitive environment
Failing to develop traditions and rituals that encourage team spirit						Creating valued and enjoyable traditions and rituals in cooperation with team members

2. When you've completed the table, look at the *X*s, and ask yourself if this is the kind of coach you want to be. If not, consider how you might change your approach.

ACTIVITY 5.3

From Words to Actions

One of the things you've learned about developing the character of your athletes is that you need to explain and discuss moral behavior. One way to do this is to label behaviors so that your athletes know what moral behavior is. Although defining moral behavior is important, you must also translate the words into actions. One way to do so is to establish team rituals and routines that make practicing the Athletes Character Code fun and enjoyable.

Instructions

1. For each of the six moral values of the Athletes Character Code listed here, write down one ritual or routine you'd like your team to adopt to start putting the words into action.

Be Respectful: _____

_____

Be Responsible: _____

_____

Be Caring: _____

_____

Be Honest: _____

_____

Be Fair: _____

_____

Be a Good Citizen: _____

_____

Coaching Diverse Athletes

LEARNING OBJECTIVES

In this unit you will learn

- factors to consider in coaching athletes with differences related to maturation, culture, and gender;
- about some of your responsibilities regarding sexual harassment, coach–player sexual relationships, and homosexuality in sport; and
- factors to consider in coaching athletes with disabilities.

WHAT TO READ

Read chapter 5, Coaching Diverse Athletes, in *Successful Coaching*.

ACTIVITY 6.1

Coaching Diverse Athletes Quiz

This activity should give you a change of pace while it allows you to review what you've learned reading chapter 5.

Instructions

1. Complete the following quiz.
2. Compare your answers to the solutions at the end of this unit. Review chapter 5 if you find you do not agree with certain answers.

▶ Coaching Diverse Athletes Quiz -

1. Scientific evidence indicates that adolescents going through the growth spurt typically lack agility, balance, and coordination.

    a. True

    b. False

2. When a coach fails to consider maturational differences in her athletes, she increases the risk of injuries to her athletes, and she sets the stage for inequitable competition.

    a. True

    b. False

3. Between the ages of 16 and 21, the range of individual differences in physical structure is greater than it is at any other time in the human life span.

    a. True

    b. False

4. The fact that men are, on average, heavier and taller than women is a sex difference.

    a. True

    b. False

5. It is irresponsible for a coach to have sex with one of her mid-teens high school athletes, but it is not illegal.

    a. True

    b. False

6. If you coach an able-bodied team, you do not have to let anyone with a disability try out for the team.

    a. True

    b. False

7. It's reasonable to assume that the percentage of homosexuals participating in sports is around 10 percent.

    a. True

    b. False

8. Cultural diversity has little to do with racism, ethnic discrimination, religious intolerance, and social class prejudice.

    a. True

    b. False

9. During middle adolescence, most teenagers become more dependent on members of the opposite sex.

   a. True

   b. False

10. Typically, girls develop breasts and begin menstruating during early adolescence.

    a. True

    b. False

11. Referring to an athlete who is blind as "an athlete with a disability" is preferred over referring to the athlete as "a disabled athlete."

    a. True

    b. False

12. You should not permit racist or sexist behavior by your athletes even if it might be the result of cultural differences.

    a. True

    b. False

13. As you develop relationships with your athletes, close is good, but intimate is not.

    a. True

    b. False

14. Although any person has the right to play on recreational sport teams, every person does not have the legal right to play on elite sport teams.

    a. True

    b. False

15. Girls and boys complete most of their physical growth during middle adolescence.

    a. True

    b. False

16. During early adolescence, most teenagers become more dependent on members of the opposite sex.

    a. True

    b. False

17. Sexual harassment by coaches may be immoral, but it is not illegal.

    a. True

    b. False

18. Attention-deficit/hyperactivity disorder (ADHD) is a mental disability.

    a. True

    b. False

19. Maturational differences relate to physical differences, not to intellectual or social differences.

    a. True

    b. False

20. In spite of all the hype, studies show that the United States is really not becoming more culturally diverse.

    a. True

    b. False

21. Sensory impairments include amputations and spinal cord injuries.

    a. True

    b. False

22. Based on auto fatality statistics, and in spite of their poor judgment and impulsiveness, teens in middle adolescence do not tend to have higher auto accident rates.

    a. True

    b. False

23. You should match athletes by physical size and apparent physical maturity if your sport involves power, speed, and strength.

    a. True

    b. False

24. Sexual harassment can occur only between a coach and an athlete of the opposite sex.

    a. True

    b. False

25. Because of their growing independence, teens typically show less respect for others during their middle adolescent years.

    a. True

    b. False

26. In spite of Title IX, studies consistently show that participating in sports has an adverse effect on women's reproductive organs.

    a. True

    b. False

27. Even if caused by cultural influences, homophobia is still harmful.
    a. True
    b. False

28. Teens typically begin setting more personal goals during their late adolescent years.
    a. True
    b. False

29. Although you may need to touch an athlete to guide the athlete's movements to learn a skill, you should still apologize if you touch an inappropriate body part.
    a. True
    b. False

30. Because of their growing independence, teens typically seek less advice from adults during their late adolescent years.
    a. True
    b. False

Unit 6 Solutions

ACTIVITY 6.1

▶ *Coaching Diverse Athletes Quiz Answers* - - - - - - - - - - - - - - - - - -

1. False	16. False
2. True	17. False
3. False	18. True
4. True	19. False
5. False	20. False
6. False	21. False
7. True	22. False
8. False	23. True
9. True	24. False
10. True	25. False
11. True	26. False
12. True	27. True
13. True	28. True
14. True	29. True
15. True	30. False

Communicating With Your Athletes

LEARNING OBJECTIVES

In this unit you will learn

- the basics of the communication process,
- eight major communication problems common to the coaching profession, and
- how to improve your communication skills for six of these problems (the other two problems will be discussed in later units).

WHAT TO READ

Read chapter 6, Communicating With Your Athletes, in *Successful Coaching.*

ACTIVITY 7.1

Communication Skills To-Do List

By now you've completed unit 6, Communicating With Your Athletes, in the classroom course, and you helped identify communication tips for eight problem coaches. You've read chapter 6 in *Successful Coaching,* so you're armed with a lot of good information about communication skills and how to improve them.

Now it's time to help yourself. On the pages following the instructions, the critical communication skills you're now familiar with are listed in tables. Each set of skills includes a reference to the problem coach you helped in the classroom. Here's what you should do with these tables.

Instructions

1. Review the communication skills in the tables that begin on the next page, and for each skill, rate yourself as follows:

   a. If you're pretty good at the skill, put a plus sign (+) next to it.

   b. If you're not so good at the skill, put a minus sign (–) next to it.

2. For each skill that you rated with a minus sign, note some things you could do to improve this skill in the empty box to the right—the "Communication skills to-do list" box. For example, you might want to read more about the skill, take an effective communication course, practice using the skill with friends, and so on.

3. After you've completed your to-do list, prioritize your to-dos.

4. Start working on your top priority communication skill to-dos.

Critical communication skills	Communication skills to-do list
Developing credibility when you communicate (Coach Incredible NOT) • Become a cooperative-style coach. • Become knowledgeable about the sport or at least honest about whatever knowledge you possess. • Be reliable, fair, and consistent. • Follow through on what you say you'll do. • Express warmth, friendliness, acceptance, and empathy. • Be dynamic, spontaneous, and open. • Remain calm under pressure. • Use the positive approach.	
Communicating with a positive approach (Coach Naysayer NOT) • Provide honest, direct, and constructive messages. • Embrace an attitude in which you look to catch your athletes doing good or right, and then tell them they've done so. • Avoid sarcasm and put-downs, but at the same time don't sugarcoat athletes' behaviors by falsely putting a positive spin on them. • Emphasize what can be done, not what cannot be done, and avoid language that dwells on problems, but instead use language that focuses on solutions. • Seek to build character rather than destroy it.	

Critical communication skills	Communication skills to-do list
Sending messages high in information (The Judge NOT) • Provide athletes with specific information that helps them correct mistakes rather than general information that judges their performance. • Be certain you understand the reason for your athletes' actions before you judge their behavior. • Avoid making evaluative comments when athletes know they've made a mistake. • Focus your comments on the athletes' behaviors, not on them as people to avoid damaging their sense of self-worth.	
Communicating with consistency (Coach Fickle NOT) • Strive hard to be consistent in your verbal messages and to ensure that your nonverbal actions are consistent with your verbal messages. • When you promise to do something, be sure to follow through. • Avoid gossiping, and discourage your athletes from gossiping. • Develop a sense of trust with your athletes by being consistent and positive. Through trust you become a coach of character.	

Critical communication skills	Communication skills to-do list
Learning how to listen (Coach Glib NOT) • Show the person speaking to you that you're interested in listening and trying to understand. • Once someone has spoken to you, check that you understand what was said by paraphrasing the message, not only the content but also the emotion behind it. • Express empathy, not sympathy, by showing that you care and respect what the person speaking to you has to say.	
Improving your nonverbal communication (Coach Stone NOT) • Recognize how much of what you communicate is in the form of nonverbal messages. • Learn how to both send and receive messages by effectively using and reading body position, body motion, voice characteristics, and touching behaviors. • Remember that it's not so much what you say but what you do that influences your athletes.	

Critical communication skills	Communication skills to-do list
Using effective instructional communication (The Professor NOT) • Use language that your athletes will understand. Keep your vocabulary simple and straightforward. • Think through your demonstrations before you present them. Break skills down into a step-by-step process and then present them in an organized sequence. • Keep cues short and simple, such as "Stay on your man" or "Arms in the air." • Use analogies that your athletes can relate to. "It's like keeping a rudder steady on a plane" won't work very well because few of your athletes have piloted a plane.	
Applying the principles of reinforcement (Coach Skinner NOT) • Before the season begins, define for yourself what you will reward and how you'll reward your athletes. Stick to this plan during the season. • Develop team rules with your athletes so that they know what is expected and what the consequences will be if they misbehave. • When an athlete misbehaves, follow through with the consequence that is listed in your player handbook. • Don't let your mood dictate how you treat athletes. The athletes' performance and behavior should be what dictates your use of rewards and consequences. • Reward athletes only when they have earned it. • Use positive discipline, which uses instruction, training, and correction, rather than negative discipline, which uses punishment.	

Motivating Your Athletes

LEARNING OBJECTIVES

In this unit you will learn

- how you can help your athletes fulfill their needs to have fun and to feel worthy,
- how optimal arousal and flow are related to fun,
- how sports can threaten self-worth and what you can do to remove the threat,
- how you can motivate athletes by helping them focus not on winning but on achieving their own performance goals, and
- how to reduce anxiety and stress in your athletes and yourself.

WHAT TO READ

Read chapter 7, Motivating Your Athletes, in *Successful Coaching*.

ACTIVITY 8.1

Optimal Arousal

In unit 7 of the classroom course, your team completed the Optimal Arousal worksheet. You should have noted several good ideas that you can use to coach your athletes toward achieving "flow." Now is a good time to review the worksheet and the activity outcome at the end of the unit and consider which of these ideas you'll want to try.

Instructions

1. Refer to the Optimal Arousal worksheet in unit 7 in the classroom portion of the study guide, review the points you noted about what coaches can do to facilitate optimal arousal in their athletes, and check the ones you want to try.

2. Refer to the outcome of Activity 7.2 Go With the Flow at the end of unit 7, review the points noted about what coaches can do to facilitate optimal arousal in their athletes, and check the ones you want to try.

ACTIVITY 8.2

Messages

One of the things you've learned in the classroom portion of Coaching Principles and by reading chapters 6 and 7 in *Successful Coaching* is the importance of messages that athletes and coaches send and receive. A lot of these messages relate to motivation.

Another thing you've learned is that some athletes think like losers, and one of your responsibilities is to guide them into thinking like winners. That's what this activity is all about.

Instructions

1. Complete the following steps to develop some messages for one of your athletes who needs to start thinking like a winner.

▶ **Step 1: Think About an Athlete-** -

Think about an athlete you've coached, or plan to coach, or one you know (including yourself). This athlete should be a person who doesn't have fun playing your sport, doesn't feel worthy, and seems to think like a loser.

Write the athlete's name, sport, and position or event (if applicable) here:

_____

_____

NOTE: To make this a little easier, from here on, we'll use an example of an athlete named Sally.

▶ Step 2: Identify a Performance Goal -

As you've learned, one of the keys to motivating athletes is to guide them to focus on performance goals, not outcome goals. A performance goal should be realistically achievable; it should represent a personal best. Achieving a personal best is a good example of a "win." An example is to reduce Sally's 100-meter sprint time by 0.5 seconds

Think about your athlete, and write one performance goal for him or her here:

_____

_____

▶ Step 3: Identify the Skills Required to Achieve the Performance Goal - - -

Athletic performance involves performing a variety of skills or techniques in a certain sequence and at the right time. These skills or techniques are the parts that together constitute the performance.

For example, to reduce Sally's 100-meter time, Sally may need to work on these skills:

- Skill A: Run on the balls of the feet with a slight forward incline of the upper body.
- Skill B: Keep the arms bent at a 90-degree angle, and swing parallel with running direction.
- Skill C: Finish strongly by leading with the chest and sprinting through the finish.

For your athlete's performance goal, write three skills required to achieve this goal here:

Skill A:

_____

_____

Skill B:

_____

_____

Skill C:

_____

_____

▶ Step 4: Identify the Behaviors and Thoughts That Reflect Your Athlete's "Not Fun," "Not Worthy," and "Loser" Attitudes - - - - - - - - -

Now that you know what you want your athlete to achieve, let's consider how you're going to motivate her or him to achieve it. In unit 7 of the classroom course, you completed the Winners and Losers worksheet by listing the attributes of athletes who think like winners and those of athletes who think like losers. The outcome for this activity is included in the Messages table on the last page of this unit (with a few changes). On this table, do the following:

- Think about your athlete, review the table, and in column 2, the "Athletes Who Think Like Losers . . ." column, check the attributes that describe your athlete.
- Add additional attributes that apply to your athlete in the boxes provided at the end of column 2.
- If you added any "loser" attributes for your athlete, add the corresponding "winner" attribute in column 1.
- Write your athlete's name at the top of column 3. Then, for each of the attributes you checked or entered in column 2, write what you think your athlete is thinking about the performance goal. For example, one of the skills Sally needs to work on is keeping her arms bent at a 90-degree angle. If Sally thinks like a loser, she's probably thinking, "I just can't run with my arms at a 90-degree angle. I'll never be able to do it."

▶ Step 5: Delivering Your Messages -

As the coach, your objective should be to transform your athlete's "loser" thoughts about the performance goal (the thoughts you noted in column 3) to "winner" thoughts (those listed in column 1). You want your athlete to start thinking like a winner while working on his or her performance goal.

For example, to counteract Sally's thinking that she's unable to run with her arms at a 90-degree angle, you'd want to say something like, "Sally, you can do it! Last week you ran with your arms almost straight, but this week you're bending your arms, and you're getting closer to the 90 degrees. Your hard work is paying off!"

This message combines some key performance information ("You're bending your arms . . . closer to 90 degrees") with some key motivational information ("Your hard work is paying off"). This is the kind of information you need to deliver to your athlete.

Now for the hard part of this activity: developing your messages. In the Messages table, do the following:

- Write your athlete's name at the top of column 4.

- For each "loser" thought you wrote in column 3, write one message in column 4 you'd like to give for one of the skills you identified. Include performance and motivational information in the message. Your message should focus on helping the athlete to think like a winner.

- Try these messages out and see how they work.

Messages

Athletes who think like winners . . .	Athletes who think like losers . . .	What _____ is thinking	My messages for _____
Blame failures on insufficient effort, not on insufficient ability; they believe they need to try harder.	Attribute failures to lack of ability.		
Take credit for their successes; accept responsibility for their failures.	Blame themselves for their failures, yet take little or no credit for their successes.		
Believe that winning is a consequence of their ability.	Believe that no matter how hard they try, the outcome will always be the same: failure.		
Believe that occasional failures are inevitable; are willing to take reasonable risks to achieve success.	Reject success because they fear they will be expected to succeed again.		
Direct their energies to the challenges of sport rather than to worry and self-doubt.	Play for extrinsic rewards rather than to attain personal goals.		

Managing Your Athletes' Behavior

LEARNING OBJECTIVES

In this unit you will learn

- what positive discipline is,
- why positive discipline is more effective than negative discipline,
- the six building blocks of preventive discipline, and
- the positive discipline guidelines for corrective discipline.

WHAT TO READ

Read chapter 8, Managing Your Athletes' Behavior, in *Successful Coaching*.

ACTIVITY 9.1

Six Steps of Preventive Discipline

Chapter 8 in *Successful Coaching* described six steps to preventing discipline problems. Let's see how good you are at using these steps.

Instructions

1. Rate yourself on each of these steps.

▶ **Step 1: Create the Right Team Culture** - - - - - - - - - - - - - - - - - - -

Creating a positive team culture by communicating your care for your athletes, providing them with a physically and psychologically safe environment, and treating them with dignity and respect and expecting them to reciprocate.

Excellent - - - - - Good - - - - - Fair - - - - - Marginal - - - - - Poor

▶ **Step 2: Hold Team Meetings** -

Conducting effective team meetings to help educate your athletes, providing them with opportunities to share in team decision making, and building team spirit.

Excellent - - - - - Good - - - - - Fair - - - - - Marginal - - - - - Poor

▶ **Step 3: Develop Team Rules** -

Developing a good set of team rules and consequences; discussing and sharing them with your athletes; and applying the consequences of broken rules consistently, fairly, and in a respectful manner.

Excellent - - - - - Good - - - - - Fair - - - - - Marginal - - - - - Poor

▶ **Step 4: Create Team Routines** -

Creating team routines, and using them to provide your players with directions about what they should do in certain situations.

Excellent - - - - - Good - - - - - Fair - - - - - Marginal - - - - - Poor

▶ *Step 5: Conduct Exciting Practices* -

Making practices exciting, interesting, and fun for your players so that they are active and motivated to participate.

Excellent - - - - - Good - - - - - Fair - - - - - Marginal - - - - - Poor

▶ *Step 6: Catch Them Doing Good* -

Catching your players doing good; providing them with positive reinforcement for skillful play and positive behaviors.

Excellent - - - - - Good - - - - - Fair - - - - - Marginal - - - - - Poor

ACTIVITY 9.2

Team Rules

Chapter 8 in *Successful Coaching* devoted a lot of attention to the importance of team rules. It discussed guidelines for creating rules, consequences for rule violations, and the importance of applying the rules consistently and fairly. It also made the point that you should strongly consider developing your team rules with input from your athletes.

Before you get your team involved, however, you should think through the kinds of rules you want to include, and you should consider the consequences for breaking these rules. That's the purpose of this activity. Chapter 8 included an outline of rules that you will likely want to address, which are based on the six moral values presented in the Athletes Character Code. This outline is included here. Use it to start developing your team rules.

Instructions

1. Start to develop your team rules using the following outline.

▶ *Rules About Being Respectful* -

Profanity

Rule: _____

Consequences

First incident: _____

Second incident: _____

Third incident: _____

Fighting

Rule: _____

Consequences

First incident: _____

Second incident: _____

Third incident: _____

Hazing

Rule: _____

Consequences

First incident: _____

Second incident: _____

Third incident: _____

Interacting with officials and opposing players

Rule: _____

Consequences

First incident: _____

Second incident: _____

Third incident: _____

Destroying property

Rule: _____

Consequences

First incident: _____

Second incident: _____

Third incident: _____

Sexual misconduct

Rule: _____

Consequences

First incident: _____

Second incident: _____

Third incident: _____

Substance abuse

Rule: _____

Consequences

First incident: _____

Second incident: _____

Third incident: _____

▶ *Rules About Being Responsible* -

Attendance and promptness

Rule: _____

Consequences

First incident: _____

Second incident: _____

Third incident: _____

Dress when practicing, competing, and traveling

Rule: _____

Consequences

First incident: _____

Second incident: _____

Third incident: _____

Insubordination (following instructions; doing what you're suppose to do)

Rule: _____

Consequences

First incident: _____

Second incident: _____

Third incident: _____

Self-discipline

Rule: _____

Consequences

First incident: _____

Second incident: _____

Third incident: _____

Academic performance

Rule: _____

Consequences

First incident: _____

Second incident: _____

Third incident: _____

Curfews

Rule: _____

Consequences

First incident: _____

Second incident: _____

Third incident: _____

Travel policies

Rule: _____

Consequences

First incident: _____

Second incident: _____

Third incident: _____

▶ *Rules About Caring* -

Respecting others

Rule: _____

Consequences

    First incident: _____

    Second incident: _____

    Third incident: _____

Helping your teammates

Rule: _____

Consequences

    First incident: _____

    Second incident: _____

    Third incident: _____

Following safety guidelines

Rule: _____

Consequences

    First incident: _____

    Second incident: _____

    Third incident: _____

▶ *Rules About Being Honest* -

Stealing

Rule: _____

Consequences

    First incident: _____

    Second incident: _____

    Third incident: _____

Cheating

Rule: _____

Consequences

First incident: _____

Second incident: _____

Third incident: _____

Lying

Rule: _____

Consequences

First incident: _____

Second incident: _____

Third incident: _____

▶ Rules About Being Fair- -

Complying with sportsmanship guidelines

Rule: _____

Consequences

First incident: _____

Second incident: _____

Third incident: _____

Blaming others

Rule: _____

Consequences

First incident: _____

Second incident: _____

Third incident: _____

Taking advantage of others

Rule: _____

Consequences

First incident: _____

Second incident: _____

Third incident: _____

Criteria for awards

NOTE: Name the awards your athletes can earn, and write the criteria for earning each award after its name.

Award 1: _____

Award 2: _____

Award 3: _____

▶ *Rules About Being A Good Citizen-* - - - - - - - - - - - - - - - - - - -

Being cooperative

Rule: _____

Consequences

First incident: _____

Second incident: _____

Third incident: _____

Obeying laws and rules

Rule: _____

Consequences

First incident: _____

Second incident: _____

Third incident: _____

Respecting authority

Rule: _____

Consequences

First incident: _____

Second incident: _____

Third incident: _____

Coaching the Games Approach Way

LEARNING OBJECTIVES

In this unit you will learn

- what technical and tactical skills are,
- the limitations of the traditional approach,
- what the games approach is all about,
- how to teach through the games approach, and
- how to make the games approach work for you.

WHAT TO READ

Read chapter 9, Coaching the Games Approach Way, in *Successful Coaching*.

ACTIVITY 10.1

Assessing Your Technical and Tactical Skill Knowledge

Starting in this unit and continuing through unit 13, you will develop a practice plan for one practice session. You'll make decisions about your practice plan starting later in this unit, and you will refine these decisions as you learn more over the next three units.

To begin, though, let's revisit a coach assessment that was included in two sections in chapter 9 of *Successful Coaching*. As you know, part of being a successful coach is being a great teacher of technical and tactical skills. Use the following assessment to identify your strengths and weaknesses in these areas. If you identify a weakness, take steps to become a better technical and tactical coach.

Instructions

1. Complete the following assessment.

▶ *Technical and Tactical Skill Knowledge Assessment* - - - - - - - - - - - - -

1. How knowledgeable are you about how to perform all of the technical skills of your sport?

| 1 | ——— | 2 | ——— | 3| ——— | 4 | ——— | 5 |
Weak   Strong

2. How skillful are you at teaching technical skills to your players? Do you know how to break down the skills into the appropriate steps to optimize learning them, and how to guide your players in putting those steps together again to execute the whole skill?

| 1 | ——— | 2 | ——— | 3| ——— | 4 | ——— | 5 |
Weak   Strong

3. How good are you at observing technique, understanding the cause of incorrect execution, and providing cues to your players to correct errors?

| 1 | ——— | 2 | ——— | 3| ——— | 4 | ——— | 5 |
Weak   Strong

4. How knowledgeable are you about the biomechanics of your sport—the science that studies the principles of movement in sport?

| 1 | ——— | 2 | ——— | 3| ——— | 4 | ——— | 5 |
Weak   Strong

5. How competent are you at reading the play, from the little cues from individual players to the patterns of team play?

| 1 | ——— | 2 | ——— | 3| ——— | 4 | ——— | 5 |
Weak   Strong

6. How skillful are you at teaching your players to read the play?

| 1 | ——— | 2 | ——— | 3| ——— | 4 | ——— | 5 |
Weak   Strong

7. How capable are you of making appropriate tactical decisions?

| 1 | ——— | 2 | ——— | 3| ——— | 4 | ——— | 5 |
Weak   Strong

8. How skillful are you at teaching tactical decision making to your players?

| 1 | ——— | 2 | ——— | 3| ——— | 4 | ——— | 5 |
Weak   Strong

9. To what extent do you plan practices to teach decision making so that your athletes can develop their tactical skills?

| 1 | ——— | 2 | ——— | 3| ——— | 4 | ——— | 5 |
Weak   Strong

ACTIVITY 10.2

Practice Planning, Part I: Who (Athletes) Will Learn to Do What (Skills)

Now let's turn to the first part of the practice planning activity. Practice planning includes six steps.

- Step 1: Identify the Skills Your Athletes Need
- Step 2: Know Your Athletes
- Step 3: Analyze Your Situation
- Step 4: Establish Priorities
- Step 5: Select the Methods for Teaching
- Step 6: Plan Practices

In this part of the activity, you will work on step 1 of practice planning. You'll revisit some of this information in later units.

Instructions

1. Provide the information requested.

Identify your team (school and sport): _____

_____.

Describe your athletes (age, sex, experience in sport, and so

forth): _____

_____.

2. In the form that starts on page 217, in the first column:
   - Write in the five critical technical skills (techniques) and five critical tactics required for your sport.
   - Identify the critical physical training, mental, communication, and character skills required for your sport by checking all that apply.
   - For now, disregard the other columns.

Identifying and Evaluating the Skills You'll Teach

Step 1: Identify the skills you'll teach	Step 2: Identify essential skills to evaluate, and rate your athletes on each essential skill		Step 4: Identify the teaching priorities for each skill, rate your athletes' readiness to learn the skill, and prioritize each skill		
	Evaluate?	Skill rating	Teaching priorities Must Should Could	Readiness to learn	Priority rating
Technical skills					
	Yes No	1 2 3 4 5	M S C	Yes No	A B C
	Yes No	1 2 3 4 5	M S C	Yes No	A B C
	Yes No	1 2 3 4 5	M S C	Yes No	A B C
	Yes No	1 2 3 4 5	M S C	Yes No	A B C
	Yes No	1 2 3 4 5	M S C	Yes No	A B C
Tactical skills					
	Yes No	1 2 3 4 5	M S C	Yes No	A B C
	Yes No	1 2 3 4 5	M S C	Yes No	A B C
	Yes No	1 2 3 4 5	M S C	Yes No	A B C
	Yes No	1 2 3 4 5	M S C	Yes No	A B C
	Yes No	1 2 3 4 5	M S C	Yes No	A B C
Physical training skills					
Strength	Yes No	1 2 3 4 5	M S C	Yes No	A B C
Speed	Yes No	1 2 3 4 5	M S C	Yes No	A B C
Power	Yes No	1 2 3 4 5	M S C	Yes No	A B C
Endurance	Yes No	1 2 3 4 5	M S C	Yes No	A B C
Flexibility	Yes No	1 2 3 4 5	M S C	Yes No	A B C
Quickness	Yes No	1 2 3 4 5	M S C	Yes No	A B C
Balance	Yes No	1 2 3 4 5	M S C	Yes No	A B C
Agility	Yes No	1 2 3 4 5	M S C	Yes No	A B C
Other	Yes No	1 2 3 4 5	M S C	Yes No	A B C

(continued)

Identifying and Evaluating the Skills You'll Teach (continued)

Step 1: Identify the skills you'll teach	Step 2: Identify essential skills to evaluate, and rate your athletes on each essential skill		Step 4: Identify the teaching priorities for each skill, rate your athletes' readiness to learn the skill, and prioritize each skill		
	Evaluate?	Skill rating	Teaching priorities Must Should Could	Readiness to learn	Priority rating
Mental skills					
Emotional control—anxiety	Yes No	1 2 3 4 5	M S C	Yes No	A B C
Emotional control—anger	Yes No	1 2 3 4 5	M S C	Yes No	A B C
Self-confidence	Yes No	1 2 3 4 5	M S C	Yes No	A B C
Motivation to achieve	Yes No	1 2 3 4 5	M S C	Yes No	A B C
Ability to concentrate	Yes No	1 2 3 4 5	M S C	Yes No	A B C
Other	Yes No	1 2 3 4 5	M S C	Yes No	A B C
Communication skills					
Sends positive messages	Yes No	1 2 3 4 5	M S C	Yes No	A B C
Sends accurate messages	Yes No	1 2 3 4 5	M S C	Yes No	A B C
Listens to messages	Yes No	1 2 3 4 5	M S C	Yes No	A B C
Understands messages	Yes No	1 2 3 4 5	M S C	Yes No	A B C
Receives constructive criticism	Yes No	1 2 3 4 5	M S C	Yes No	A B C
Receives praise and recognition	Yes No	1 2 3 4 5	M S C	Yes No	A B C
Credibility with teammates	Yes No	1 2 3 4 5	M S C	Yes No	A B C
Credibility with coaches	Yes No	1 2 3 4 5	M S C	Yes No	A B C
Character skills					
Trustworthiness	Yes No	1 2 3 4 5	M S C	Yes No	A B C
Respect	Yes No	1 2 3 4 5	M S C	Yes No	A B C
Responsibility	Yes No	1 2 3 4 5	M S C	Yes No	A B C
Fairness	Yes No	1 2 3 4 5	M S C	Yes No	A B C
Caring	Yes No	1 2 3 4 5	M S C	Yes No	A B C
Citizenship	Yes No	1 2 3 4 5	M S C	Yes No	A B C

Teaching Technical Skills

LEARNING OBJECTIVES

In this unit you will learn

- how athletes learn technical skills by developing motor programs,
- the three stages of learning technical skills and your coaching role when players are in each of these stages,
- the four steps to teaching technical skills effectively, and
- a set of principles for conducting better practices.

WHAT TO READ

Read chapter 10, Teaching Technical Skills, in *Successful Coaching*.

ACTIVITY 11.1

Teaching Evaluation Scale

As you know, coaching is about teaching. It's also about learning. Your athletes will learn to be better at what they do, and so will you.

One way to get better as a coach is to evaluate how you did after every practice. We'll discuss this more in unit 13. As you determine how you'll teach a technical skill—which is the primary activity in this unit—you should think through some of the characteristics of a good teacher, and a good coach. Spending a few minutes thinking about the Teaching Evaluation Scale in this unit will help.

The scale is designed to help you evaluate how well you apply some of the things you've learned in the Coaching Principles course. One way to use it is to sit down immediately after practice and fill it out yourself. Even better is to have another person who coaches complete it after observing you in a practice situation. Discuss the results with your evaluator and use them as a guide to improve your teaching.

Instructions

1. Think about the last practice you conducted, and rate how well you did using the Teaching Evaluation Scale that follows these instructions. If you haven't taught a sport skill yet, review the scale anyway, and rate how well you think you'll do.

2. Place a check mark in the appropriate column to the right of each phrase, using this scale: 1 = always; 2 = usually; 3 = sometimes; 4 = never; 5 = not applicable to this practice.

Teaching Evaluation Scale

	Rating scale				
	1	2	3	4	5
Introducing the skill					
Identifies the skill to be taught					
Indicates why the skill is important to learn					
Introduces the skill in less than 3 minutes					
Is enthusiastic in actions and words					
Avoids sarcasm, annoying mannerisms, and abusive language					
Uses terminology athletes can understand					
Speaks clearly					
Faces the team when speaking to them, and makes good eye contact					
Controls temper					
Models poise when dealing with inattentive athletes					
Ensures that all can see and hear the demonstration					
Demonstrating and explaining the skill					
Directs the team's attention to the demonstration					
Explains how the demonstration will proceed					
Demonstrates the whole skill as it would be performed in competition					
Demonstrates skillfully					
Demonstrates the skill several times					
Demonstrates the skill so that athletes can view it from different angles					

	Rating scale				
	1	**2**	**3**	**4**	**5**
Demonstrates the skill slower if necessary					
Explains the major sequence of actions that comprise the skill when it is demonstrated slowly					
Points out the most relevant cues					
Keeps explanations simple and brief					
Demonstrates parts of the skill when appropriate					
Briefly demonstrates or explains the similarities between skills					
Repeats questions asked and answers relevant questions so all can hear					
Practicing the skill					
Begins skill practice as soon as possible after the demonstration					
Uses the games approach effectively					
Uses drills that emphasize the skill being taught					
Eliminates or minimizes any danger involved in performing the skill					
Creates an atmosphere to minimize fear of failure					
Is in control of the team during practice					
Checks to be certain all are proceeding through the drill correctly					
Repeats the demonstration and explanation if the team cannot perform the skill effectively					
Uses key terms step-by-step if the team cannot perform the skill effectively					
Checks after each step to be sure that everyone is performing correctly when initial teaching has been unsuccessful					
Repeats questions asked and answers relevant questions so all can hear					
Divides the skill into parts when athletes have difficulty mastering the whole skill					
Stops practice and corrects common errors when necessary					
Presents brief explanations and demonstrations of errors and their corrections when confronted with common errors					
Providing feedback to correct errors					
Observes and evaluates performance					
Compliments efforts and parts of the skill that were performed correctly					
Corrects one error at a time					
Gives specific positive feedback					
Gives specific negative feedback					
Uses visual feedback of errors and corrections					
Makes certain athletes understand the information given					
Shows patience with athletes					
Encourages athletes to continue to practice and improve					

ACTIVITY 11.2

Practice Planning, Part II: What (Technical Skills) Will be Taught How (Teaching Methods)

In this activity you'll continue with your practice plan. You'll work on these practice planning steps:

- Step 1: Identify the Skills Your Athletes Need
- Step 5: Select the Methods for Teaching

You've already done a similar activity in the classroom. Don't reuse the skill you used in the classroom. Try a new skill.

Instructions

1. Provide the information requested.

▶ **Technical Skills Planning Sheet-** -

1. Choose one skill from the list of technical skills for your sport that you developed in unit 10 in the classroom course.

_____

2. Determine whether you will teach the whole skill, or break it into parts and teach the parts. If you decide to break it into parts, describe the parts here.

_____

_____

_____

_____

3. Determine the overall approach you will use to teach the skills. Will you use the traditional approach, the games approach, or both? Whichever you choose, describe what your approach will look like—what drills you will use or what games you might play.

_____

_____

_____

_____

4. Determine teaching tips to use while teaching during the mental stage of learning the skill, and list those here.

_____

_____

_____

_____

5. Determine teaching tips to use while teaching during the practice stage of learning the skill, and list those here.

_____

_____

_____

_____

6. Identify the types of errors you expect to see, and explain the feedback approaches you'll use for those errors.

_____

_____

_____

_____

7. Outline the technical skills practice plan for these steps:

Step 1: Introduce the skill

_____

_____

_____

Step 2: Demonstrate and explain the skill

_____

_____

_____

Step 3: Have the athletes practice the skill

_____

_____

_____

Teaching Tactical Skills

LEARNING OBJECTIVES

In this unit you will learn

- what tactics and tactical skills are,
- what's involved in "reading the situation" during play,
- what knowledge your athletes need to make good tactical decisions,
- factors that influence tactical decision making, and
- how to teach tactical skills.

WHAT TO READ

Read chapter 11, Teaching Tactical Skills, in *Successful Coaching*.

ACTIVITY 12.1

Evaluating Your Tactical Skills

It's widely known that in practices coaches give far greater emphasis to technical skill development and physical training than they do to tactical skill development. In chapter 11 you learned the importance of teaching tactical skills and what is involved in doing so. Unlike knowledge about technical skills and physical training, knowledge about tactical skills is not readily available. So to help you become a better tactical skill coach, let's begin by assessing your own tactical skills as a player and coach.

Instructions

1. Rate yourself as a player and coach on the 1 to 5 scale in the table on the next page for each of the three elements of tactical skills.

Rating Yourself

Tactical skill	... As a player					... As a coach				
Ability to read the play	1 Low	2	3	4	5 High	1 Low	2	3	4	5 High
Knowledge to make appropriate tactical decisions	1 Low	2	3	4	5 High	1 Low	2	3	4	5 High
Decision-making skill during the contest	1 Low	2	3	4	5 High	1 Low	2	3	4	5 High

ACTIVITY 12.2

Tactical Skill Development Plan for Coaches

Some tactical decisions only players can make, although some coaches try to make those decisions themselves, usually doing more harm than good. The tactical decisions that coaches usually make are related to team tactics rather than individual tactics. How much do you know about team tactics?

Instructions

1. Describe the five most important tactical decisions that you must make as a coach.
2. Identify the cues that you must attend to in those situations to indicate a course of action.
3. Explain the tactical options in those situations.

▶ *Tactical Decisions* -

TACTICAL DECISION 1

Decision: _____

Cues: _____

_____

Options: _____

_____

TACTICAL DECISION 2

Decision: _____

Cues: _____

_____

Options: _____

_____

TACTICAL DECISION 3

Decision: _____

Cues: _____

_____

Options: _____

_____

TACTICAL DECISION 4

Decision: _____

Cues: _____

_____

Options: _____

_____

TACTICAL DECISION 5

Decision: _____

Cues: _____

_____

Options: _____

_____

ACTIVITY 12.3

Practice Planning, Part III: What (Tactical Skill) Will be Taught How (Teaching Methods)

In this activity you'll continue with your practice plan. You'll work on these practice planning steps:

- Step 1: Identify the Skills Your Athletes Need
- Step 5: Select the Methods for Teaching

You've already done a similar activity in the classroom. Don't reuse the tactical skill you used in the classroom. Try a new skill.

Instructions

1. Provide the information requested.

▶ *Tactical Skills Planning Sheet* -

1. Choose one skill from the list of tactical skills for your sport that you developed in unit 10 in the classroom course.

_____

2. What tactical decisions do your players need to make to perform the tactical skill?

_____

_____

_____

3. What knowledge do your athletes need to decide when to use the tactical skill?

_____

_____

_____

_____

4. Given a situation in which your athletes might use this tactical skill, what cues should your athletes attend to? What cues should they not attend to? List both here.

_____

_____

5. What tactical options, guidelines, or rules should your players follow to use the tactical skill appropriately?

_____

_____

6. Design one practice game that would give your athletes the opportunity to work on reading the situation and selecting the appropriate tactic.

_____

_____

7. Identify the types of errors you expect to see while your athletes are learning this tactical skill, and explain the feedback approaches you'll use for those errors.

_____

_____

_____

8. Outline the tactical skill practice plan according to these methods:

Method 1: Teach the tactics in whole, then the parts.

_____

Method 2: Have players observe decision making in others.

_____

Method 3: Have players observe themselves.

_____

Method 4: Vary practices.

_____

Planning for Teaching

LEARNING OBJECTIVES

In this unit you will learn

- how to develop instructional plans for the season and
- how to prepare instructional plans for each practice.

WHAT TO READ

Read chapter 12, Planning for Teaching, in *Successful Coaching*.

ACTIVITY 13.1

Coaching Time Allotted to Six Major Skills

Take a moment to reflect on how your team spends its practice time.

Instructions

1. For each skill category listed in the following table, indicate the percent of practice time devoted to it over the course of the season, first for what you've done in the past, and second for what you plan to do in the future.

Percentages of How Practice Time Is Spent

Skill category	% of time for past seasons	% of time for future seasons
Technical		
Tactical		
Physical training		
Mental		
Communication		
Character		
Sum to 100%		

ACTIVITY 13.2

Identifying and Evaluating the Skills You'll Teach

In unit 10 you completed the first column of the form Identifying and Evaluating the Skills You'll Teach. When you start to apply what you've learned in the classroom and from reading chapter 12 of *Successful Coaching,* you should start to see how useful this form can be.

The purpose of the form is to help you complete these steps in practice planning:

- Step 1: Identify the Skills Your Athletes Need
- Step 2: Know Your Athletes
- Step 4: Establish Priorities

You would complete the form during the preseason, as follows:

- Step 1: Identify the skills you'll teach. You practiced doing this in unit 10 for the six constellations of skills included in the form. Your technical and tactical skills lists could be very long, depending on your sport. Initially, you can use the other constellations of skills listed, but if you have the knowledge, or when you learn more, replace these with more specific skills for your sport.

- Step 2: Identify essential skills to evaluate, and rate your athletes on each essential skill. For each skill you listed in step 1, determine whether you will evaluate your athletes on this skill in the preseason, and if you do, rate their skill levels from weak to strong.

- Step 4: Identify the teaching priorities for each skill, rate your athletes' readiness to learn the skill, and prioritize each skill.

  - In the "Teaching priorities" column, if the skill *must* be taught, circle "M." If the skill *should* be taught, circle "S." If the skill *could* be taught, circle "C."

  - In the "Readiness to learn" column, and based on your preseason evaluations, circle "Yes" if you think the majority of your athletes are ready to learn the skill, and circle "No" if they are not.

  - In the "Priority rating" column, and for the skills that your athletes are ready to learn, rate the skills that *must* be taught an "A," rate the skills that *should* be taught a "B," and rate the skills that *could* be taught a "C." Typically, "A" skills are prerequisites for learning "B" skills, and "A" and "B" skills are prerequisites for learning "C" skills.

Identifying and Evaluating the Skills You'll Teach

Step 1: Identify the skills you'll teach	Step 2: Identify essential skills to evaluate, and rate your athletes on each essential skill		Step 4: Identify the teaching priorities for each skill, rate your athletes' readiness to learn the skill, and prioritize each skill		
	Evaluate?	Skill rating	Teaching priorities Must Should Could	Readiness to learn	Priority rating
Technical skills					
	Yes No	1 2 3 4 5	M S C	Yes No	A B C
	Yes No	1 2 3 4 5	M S C	Yes No	A B C
	Yes No	1 2 3 4 5	M S C	Yes No	A B C
	Yes No	1 2 3 4 5	M S C	Yes No	A B C
	Yes No	1 2 3 4 5	M S C	Yes No	A B C
Tactical skills					
	Yes No	1 2 3 4 5	M S C	Yes No	A B C
	Yes No	1 2 3 4 5	M S C	Yes No	A B C
	Yes No	1 2 3 4 5	M S C	Yes No	A B C
	Yes No	1 2 3 4 5	M S C	Yes No	A B C
	Yes No	1 2 3 4 5	M S C	Yes No	A B C
Physical training skills					
Strength	Yes No	1 2 3 4 5	M S C	Yes No	A B C
Speed	Yes No	1 2 3 4 5	M S C	Yes No	A B C
Power	Yes No	1 2 3 4 5	M S C	Yes No	A B C
Endurance	Yes No	1 2 3 4 5	M S C	Yes No	A B C
Flexibility	Yes No	1 2 3 4 5	M S C	Yes No	A B C
Quickness	Yes No	1 2 3 4 5	M S C	Yes No	A B C
Balance	Yes No	1 2 3 4 5	M S C	Yes No	A B C
Agility	Yes No	1 2 3 4 5	M S C	Yes No	A B C
Other	Yes No	1 2 3 4 5	M S C	Yes No	A B C

(continued)

Identifying and Evaluating the Skills You'll Teach *(continued)*

Step 1: Identify the skills you'll teach	Step 2: Identify essential skills to evaluate, and rate your athletes on each essential skill							Step 4: Identify the teaching priorities for each skill, rate your athletes' readiness to learn the skill, and prioritize each skill					
	Evaluate?		Skill rating					Teaching priorities Must Should Could			Readiness to learn		Priority rating
Mental skills													
Emotional control—anxiety	Yes	No	1	2	3	4	5	M	S	C	Yes	No	A B C
Emotional control—anger	Yes	No	1	2	3	4	5	M	S	C	Yes	No	A B C
Self-confidence	Yes	No	1	2	3	4	5	M	S	C	Yes	No	A B C
Motivation to achieve	Yes	No	1	2	3	4	5	M	S	C	Yes	No	A B C
Ability to concentrate	Yes	No	1	2	3	4	5	M	S	C	Yes	No	A B C
Other	Yes	No	1	2	3	4	5	M	S	C	Yes	No	A B C
Communication skills													
Sends positive messages	Yes	No	1	2	3	4	5	M	S	C	Yes	No	A B C
Sends accurate messages	Yes	No	1	2	3	4	5	M	S	C	Yes	No	A B C
Listens to messages	Yes	No	1	2	3	4	5	M	S	C	Yes	No	A B C
Understands messages	Yes	No	1	2	3	4	5	M	S	C	Yes	No	A B C
Receives constructive criticism	Yes	No	1	2	3	4	5	M	S	C	Yes	No	A B C
Receives praise and recognition	Yes	No	1	2	3	4	5	M	S	C	Yes	No	A B C
Credibility with teammates	Yes	No	1	2	3	4	5	M	S	C	Yes	No	A B C
Credibility with coaches	Yes	No	1	2	3	4	5	M	S	C	Yes	No	A B C
Character skills													
Trustworthiness	Yes	No	1	2	3	4	5	M	S	C	Yes	No	A B C
Respect	Yes	No	1	2	3	4	5	M	S	C	Yes	No	A B C
Responsibility	Yes	No	1	2	3	4	5	M	S	C	Yes	No	A B C
Fairness	Yes	No	1	2	3	4	5	M	S	C	Yes	No	A B C
Caring	Yes	No	1	2	3	4	5	M	S	C	Yes	No	A B C
Citizenship	Yes	No	1	2	3	4	5	M	S	C	Yes	No	A B C

Instructions

1. Normally, you'd complete steps 2 and 3 of the form during the preseason. However, for practice, turn to the form in unit 10 and, based on your knowledge of your team, complete steps 2 and 3 for the technical and tactical skills you developed a practice plan for in units 11 and 12. (The form on the previous pages is for your future use.)

ACTIVITY 13.3

Practice Planning, Part IV: What Will be Taught How, When, by Whom

Starting in unit 10, and including the previous activity, you've completed these practice planning steps:

- Step 1: Identify the Skills Your Athletes Need
- Step 2: Know Your Athletes
- Step 4: Establish Priorities
- Step 5: Select the Methods for Teaching

You've also completed a practice plan outline for one technical skill and one tactical skill, so you've completed part of step 6, Plan Practices. Now it's time to address step 3, Analyze Your Situation, and to complete step 6.

In step 3, Analyze Your Situation, you need to determine what your practice environment will be like. For example, you need to answer the questions in form 12.4, Evaluating Your Team Situation, on pages 247 and 248 in Successful Coaching.

Once you've completed steps 1 through 5, you need to complete step 6, Plan Practices. In unit 12 of the classroom course, you evaluated some practice plans. You learned that the basic elements of a practice plan are these:

- Date, time of practice, and length of practice session
- Objective of the practice
- Equipment needed
- Warm-up
- Practicing previously taught skills
- Learning and practicing new skills
- Cool-down
- Coach's comments
- Evaluation of practice

Now it's time for you to create a practice plan.

Instructions

1. Create a practice plan using the practice plan form on the next page.

2. Include a summary of the practice plan outlines you completed for a technical skill in unit 11 and for a tactical skill in unit 12.

3. Include time for Coach's comments. Use this time at the close of practice to review how the team practiced, directing your comments to the whole team and recognizing any outstanding efforts or performances by individuals.

4. You don't need to include time for evaluating the practice, but remember: You should evaluate each practice as soon after its conclusion as possible. Discuss the practice with your assistant coaches, evaluate whether the practice objectives were achieved, and note athletes who may need special assistance in future practices.

5. When you've completed your practice plan, review it, and ask yourself if it was consistent with the following principles:

   Principle 1: Have athletes practice the right tactical skill.

   Principle 2: Have athletes practice the technique in gamelike conditions.

   Principle 3: Keep practices short and frequent when teaching new tactical skills.

   Principle 4: Use practice time efficiently.

   Principle 5: Make optimal use of facilities and equipment.

   Principle 6: Make sure athletes experience a reasonable amount of success at each practice.

   Principle 7: Make practice fun.

Practice Plan #_____

DATE: _____

PRACTICE START TIME: _____

LENGTH OF PRACTICE: _____

PRACTICE OBJECTIVES: _____

_____

EQUIPMENT: _____

_____

Practice Activities

Time	Name of activity	Description	Key teaching points

Training Basics

LEARNING OBJECTIVES

In this unit you will learn

- how the body works,
- the basics about energy and muscular fitness,
- your role in developing and conducting physical training programs, and
- the principles of physical training.

WHAT TO READ

Read chapter 13, Training Basics, in *Successful Coaching*.

ACTIVITY 14.1

Chapter 13 Quick Quiz

Instructions

1. Complete the following quiz.

▶ **Chapter 13 Quick Quiz** -

1. Which of the following describe the anaerobic energy system, and which describe the aerobic energy system? Write *a* for anaerobic and *b* for aerobic.

___ Means "without oxygen"

___ Energy system for enduring and less intense activity

___ Means "with oxygen"

___ Energy system for immediate movement and intense exercise

___ Source for activities such as sprinting, power lifting, or hitting a baseball

___ Source for activities such as long-distance running events

2. Enter the letter for the fitness component each definition describes, using *a* for muscular strength, *b* for muscular endurance, *c* for speed, *d* for muscular power, *e* for flexibility, and *f* for agility.

___ The range of motion through which the joints of the body are able to move

___ The ability to move the body or parts of it quickly

___ The maximum amount of force that a muscle can generate in a single effort

___ The ability to exert muscular strength quickly— strength and speed combined

___ The ability of a muscle to contract repeatedly or sustain a continuous contraction involving less than maximum force

___ The ability to start, stop, and change speed and direction quickly and with precision

3. Indicate which of the following statemants are true and which are false, using *t* for true and *f* for false.

___ Strength training in prepubescent athletes does not produce appreciable increases in strength.

___ Lactic acid causes muscle soreness.

___ The recommended minimum percentage of body fat for male athletes is 5 to 10 percent.

___ Plyometrics refers to a set of exercises used to develop strength and endurance in the muscles.

___ An ideal diet for athletes consists of 20 percent fat, 15 percent protein, and 65 percent carbohydrate.

4. Which of the following are benefits of warming up before rigorous exercise? Circle all that apply.

a. decreased risk of injury to the muscles

b. increased muscle mass

c. improvement of range of motion because of decreased viscosity of joint fluids

d. increased blood flow through the muscles

e. early onset of fatigue

f. increased rate of energy release from cells

5. Elena is a basketball player who will be working on breaking a press during the coming practice. Circle her proper warm-up sequence from the following options.

   a. stretch, jog, dribbling drill

   b. dribbling drill, jog, stretch

   c. jog, stretch, dribbling drill

6. After a workout, which one of the following cool-down options represents the best option? Circle your answer.

   a. Stretch first and then do an aerobic, low-intensity exercise.

   b. Do an aerobic, low-intensity exercise followed by stretching.

   c. Stretch only.

   d. Do the aerobic exercise only.

7. Cooling down for 10 to 15 minutes can speed recovery for the next workout by removing which of the following? Circle all that apply.

   a. fat

   b. blood

   c. creatine

   d. lactic acid

8. Which of the following characterizes the demand for *power* for an athlete competing in a short-distance swimming race? Circle all that apply.

   a. low

   b. medium

   c. medium high

   d. high

ACTIVITY 14.2

Training Principles

Chapter 13 in *Successful Coaching* introduced you to eight cardinal training principles that will help you design a training program for your athletes. For the final activity in this unit, you'll meet Coach Park, a soccer coach who is having some trouble making good decisions about training his athletes. His decisions relate to typical factors a coach should consider in designing a training program—for example, intensity of exercise and length of rest period.

Your job is to help him decide on a training principle to apply and then explain what he needs to do differently. The training principles you can select from to help Coach Park are these:

- Specificity
- Overload
- Progression
- Diminishing returns
- Variation
- Reversibility
- Individual differences
- Moderation

Instructions

1. Read the accounts of Coach Park conducting part of his training program. Each account begins with the factor Coach Park considered when he made his decision.

2. For each account, write in the training principle that Coach Park needs to apply, and write in your suggestions about how he needs to change his actions.

3. After you've noted your recommendations, check them against the activity solutions at the end of the unit. Remember, though, that your answers could be valid even if they don't match the ones listed in this unit exactly. The point is to get you thinking about the principles and how you can apply them.

▶ Coach Park's Decision: Intensity of Exercises - - - - - - - - - - - - - - -

During the first day of practice, Coach Park demands that his players run full speed throughout an hour-long scrimmage. He yells at anyone who slacks off. At the end of the practice, some of his players look physically ill from exhaustion.

Training principle to be applied:

_____

What Coach Park needs to do differently:

_____

_____

▶ Coach Park's Decision: Length of Rest Period - - - - - - - - - - - - - - -

After stressing strength training of the legs for the first few weeks of the season, Coach Park doesn't do it again for another two months. His players lose strength in their legs midway through the season.

Training principle to be applied:

_____

What Coach Park needs to do differently:

_____

_____

▶ *Coach Park's Decision: Volume of Exercises* - - - - - - - - - - - - - - - -

To improve his players' energy fitness, Coach Park has them run the same distance within the same amount of time every day for two months.

Training principle to be applied:

_____

What Coach Park needs to do differently:

_____

_____

▶ *Coach Park's Decision: Frequency of Training* - - - - - - - - - - - - - - -

Wanting his goalkeeper to improve his leaping ability, every day Coach Park has the athlete carry out exercises to strengthen his calves and perform drills to improve his reflexes. After a few weeks, the goalkeeper has shown marked improvement. Coach Park instructs the athlete to continue the exercises every day, but is frustrated when the goalkeeper's ability remains the same a month later.

Training principle to be applied:

_____

What Coach Park needs to do differently:

_____

_____

▶ Coach Park's Decision: Order of Exercises - - - - - - - - - - - - - - - - - -

Upset by the way his team seems to be getting pushed around on the field, Coach Park decides to emphasize upper body muscular fitness. He asks his athletes to do only arm curls every day for two weeks to strengthen their biceps and then switch to doing only bench presses for another two weeks to target their pectorals.

Training principle to be applied:

_____

What Coach Park needs to do differently:

_____

_____

▶ Coach Park's Decision: Choice of Exercise - - - - - - - - - - - - - - - - - -

Coach Park wants to help his athletes improve their ability to dribble the ball and sprint at the same time. He has them train by lifting weights to strengthen their back muscles.

Training principle to be applied:

_____

What Coach Park needs to do differently:

_____

_____

Unit 14 Solutions

ACTIVITY 14.1

▶ **Chapter 13 Quick Quiz** -

1. a, b, b, a, a, b
2. e, c, a, d, b, f
3. f, f, t, f, t
4. a, c, d, f
5. c
6. b
7. d
8. d

ACTIVITY 14.2

Training Principles

▶ **Coach Park's Decision: Intensity of Exercises** - - - - - - - - - - - - - - - - -

Training principle to be applied: Moderation
What Coach Park needs to do differently: Coach Park may need to give some of his athletes time to progress. At the beginning of the season, some of them might need to build up their fitness levels to meet the demands of game situations.

▶ **Coach Park's Decision: Length of Rest Period** - - - - - - - - - - - - - - - - -

Training principle to be applied: Reversibility
What Coach Park needs to do differently: Coach Park is forgetting that whatever progress his athletes made in building their muscles can quickly diminish if training does not continue. He should have his athletes continue the strength training for their legs.

▶ *Coach Park's Decision: Volume of Exercises* - - - - - - - - - - - - - - -

Training principle to be applied: Overload
What Coach Park needs to do differently: He needs to increase the duration or intensity of their current routine if he wants to see improvement in their fitness level.

▶ *Coach Park's Decision: Frequency of Training* - - - - - - - - - - - - - -

Training principle to be applied: Diminishing returns
What Coach Park needs to do differently: Coach Park should remember that he can expect the same rate of return on a continuing basis. He should focus on helping the goalkeeper maintain his improved skills.

▶ *Coach Park's Decision: Order of Exercises* - - - - - - - - - - - - - - - -

Training principle to be applied: Variation
What Coach Park needs to do differently: Coach Park needs to vary the exercises that his athletes are performing so that they don't overstress one part of their bodies.

▶ *Coach Park's Decision: Choice of Exercise* - - - - - - - - - - - - - - - -

Training principle to be applied: Specificity
What Coach Park needs to do differently: Coach Park needs to have his athletes train the muscles and energy systems that they will use to dribble and sprint.

Training for Energy Fitness

LEARNING OBJECTIVES

In this unit you will learn

- the basic physiology of the body's energy systems,
- how to determine the energy demands of your sport,
- how to assess and monitor energy fitness, and
- how to design an energy fitness training program.

WHAT TO READ

Read chapter 14, Training for Energy Fitness, in *Successful Coaching*.

ACTIVITY 15.1

Chapter 14 Quick Quiz

Instructions

1. Complete the following quiz by circling all answers that apply.

▶ *Chapter 14 Quick Quiz* -

1. What is the daily caloric requirement for high school athletes in intense training?
   a. 2,000 to 2,500
   b. 3,000 to 4,000

    c. 4,000 to 5,000

    d. 5,000 to 6,000

2. What is the only fuel a cell can use to contract muscle?

    a. phosphocreatine (PCr)

    b. adenosine triphosphate (ATP)

    c. glucose

    d. lactic acid

3. You should understand the blood lactate threshold so that you know when the body switches from

    a. aerobic to primarily anaerobic activity

    b. the ATP-PCr system to the anaerobic glycolysis system

    c. 50 percent to 60 percent of its maximum capacity

    d. 70 percent to 80 percent of its maximum capacity

4. What is the main purpose for a cool-down period after an intense workout?

    a. to extend the workout period

    b. to increase the production of ATP

    c. to remove lactic acid from the body

    d. to decrease the body's core temperature gradually

5. What is the primary energy system required when a softball player hits a home run?

    a. the ATP-PCr system

    b. the anaerobic glycolysis system

    c. the aerobic system

    d. the Neanderthal system

6. What happens when athletes use protein as an energy source?

    a. They speed up the conversion to ATP.

    b. They build muscle tissue while they exercise.

    c. They cannibalize their muscle tissue and overwork their kidneys.

    d. They are able to participate in sustained activities for a longer period.

7. What is the most accurate way to measure an athlete's muscle fiber type?

    a. Perform the skinfold test.

    b. Perform a muscle biopsy.

    c. Administer the vertical jump test.

    d. Divide the athlete's weight by his or her height.

ACTIVITY 15.2

Energy Fitness Evaluation

You spent some time thinking about the energy demands of your sport in the classroom course and when you read chapter 14 in *Successful Coaching*. Before you can design an effective energy fitness training program, however, you need to understand the energy requirements of your sport and the energy fitness level of each of your athletes. Expecting an overweight, out-of-shape team member to perform at the same level as those who have trained well in the preseason won't help anybody and may discourage the less fit athlete from participating at all.

In this activity you'll evaluate four athletes—Paulo, Mark, Shari, and Vickie—at the beginning of the year in each of the following areas: body type, body fat, and aerobic fitness. Later in this unit you'll use this information to design a customized energy training program for each athlete.

As you work through the activity, you should refer to the following items in chapter 14 as needed:

- Fitness Assessment for SporT (FAST) form
- Evaluation of Weight/Height Index Scores, table 14.4
- Percent Body Fat Recommendations for Athletes, table 14.5
- Aerobic Fitness Categories for the 1.5-Mile Test, table 14.7
- Training Pyramid, figure 14.8

Normally, you should use the Fitness Assessment for SporT (FAST) form to record your athlete evaluations. However, for the activities that follow, write your answers in the following table:

Energy Fitness Evaluation

Athlete	Paulo	Mark	Shari	Vickie
Sport				
Weight (lb)				
Height (in.)				
Body type assessment				
Body type evaluation				
% body fat				
Body fat evaluation				
1.5-mile test				
Aerobic fitness evaluation				

▶ Part 1 --

This is what you know about your athletes:

- Paulo: basketball; weight = 184 pounds; height = 73 inches
- Mark: football; weight = 229 pounds; height = 71 inches
- Shari: track; weight = 111 pounds; height = 67 inches
- Vickie: volleyball; weight = 186 pounds; height = 64 inches

PART 1 INSTRUCTIONS

1. Record your athletes' sports, weight, and height in the Energy Fitness Evaluation table.
2. Calculate the body type assessment for each athlete by dividing weight by height, and record this information in the Energy Fitness Evaluation table.
3. Determine the body type evaluation for each athlete by referring to the Evaluation of Weight/Height Index Scores, and record this information in the Energy Fitness Evaluation table.

▶ Part 2 --

The next part of your energy fitness evaluation includes an assessment for body fat percentage. Because you are in close proximity to the university in your city, you have each athlete hydrostatically weighed, an accurate process in which athletes are submerged in water.

Here are the results:

- Paulo: 8 percent body fat
- Mark: 11 percent body fat
- Shari: 13 percent body fat
- Vickie: 20 percent body fat

PART 2 INSTRUCTIONS

1. Record each athlete's body fat percentage in the Energy Fitness Evaluation table.
2. Refer to the Percent Body Fat Recommendations for Athletes table; determine whether each athlete is below, within, or above the recommendation for the given sport; and record this body fat evaluation information in the Energy Fitness Evaluation table.

▶ **Part 3** -

The last part of the energy test is an assessment of aerobic fitness. Here are the results of the 1.5-mile test:
- Paulo: 10:14
- Mark: 12:20
- Shari: 9:20
- Vickie: 11:53

PART 3 INSTRUCTIONS

1. Record the 1.5-mile test times for each athlete in the Energy Fitness Evaluation table.
2. Refer to the Aerobic Fitness Categories for the 1.5-Mile Test table, determine each athlete's aerobic fitness category, and record this information in the Energy Fitness Evaluation table.

ACTIVITY 15.3

Energy Fitness Training Plan

To develop an energy fitness training plan for each of your athletes, you should use the training pyramid, making sure to consider the athlete's current fitness level and the athlete's goals. The main idea is to start with a good aerobic base and increase the intensity or duration of the training to apply the overload and progression principles discussed in *Successful Coaching*.

For now, let's test your understanding of some of the concepts involved in developing an energy fitness training plan with the following questions.

Instructions

1. Answer the following questions by entering the information requested or by circling all answers that apply. The athletes named are the ones you considered in the previous activity.

▶ *Fitness Training Plan Quiz* -

1. Mark is 17 years old, his resting heart rate (HR) is 70, and you want him to exercise at 75 percent of his maximum hear rate (max HR). Determine his training target heart rate, and write it here: _____.

2. Which type of training will best help Shari increase her lactate threshold?

   a. long, slow distance training

   b. pace or tempo training

   c. interval training

   d. fartlek training

   e. sprints

3. Vickie has a solid aerobic base and wants to work more on increasing her speed. Which two types of training should you incorporate into the practice games to help her develop her anaerobic energy?

   a. long-distance training

   b. pace or tempo training

   c. interval training

   d. fartlek training

   e. sprints

4. Paulo generally works hard during basketball practice and makes progress in his skills during the first few weeks of the season. Over time, however, Paulo's coordination declines, and he complains of muscle soreness and headaches. What is the most likely cause of Paulo's condition?

   a. illegal drugs

   b. caffeine

   c. overtraining

   d. not enough sprint training

ACTIVITY 15.1

1. c
2. b
3. a
4. c
5. a
6. c
7. b

ACTIVITY 15.2

▶ **Energy Fitness Evaluation** -

Energy Fitness Evaluation

Athlete	Paulo	Mark	Shari	Vickie
Sport	Basketball	Football	Track	Volleyball
Weight (lb)	184	229	111	186
Height (in.)	73	71	67	64
Body type assessment	2.5 lb/in.	3.2 lb/in.	1.8 lb/in.	2.9 lb/in.
Body type evaluation	Mesomorph	Endomorph	Ectomorph	Endomorph
% body fat	8	11	13	20
Body fat evaluation	Within	Within	Within	Above
1.5-mile test	10:14	12:20	9:20	11:53
Aerobic fitness evaluation	Average	Low	High	High

ACTIVITY 15.3

1. 170 beats per minute

    Use the following formula to determine Mark's training target heart rate (TTHR), using .75 as the percentage of max HR. Round to the nearest whole number.

$$220 - \underset{\substack{\text{(age} \\ \text{in years)}}}{\underline{\hspace{1cm}}} = \underset{\text{(max HR)}}{\underline{\hspace{1.5cm}}} - \underset{\text{(resting HR)}}{\underline{\hspace{1.5cm}}} = \underset{\text{(exercise HR)}}{\underline{\hspace{1.5cm}}} \times \underset{\substack{\text{(\% of training} \\ \text{intensity as} \\ \text{measured by} \\ \text{\% of max HR)}}}{\underline{\hspace{1.5cm}}} + \underset{\text{(resting HR)}}{\underline{\hspace{1.5cm}}} = \underset{\text{(TTHR)}}{\underline{\hspace{1.5cm}}}$$

    To exercise at 75 percent of his maximum heart rate, Mark needs to get his heart rate up to 170 beats per minute. You might want to administer the 1.5-mile test again at the beginning of the season to see how much improvement he's made.

2. b. Pace or tempo training allows Shari to increase her training heart rate gradually from 70 percent of max HR to 85 percent of max, which shifts the focus from aerobic fitness to lactate threshold training.

3. c and e. Interval training and sprints are most effective for developing the anaerobic energy system.

4. c. That's right! Frequent headaches, increased muscle soreness, and loss of coordination are classic signs of overtraining. You might want to see if he's participating in any training outside of basketball practice and make adjustments accordingly.

Training for Muscular Fitness

LEARNING OBJECTIVES

In this unit you will learn

- what muscular fitness is,
- how muscles work and the effect training has on muscles,
- how to determine the muscular demands of your sport and assess muscular fitness, and
- how to design a muscular fitness training program.

WHAT TO READ

Read chapter 15, Training for Muscular Fitness, in *Successful Coaching*.

ACTIVITY 16.1

Chapter 15 Quick Quiz

Instructions

1. Complete the following quiz by filling in the blanks or circling all answers that apply.

▶ Chapter 15 Quick Quiz -

1. The maximum amount of force that a muscle can generate in a single effort is called _____.

2. The ability of a muscle to contract repeatedly or sustain a continuous contraction involving less than maximum force is called _____.

3. Having enough strength, endurance, speed, power, and flexibility to meet the demands of a given sport is called _____.

4. During the upward movement of a biceps curl, which action does the biceps require?

   a. concentric action

   b. eccentric action

   c. isometric action

5. For endurance sports, strength should be at least _____ times the resistance encountered.

   a. 2

   b. 2.5

   c. 5

   d. 5.5

6. For power sports, strength should be at least _____ times the force required to perform the action.

   a. 2

   b. 2.5

   c. 5

   d. 5.5

7. Lactic acid causes muscle soreness.

   True

   False

8. Two methods for testing muscular endurance include the push-up test and the curl-up test.

   True

   False

9. How often should a beginning athlete train per week?

   a. two to three times

   b. three to four times

   c. four to six times

   d. seven times

10. What is not a way to improve an athlete's speed?

   a. Shorten the reaction time to the stimulus.

   b. Increase the acceleration time to reach full speed faster.

   c. Improve the ability to maintain speed for the required distance.

   d. Decrease the length of the stride while maintaining the pace of the stride.

ACTIVITY 16.2

Muscular Fitness Evaluation

As with energy fitness, you need to know the current strengths and weaknesses of an athlete before you can design a muscular fitness plan tailored to his or her specific needs. In this activity we'll cover testing athletes in the following three areas:

- Flexibility
- Strength
- Power

As you work through the activity, you should refer to the following items in chapter 15 as needed:

- 10 Commandments for Stretching
- Estimating the Muscular Demands of Your Sport, table 15.1
- Evaluation of the Sit-and-Reach Test Scores, table 15.3
- Essential Eight Resistance Exercises, table 15.4
- Estimating 1RM From the Essential Eight Test, table 15.5
- Average Strength of Athletes As a Percentage of Their Body Weight for the Essential Eight Strength Test Scores, table 15.6
- Evaluation of Stair Sprint Test Scores, table 15.10
- Determing the Starting Resistance or Load for Strength Training, table 15.11

Do you remember the four athletes you worked with in unit 15? You'll continue working with them throughout this unit. Here's a summary of the information you've gathered so far.

Energy Fitness Evaluation

Athlete	Paulo	Mark	Shari	Vickie
Sport	Basketball	Football	Track	Volleyball
Weight (lb)	184	229	111	186
Height (in.)	73	71	67	64
Body type assessment	2.5 lb/in.	3.2 lb/in.	1.8 lb/in.	2.9 lb/in.
Body type evaluation	Mesomorph	Endomorph	Ectomorph	Endomorph
% body fat	8	11	13	20
Body fat evaluation	Within	Within	Within	Above
1.5-mile test	10:14	12:20	9:20	11:53
Aerobic fitness evaluation	Average	Low	High	High

Assume that you administered the sit-and-reach test for flexibility to your four athletes. These are the results:

Sit-and-Reach Test Results

	Test 1	Test 2	Test 3
Paulo	17.50 in.	17.75 in.	18 in.
Mark	14 in.	14.25 in.	14.25 in.
Shari	10.75 in.	11 in.	11.25 in.
Vickie	18 in.	18.50 in.	18.25 in.

Instructions

1. Complete the following muscular fitness assessment by filling in the blanks or circling all answers that apply.

▶ *Muscular Fitness Assessment* -

1. Based on the Evaluation of the Sit-and-Reach Test Scores table in chapter 15, which one of your athletes needs the most work in this area? _____

2. Assume that Paulo can bench press 100 pounds for 10 reps. Based on the Estimating 1RM table in chapter 15, what is Paulo's 1RM for the bench press?

    a. 118 pounds

    b. 125 pounds

    c. 133 pounds

    d. 149 pounds

3. Vickie can leg press 150 pounds for eight reps. Based on the Estimating 1RM table in chapter 15, what is Vickie's 1RM for the leg press?

    a. 176 pounds

    b. 188 pounds

    c. 200 pounds

    d. 224 pounds

4. Mark can curl a 45-pound dumbbell for 12 reps. Based on the Estimating 1RM table in chapter 15, what is Mark's 1RM?

    a. 56 pounds

    b. 60 pounds

    c. 67 pounds

    d. 69 pounds

5. Now let's evaluate our athletes for power by using the stair sprint test. We're running the test on stairs that have a 7-inch rise and enough room at the top for the athletes to stop, and we've already marked steps 2 and 10. The athletes will start 10 feet from the first stair and then run as fast as possible up the stairs, using only even-numbered steps. We'll start the clock when the athlete reaches stair 2 and stop it on stair 10. How many steps should you multiply by 7 inches to get the vertical distance?

    a. 5

    b. 7

    c. 8

    d. 10

Now that you know the vertical distance, 4.67 feet, you can plug values into the following equation to find each athlete's power score:

$$\text{Power} = \frac{\text{body weight (in pounds)} \times \text{vertical distance (in feet)}}{\text{time (in seconds)}}$$

6. Using the power score equation and the Evaluation of Stair Sprint Test Scores in chapter 15, calculate Paulo's power score, and determine his power evaluation.

Paulo's power score: _____

Paulo's power evaluation: _____

7. Using the power score equation and the Evaluation of Stair Sprint Test Scores in chapter 15, calculate Mark's power score, and determine his power evaluation.

Mark's power score: _____

Mark's power evaluation: _____

8. Using the power score equation and the Evaluation of Stair Sprint Test Scores in chapter 15, calculate Shari's power score, and determine her power evaluation.

Shari's power score: _____

Shari's power evaluation: _____

ACTIVITY 16.3

Muscular Fitness Training Plan

Now that you know more about each athlete's flexibility, strength, and power, you're ready to help them with a muscular fitness training plan. Let's start on that now. You won't complete an entire plan, but you can start thinking about how you would complete one.

Instructions

1. Answer the following questions by entering the information requested or by circling all answers that apply. The athletes named are the ones you considered in the previous activity.

▶ *Muscular Fitness Training Plan* -

One of Paulo's training goals is to develop a strength base in his lower body for layups and rebounds. His 1RM on the leg press is 200 pounds, and you want him to use a resistance of 80 percent for six to eight repetitions.

1. Using the Determing the Starting Resistance or Load for Strength Training table in chapter 15, calculate Paulo's appropriate starting weight.

Starting weight: _____

Paulo's second training goal is to increase his power when passing the ball to other players. His 1RM on the bench press is 133 pounds, and he wants to use three to five repetitions per set with a resistance of 75 percent.

2. Using the Determing the Starting Resistance or Load for Strength Training table, calculate Paulo's appropriate starting weight.

Starting weight: _____

Vickie hasn't done any resistance training in the last three months, so your primary goal when working with her is building strength. Her 1RM for arm curls is 27 pounds. You decide to have her start at 75 percent for 8 to 10 reps.

3. Using the Determing the Starting Resistance or Load for Strength Training table, calculate Vickie's appropriate starting weight.

Starting weight: _____

Mark needs explosive power as a defensive tackle. His 1RM for the biceps curl is 67. You decide to start him at 85 percent for one to two reps per set.

4. Using the Determing the Starting Resistance or Load for Strength Training table, calculate Mark's appropriate starting weight.

Starting weight: _____

Unit 16 Solutions

ACTIVITY 16.1

▶ **Chapter 15 Quick Quiz** -

1. strength
2. endurance
3. fitness
4. a
5. b

6. c
7. False
8. True
9. a
10. d

ACTIVITY 16.2

▶ **Muscular Fitness Evaluation** -

1. Shari needs the most work in this area, and you might want to recommend that she stretch twice a day instead of only once. You should probably work closely with her at first, in case she simply isn't using the proper technique.
2. 133 pounds
3. 188 pounds
4. 67 pounds
5. 8 steps. If you multiply the eight steps by 7 inches, the vertical distance traveled during the test is 56 inches, or 4.67 feet.
6. Paulo's power score: 728; Paulo's power evaluation: average
7. Mark's power score: 835; Mark's power evaluation: high
8. Shari's power score: 762; Shari's power evaluation: high

ACTIVITY 16.3

▶ **Muscular Fitness Training Plan** -

1. Paulo's starting weight: 150 to 170 pounds
2. Paulo's starting weight: 100 pounds
3. Vickie's starting weight: 22.5 pounds
4. Mark's starting weight: 55 pounds

SELF-STUDY UNIT

Fueling Your Athletes

LEARNING OBJECTIVES

In this unit you will learn

- what athletes should eat;
- how carbohydrates, fat, and protein nourish the body;
- the role of nutritional supplements in the athlete's diet;
- how to keep your athletes hydrated and avoid heat illnesses;
- how much your athletes should eat for maintaining, losing, and gaining weight;
- when and what your athletes should eat before, during, and after competition; and
- how to deal with eating disorders.

WHAT TO READ

Read chapter 16, Fueling Your Athletes, in *Successful Coaching*.

ACTIVITY 17.1

Chapter 16 Quick Quiz

Instructions

1. Complete the following quiz by circling all answers that apply.

► *Chapter 16 Quick Quiz* -

1. Which nutrient helps the eyes work correctly, helps the cells burn energy, and protects the cells from damage?
   a. minerals
   b. vitamins
   c. protein
   d. fat

2. For which category is popcorn a good way to get servings?
   a. fats, oils, and sweets
   b. milk, yogurt, and cheese
   c. breads, cereals, rice, and pasta
   d. meats, poultry, fish, dry beans, eggs, and nuts

3. Which snack is most appropriate before a competition or workout? (Consider glycemic level.)
   a. carrots
   b. muffins
   c. potatoes
   d. yogurt

4. When athletes go from rest to exercise, how much more heat can their muscles generate?
   a. twice as much
   b. 5 times as much
   c. 10 times as much
   d. 20 times as much

ACTIVITY 17.2

Nutrients

In chapter 16 you learned about the six basic nutrients that fuel, strengthen, and heal the human body, and you probably know how challenging it is for athletes to get all the nutrition they need for proper conditioning and maintenance.

Take a little time now to make sure that you have a solid understanding of the six basic nutrients.

Instructions

1. Write the name of the nutrient described next to the description.

▶ Understanding the Six Basic Nutrients -

1. This nutrient is much healthier when it comes from plants (except for some tropical plants). _____

2. This nutrient is found in potatoes, pasta, bread, cereal, and beans. _____

3. Eggs have lots of cholesterol, but they also provide lots of this nutrient. _____

4. This nutrient is responsible for carrying other nutrients to the body's cells. _____

5. This nutrient is responsible for controlling the water level inside and outside the cells. _____

6. Calcium, which keeps bones strong, is an example of this nutrient. _____

7. This nutrient can't be stored in the body, so people should consume it daily. _____

8. A diet too high in protein usually means a diet too low in this nutrient. _____

9. This nutrient regulates your immune system, your nervous system, your energy burning, and even the function of your eyes. _____

10. This nutrient, which can be stored, provides energy for long-term aerobic activity. _____

ACTIVITY 17.3

The Food Guide Pyramid

Your knowledge of the sources and functions of the six basic nutrients puts you in an excellent position to advise your athletes on their daily meal and snack choices. But you also need information on balancing an athlete's diet for high performance.

Coaches today have access to more information about nutrition and performance than ever before. For this reason, an increasing number of coaches are discussing nutrition in their preseason conferences with parents or working the halls of their schools to encourage athletes to make good choices over the lunch hour.

The United States Department of Agriculture (USDA) developed the Food Guide Pyramid based on the foods that Americans eat. The pyramid depicts daily food choices that ensure a balanced, healthy diet low in fats. Your active, growing athletes may need a higher caloric intake than this pyramid suggests, so they would require even more servings than the pyramid recommends.

Now try to apply your knowledge of nutrition and USDA recommendations to some daily meal choices. The series of questions that follow will ask you to consider the diet of some of your athletes. How do their choices register on the Food Guide Pyramid, and what advice can you give them to ensure healthy eating?

Instructions

1. Circle all answers that apply.

▶ *Food Guide Pyramid* -

1. Why does the USDA place fats, oils, and sweets at the top of the Food Guide Pyramid?

   a. The top segment of a pyramid is smaller than the bottom; people should consume the smallest possible amounts of fats, oils, and sweets.

   b. These three nutrients, in moderation, are the most important part of a healthy diet.

   c. People can't store fats, oils, and sweets so those foods should be part of each daily meal.

2. How many servings of milk, yogurt, and cheese should most athletes in training eat each day?

   a. 2 to 3

   b. 3 to 5

   c. 6 to 11

3. In one day, an athlete should eat

   a. eight eggs

   b. 7 ounces (196 grams) of meat, chicken, turkey, or fish

   c. three 7-ounce cuts (588 grams total) of meat, chicken, turkey, or fish

4. A basketball player has one banana and one cup of fruit juice for lunch. The player has

   a. met the minimum recommended daily amount of fruits

   b. exceeded the maximum recommended daily amount of fruits

   c. not met the minimum recommended daily amount of fruits

5. One of your runners has two cheese sandwiches on wheat bread and four medium-sized cookies for lunch. How many

servings of "bread, cereal, rice, and pasta" has the runner consumed?

a. two

b. four

c. six

ACTIVITY 17.4

Hydration

Insufficient fluid intake is the most common nutritional problem that athletes face. Every function of the body relies on proper hydration. Athletes who aren't properly hydrated suffer from fatigue, impaired performance, and increased body temperature.

Your athletes also run a much higher risk of heat illness when they're not properly hydrated. You need to control the conditions that can lead to heat illness and learn to recognize and respond to the symptoms.

On a daily basis, you must encourage your athletes to drink the right beverages in the right amounts, and at the right times. Now try your hand at a quick exercise in beverage choices.

Instructions

1. Write the name of the beverage described next to the description, using these beverage names: soft drink, diet soft drink, water, sport drink, fruit juice, and coffee.

▶ **Beverage Choices** -

1. This beverage contains water, sugar, and sometimes sodium, but no other nutrients. _____

2. This beverage has no caffeine, no sugar, and only one important nutrient. _____

3. This beverage can stimulate the nervous system and increase performance, but it can also cause increased urination, leading to dehydration. _____

4. This drink can speed up rehydration in your athletes and replace vital nutrients that they lose through sweat. _____

5. This drink provides water as well as other nutrients, but it doesn't replace nutrients lost through sweat, and it takes a while to absorb into the bloodstream. _____

Unit 17 Solutions

ACTIVITY 17.1

▶ **Chapter 16 Quick Quiz** -

1. b
2. c
3. d
4. d

ACTIVITY 17.2

▶ **Nutrients-** -

1. fat
2. carbohydrates
3. protein
4. water
5. protein

6. minerals
7. protein
8. carbohydrates
9. vitamins
10. fat

ACTIVITY 17.3

▶ **he Food Guide Pyramid** -

1. a
2. b
3. b

4. c
5. c

ACTIVITY 17.4

▶ **Hydration** -

1. soft drink
2. water
3. coffee

4. sport drink
5. fruit juice

SELF-STUDY UNIT

Battling Drugs

LEARNING OBJECTIVES

In this unit you will learn what you can do to

- become sufficiently knowledgeable about drugs so that you are in a position to help;
- develop and enforce a drug-free participation policy;
- provide your players with preventive education about substance abuse;
- detect the signs of substance abuse among your athletes; and
- counsel your athletes and, when necessary, help them obtain professional help.

WHAT TO READ

Read chapter 17, Battling Drugs, in *Successful Coaching*.

ACTIVITY 18.1

Chapter 17 Quick Quiz

Instructions

1. Complete the following quiz by circling all answers that apply, or by writing the correct responses as directed.

▶ Chapter 17 Quick Quiz -

1. Heroin, morphine, and codeine are examples of
   a. hallucinogens
   b. narcotics
   c. depressants
   d. inhalants

2. Which of the following has not been attributed to the habitual use of alcohol?
   a. weight gain
   b. damage to the central nervous system
   c. sexual impotence
   d. anemia

3. A hallucinogen commonly known as the date-rape drug is
   a. psilocybin
   b. PCP
   c. nitrous oxide
   d. Rohypnol

4. Identify the following street names by writing the letter of the drug it refers to in the appropriate box. Drug name or types—a: marijuana; b: cocaine; c: depressants; d: LSD; e: inhalants; f: methadone
   ____ huff
   ____ grass
   ____ blues
   ____ dollies
   ____ snow
   ____ acid

5. Which of the following types of performance-enhancing drugs can mask the use of other unauthorized drugs?
   a. diuretics
   b. stimulants
   c. anabolic agents
   d. peptide hormones

6. Which of the following is a performance effect attributed to erythropoietin (a peptide hormone)?
   a. increased muscle mass and decreased body fat
   b. anti-inflammatory effects
   c. increased aerobic power and endurance
   d. soothing coating of the stomach to aid indigestion

7. Which of the following could be true of both the performance effects and negative consequences of taking anabolic steroids?

   a. You might have increased energy and alertness, but you could become more nervous and anxious.

   b. You could see an increase in strength and power, but you could experience premature balding.

   c. You may lose weight, but you could become dehydrated.

8. Identify whether the following statements from student-athletes indicate a reason to use drugs or a reason not to use drugs. Use *a* for "why I use drugs" and *b* for "why I don't use drugs."

   ____ I need help coping with stress.

   ____ My religious beliefs dictate my moral decisions.

   ____ I don't like being out of control.

   ____ I get a kick out of taking risks.

   ____ I'm concerned about negative health effects.

   ____ I want to fit in with my friends.

ACTIVITY 18.2

Your Attitude Toward Drugs

You can't solve the problem of substance abuse alone, and no one expects you to, but you can be a part of the solution. A good first step is knowing where you stand on the issue.

In this activity you'll take a quick survey to discover what your attitude is toward athletes' use of alcohol, tobacco, and illicit drugs.

Instructions

1. For each question on the survey, circle the rating that best matches your attitude.

   • Circle 1 if you are not opposed to the statement.

   • Circle 3 if you are opposed to the statement.

   • Circle 5 if you're strongly opposed to the statement.

   • Circle 2 or 4 if you fall somewhere between these ratings.

2. Answer honestly, not as you think someone wants you to answer. You will not be asked to share your results.

▶ Coach's Attitude Toward Drugs Survey - - - - - - - - - - - - - - - - - -

1. Athletes' use of illicit drugs at any time

| 1 | ——— | 2 | ——— | 3| ——— | 4 | ——— | 5 |
Not opposed   Opposed   Strongly opposed

2. Athletes receiving special consideration from coaches, administrators, and law enforcement officers if caught using illicit or performance-enhancing drugs

| 1 | ——— | 2 | ——— | 3| ——— | 4 | ——— | 5 |
Not opposed   Opposed   Strongly opposed

3. Athletes' use of drugs that are banned by a regulating governing body of sports

| 1 | ——— | 2 | ——— | 3| ——— | 4 | ——— | 5 |
Not opposed   Opposed   Strongly opposed

4. Athletes' use of these banned substances even when participating in competitive events in which no rules against the use of these drugs exist

| 1 | ——— | 2 | ——— | 3| ——— | 4 | ——— | 5 |
Not opposed   Opposed   Strongly opposed

5. Use of tobacco when an athlete is a minor

| 1 | ——— | 2 | ——— | 3| ——— | 4 | ——— | 5 |
Not opposed   Opposed   Strongly opposed

6. Use of tobacco when an athlete is an adult

| 1 | ——— | 2 | ——— | 3| ——— | 4 | ——— | 5 |
Not opposed   Opposed   Strongly opposed

7. Allowing the use of tobacco and alcohol at sport events in which minors are participating

| 1 | ——— | 2 | ——— | 3| ——— | 4 | ——— | 5 |
Not opposed   Opposed   Strongly opposed

8. Use of alcohol when an athlete is a minor

| 1 | ——— | 2 | ——— | 3| ——— | 4 | ——— | 5 |
Not opposed   Opposed   Strongly opposed

9. Use of alcohol when an athlete is an adult

| 1 | ——— | 2 | ——— | 3| ——— | 4 | ——— | 5 |
Not opposed   Opposed   Strongly opposed

ACTIVITY 18.3

A Problem With Alcohol

Despite all your efforts in preventing drug and alcohol use among your athletes, you may at times encounter an athlete with a problem. As you learned in chapter 17, the following steps can help you respond appropriately, responsibly, and professionally to such a situation.

- Recognize the signs.
- Choose to respond.
- Share your concern.
- Get help.
- Show support once the athlete has been referred for help.

Let's explore some scenarios that will give you practice determining how to respond to an athlete with an alcohol problem. Imagine that you're the cross country coach for boys and girls, and your high school has not adopted drug testing of athletes. How would you respond to the following circumstances?

Instructions

1. Read each scenario and some possible responses to it.
2. Circle the response that most closely represents what you would do.
3. Then review the assessment for each response.
4. You don't have to agree with the responses or the assessments. If your response would be very different from those listed, write it in the space provided, and then assess the effectiveness of your response in the space provided.

▶ *Scenario 1* -

One Wednesday night as you're about to go into the school auditorium for a concert, you see Angie, one of the runners on your team, in the parking lot. Angie's always been a good kid. As you approach to say hi, you catch a whiff of alcohol. Angie says hello and then runs off, apparently embarrassed. How would you respond?

YOUR RESPONSE

a. Don't handle it at all for now. She hasn't had any problems with alcohol or drug use in the past.

b. Lecture her during practice the next day.

c. Call her into your office for a chat.

d. _____

_____

ASSESSMENTS

a. This may be the easiest choice to make, but it's probably not the wisest. The incident may well be an isolated event, but you don't know that yet. You have an obligation to respond.

b. You're not ignoring the situation here, but a private setting is the appropriate place to discuss Angie's problem.

c. By making this choice, you'll be able to discuss the problem one-on-one with Angie.

d. _____

_____

▶ Scenario 2 -

Angie comes to your office to discuss what happened in the parking lot. She knows why she's there and starts by owning up to the fact that she drank that night because of peer pressure. She insists that she drank only that one time this year. What can you say to her now to share your concern?

YOUR RESPONSE

a. "I'm disappointed that you chose to drink when you know it's illegal and clearly against our team rules."

b. "I don't know what's wrong with you. Why didn't you think before you did something like this?"

c. _____

_____

ASSESSMENTS

a. This is a good choice. You're expressing the way Angie's behavior makes you feel, showing her that she's affecting more people than just herself.

b. You're expressing your frustration in an attacking and judgmental manner rather than simply stating that Angie's behavior has frustrated and worried you.

c. _____

_____

► Scenario 3 -

You've shared your concern with Angie, and she has admitted her mistake and expressed regret. She's violated the team's drug and alcohol policy, although she insists that the drinking was an isolated incident. Now consider your choices of how to get help for Angie.

YOUR RESPONSE

a. Contact Angie's parents and apply the appropriate consequences, as stipulated in your team drug policy. Assist with a plan to provide professional help if needed.

b. Refer Angie to the school counselor, but tell her parents only if the counselor feels that they should know.

c. _____

_____

ASSESSMENTS

a. Angie will be able to get the help she needs, and her parents will be able to offer her support at home. She will have to deal with the consequences of her actions, but because you have a written policy, she will also know where she stands and how she can regain her previous standing with the team.

b. You should inform Angie's parents of the situation because she has violated your team's drug policy.

c. _____

_____

► Scenario 4 -

Now consider a situation after you've sought help for Angie. She's faced some consequences for her choices and is now back with the team. On a Friday before a long weekend, you hear some students at the school talking about a big party planned for that night. During practice you feel inclined to emphasize the team's commitment to your drug policy.

YOUR RESPONSE

    a. Mention Angie's previous infraction of the team's rules, and warn your athletes not to make the same mistake she did.

    b. Point out that you know there will be a lot of parties this weekend and that you expect the athletes to adhere to the team's policy.

    c. _____

    _____

ASSESSMENTS

    a. Angie will likely feel targeted and belittled by these actions. She needs you to show support for her after she has gotten help for her problem or paid her dues for violating team policy.

    b. This cautionary statement will remind Angie and her teammates of the rules that they have all agreed to. You don't have to single out Angie to emphasize the athletes' need to maintain their integrity.

    c. _____

    _____

Unit 18 Solutions

ACTIVITY 18.1

▶ *Chapter 17 Quick Quiz* -

    1. b
    2. d
    3. d
    4. e, a, c, f, b, d
    5. a
    6. c
    7. b
    8. a, b, b, a, b, either a or b

Managing Your Team

LEARNING OBJECTIVES

In this unit you will learn about your

- policy management responsibilities,
- information management responsibilities,
- personnel management responsibilities,
- instructional management responsibilities,
- event and contest management responsibilities,
- logistics management responsibilities, and
- financial management responsibilities.

WHAT TO READ

Read chapter 18, Managing Your Team, in *Successful Coaching,* but before you start, see Activity 19.1.

ACTIVITY 19.1

Manager To-Do List

As you'll learn when you read chapter 18, being a coach means wearing a lot of manager hats. Depending on your school and the size of the coaching staff, you may be managing any or all of the following:

- Policy
- Information
- Personnel

- Instruction
- Events and contests
- Logistics
- Finances

Do not despair. Chapter 18 provides a comprehensive summary of what you'll need to do, no matter what hat you're wearing. As you read through the chapter, take this opportunity to start a to-do list for one of your manager roles. If you're new to coaching, pick either the information manager role or the personnel manager role. If you're an experienced coach, pick the one role you never seem to find time to tackle. Then, for the role you selected, do the following.

Instructions

1. Write the name of the manager role at the top of the table on the next page.
2. Identify the 10 most important or highest priority tasks you must get done, and note them in column 1 of the table.
2. Enter the dates when the task needs to be finished in column 2. If you're not sure about specific dates, put in the month or the season (preseason, in-season, or postseason); or if the task is continuous, put in its frequency (daily, weekly, monthly, yearly).
3. Identify the information you'll need to complete the task, and note it in column 3.
4. Identify who you can or should contact to get help or guidance for the task, and note the names of these contacts in column 4.
5. When you've completed your to-do list, review it, and prioritize the tasks from 1 to 10. You should be ready to start working on one of your important manager roles.

Manager To-Do List

Task	Done when	Information needed	Contacts

Managing Relationships

LEARNING OBJECTIVES

In this unit you will learn

- how to manage relationships by mastering four interpersonal skills that are vital to your coaching success and
- how to work more effectively with your fellow coaches, administrators, medical personnel, officials, the parents of your players, and the media.

WHAT TO READ

Read chapter 19, Managing Relationships, in *Successful Coaching*.

ACTIVITY 20.1

Resolving Conflict Like Animals

Chapter 19 illustrates five styles of conflict management by drawing parallels from the animal kingdom. Which animal do you most closely resemble?

- Turtle: Because the relationship is of little consequence and their goals are also of low importance, turtles withdraw from conflicts and avoid any type of confrontation. Turtles often see resolving the conflict as hopeless, and they feel helpless about changing the situation. Being aware that you have an inclination to react like the turtle (tending to withdraw and avoid confrontation when conflict arises) can help you assess whether you need to change your approach generally or in specific circumstances.

- Shark: Because they value their goals highly and give low priority to retaining relationships, sharks respond to conflict by attacking, overpowering, and intimidating others, forcing them to accept their solution to the conflict. Sharks consider conflicts to be contests in which one person wins and the other loses, and they want to win. Reacting like the shark (attacking and forcing others to accept your solution to conflict) is the strategy that you will find least effective in the long run. That approach can end up being detrimental to your relationships.

- Teddy Bear: To teddy bears the relationship is extremely important, and thus they're willing to give up their own goals. They have a high need to be accepted and liked, and they avoid conflict because they believe that they can't address conflicts without damaging relationships. Being aware that you have an inclination to react like the teddy bear (avoiding conflict in an attempt to prevent damage to a relationship) can help you assess whether you need to change your approach generally or in specific circumstances.

- Fox: Foxes are moderately concerned with achieving their goals and maintaining a good relationship. Consequently, they seek compromise. They're willing to give up part of their goals if the other person will too; in that way both sides gain something. Having an inclination to react like the fox (seeking compromise when necessary in accomplishing moderately important goals) will be beneficial to you in most cases.

- Owl: Owls value their goals as well as the relationship with the other person. Consequently, their solution is to confront the other person to seek a solution that achieves the goals of both themselves and the other person. Having an inclination to react like the owl (facing confrontation head on, but seeking a win–win solution) will be beneficial to you in most cases.

Now let's see how coaches with these animal characteristics might respond to some conflict situations, and let's see what the assessments of their responses might be. Let's not change a good thing: we'll call these coaches Coach Turtle, Coach Shark, Coach Teddy Bear, Coach Fox, and Coach Owl.

Instructions

1. Read each scenario and the responses to it by a few coaches.
2. Circle the name of the coach who you think had the best response.
3. Then review the assessment of each coach's response.

4. You don't have to agree with the responses or the assessments. If your response would be very different from those listed, write it in the space provided, and then assess the effectiveness of your response in the space provided.

▶ Scenario 1 -

An athlete on your team is having problems keeping up his grades in the classroom and is on the verge of losing eligibility to play. He doesn't seem committed to improving scholastically, but he tells you that he really wants to stay on the team.

RESPONSES

- Coach Teddy Bear: Let him deal with the classroom in his own way. Your relationship with the athlete is too important to risk becoming involved.
- Coach Fox: Work out a compromise regarding his eligibility so that he can remain on the team.
- Coach Owl: Confront him about the problem and work out a solution in private. Focus on getting him to improve his grades while staying a part of the team.

- _____

_____

ASSESSMENTS

- Coach Teddy Bear: You need to be a little firmer in this case. True, your relationship with the athlete is important, but so is helping him take advantage of his educational opportunities (and stay eligible to play for your team). You can't let only his wants control the situation.
- Coach Fox: Although compromise is often a good strategy, in this case you need to deal with the problem head on. You don't have much room for negotiation here. If the athlete doesn't improve his grades, he will become ineligible, and you don't have the power to change eligibility requirements as part of the bargain.
- Coach Owl: There's no reason to think that this athlete can't agree to try harder in school so that he can remain on the team (a win–win situation). Face the conflict head on and, like a wise owl, reach an agreement with the athlete on how to resolve the problem.

- _____

_____

▶ Scenario 2 -

You want a parent of one of your athletes to help with a fundraiser by staffing a concession stand on Friday night, but she says she's too busy and would rather just make a financial contribution.

RESPONSES

- Coach Turtle: Tell her not to worry about it and withdraw from the situation without accepting her money.
- Coach Teddy Bear: Accept her suggestion of giving a contribution and find another way to staff the concession stand.
- Coach Fox: Try to persuade her to accept a compromise by suggesting that she work half the time on Friday night and give only half the contribution she had planned to give.

- _____

_____

ASSESSMENTS

- Coach Turtle: You are wise not to push her to do what you want in this situation, but simply walking away shows that you don't value the relationship.
- Coach Teddy Bear: Your relationship with the parent of an athlete is important, whereas having her staff the concession stand is not. Reacting like the teddy bear by giving up what you want is a good choice here. Besides, she's planning to participate in the fund-raising in a way that works better for her.
- Coach Fox: If your goal to have her staff the concession stand were really important, seeking a compromise would be a good strategy.

- _____

_____

▶ Scenario 3 -

You're in a convenience store buying a bag of chips and a soda. The guy behind you in line says, "I know you! You coach at the high school. The way your team played this year, you won't have that job for very long."

RESPONSES

- Coach Turtle: Tell him that everyone's entitled to an opinion; then walk away and avoid further confrontation.
- Coach Shark: Give him a piece of your mind. And while you're at it, explain the stats that prove you deserve the position you're in.
- Coach Owl: Invite him to take a walk and talk calmly with the man until you can determine his specific complaints. Let him know that you're always trying to improve and see if you can both reach the goals that you're seeking.

- _____

_____

ASSESSMENTS

- Coach Turtle: Walking away can be the right choice at times like this, when the relationship and your goal (convincing him that you really are a good coach) are relatively unimportant.
- Coach Shark: Few if any circumstances in coaching would justify reacting like the shark. You may not value this relationship much, but attacking him isn't likely to do any good.
- Coach Owl: This guy is attacking you out of nowhere. Is the relationship important enough to spend all that time trying to convince him that you're a good coach?

- _____

_____

▶ *Scenario 4* -

You and the coach of another team at your school want to reserve the weight room for your teams on the same days of the week.

RESPONSES

- Coach Shark: Demand that you get the weight room when you need it and seek an administrator if she doesn't cave in.
- Coach Fox: Seek a compromise that may involve sacrifice on both sides but will allow you to achieve your goals regardless.

• Coach Teddy Bear: Yield to the other coach. She'll appreciate your cooperation, and your relationship will benefit from it.

• _____

_____

ASSESSMENTS

• Coach Fox: In this situation both the goal and the relationship are important. Seeking a compromise is a good way of dealing with this potential conflict.

• Coach Shark: Few if any circumstances in coaching would justify reacting like the shark. Attacking the coach of the other team will set a bad example for your athletes and damage a relatively important relationship.

• Coach Teddy Bear: Not wanting to damage your relationship with the other coach is commendable, but your goal of using the weight room is important for the growth of your team. Don't give in so easily here.

• _____

_____

ACTIVITY 20.2

Resolving Conflict Your Way

Now try your hand with some more conflict scenarios, focusing more on your way for dealing with the situations.

Instructions

1. Read each scenario and some possible responses to it.

2. Circle the response that most closely represents what you would do.

3. Then review the consequences of each response.

4. You don't have to agree with the responses or the consequences. If your response would be very different from those listed, write it in the space provided, and then write the possible consequences of your response in the space provided.

▶ Scenario I -

An official makes what you feel are a series of horrible calls that affect the outcome of a contest. As you approach him during a stop in the action and begin to express your concern, his reaction is terse, rude, and dismissive. What do you do?

YOUR RESPONSE

    a. State your case briefly and clearly and then focus your athletes on controlling their efforts to do their best. Following the contest, file a report concerning the official's poor performance.

    b. Tell him how poorly he's officiating the contest. Admonish him for as long as possible to drive your point home.

    c. _____

    _____

CONSEQUENCES

    a. The official continues to make some questionable calls during the contest, but he seems to pay slightly more attention to your concerns. The official does not participate in another contest with your team that season.

    b. The official appears frazzled for a few minutes following your confrontation. He seems more hesitant to blow the whistle for the remainder of the contest and continues to make some questionable calls. In subsequent contests he treats you coldly and remains aloof.

    c. _____

    _____

▶ Scenario 2 -

A reporter for the local newspaper has written some critical stories lately about your team, particularly about your game-day decisions. He comes up after practice and wants to ask you some questions for a story. What do you do?

YOUR RESPONSE

    a. Grant him an interview and try to express your side of the story as clearly as possible.

b. Tell him that you're not giving any interviews for a while and walk away.

c. _____

_____

CONSEQUENCES

a. The story in the next day's newspaper includes this commentary: "Even though the team has performed below expectations so far, this coach remains optimistic about the remainder of the season."

b. The story in the next day's newspaper includes this commentary: "With the incredible disappointment that is this season, the coach seems either too embarrassed or too angry to answer questions about the team."

c. _____

_____

▶ Scenario 3 -

Mr. Willis is the father of Tanya, an athlete on your team. He comes into your office one day and begins complaining that Tanya is not getting enough exposure. "She needs to see more action, Coach. I mean, with her skills, she should be out there as much as possible, yet you continue to use other kids in her place. I don't want her to lose a chance at a scholarship." What do you do?

YOUR RESPONSE

a. Tell Mr. Willis that parents don't have the experience to decide these things and that if Tanya deserved a scholarship, she would be playing more.

b. Tell Mr. Willis that you and your staff are making the best decisions you can about who gets to play and when. Then subtly remind him that he should leave the coaching to you.

c. Tell Mr. Willis that you'll try to increase Tanya's playing time but that you can't give any guarantees.

d. _____

_____

CONSEQUENCES

a. "Listen, she's Division I caliber," says Mr. Willis as he gets up to leave. "If you can't see that, you're not the coach I thought you were. Believe me, I know my daughter's skills better than you do."

b. Mr. Willis says, "Well, I guess there's nothing else I can do. You know how I feel, and you can make the call. I just want her to have the chance to go to college."

c. Mr. Willis thanks you and leaves. Two weeks later, however, he is back in your office complaining that you haven't made good on your promise to play Tanya more.

d. _____

_____

▶ *Scenario 4* -

Mrs. Poole has had three sons participate in your program. Her fourth son, John, is now on the team. John's not as athletic or skilled as his brothers were, but he puts forth an honest effort and seems to enjoy being part of the group. Mrs. Poole pulls you aside one day and tells you, "John isn't happy with his role on the team. He really should get more opportunities to compete, you know." How do you respond to Mrs. Poole?

YOUR RESPONSE

a. "To be frank, Mrs. Poole, it's none of your business whether I give John playing time or not."

b. "I'll talk to John about his role and his playing time. Thanks for sharing your concern."

c. _____

_____

CONSEQUENCES

a. Mrs. Poole is clearly offended and doesn't know what to say. She quickly excuses herself and doesn't speak to you again for the rest of the season.

b. Mrs. Poole says, "Well, OK. But don't tell him I came to you. He'd be so embarrassed. You see, he hasn't actually said anything to me. I can just tell he'd like to play more by the way he acts."

c. _____

_____

► *Scenario 5* -

Another coach at your school tells you that the athletic director (AD) is concerned that coaches are verbally abusing student-athletes during practices. Several other teams are currently holding practices, so you can't be sure if she is concerned about your team or not. What action do you take?

YOUR RESPONSE

a. Talk to the other coaches about the situation and ask them if they think that the athletic director's statement is fair.

b. Invite the athletic director to observe some of your practices and provide an objective view of the interactions you and your staff have with your athletes.

c. _____

_____

CONSEQUENCES

a. Some of the other coaches haven't heard anything about the AD's displeasure with the treatment of athletes. Some of them become upset and want to complain to the AD. You realize too late that you've become part of spreading a rumor.

b. The AD accepts your offer and attends a couple of your practices. She doesn't mention anything about verbal abuse of your athletes, but she does end up giving you and your staff some valuable pointers about other matters.

c. _____

_____

Managing Risk

LEARNING OBJECTIVES

In this unit you will learn about

- our legal system and the definition of negligence,
- what risk management means for coaches,
- immunity laws, and
- your nine legal duties as a coach.

WHAT TO READ

Read chapter 20, Managing Risk, in *Successful Coaching*.

ACTIVITY 21.1

Chapter 20 Quick Quiz

Instructions

1. Complete the following quiz by circling all answers that apply.

▶ *Chapter 20 Quick Quiz* -

1. If an athlete is injured and you have failed to fulfill your legal duty, yet the athlete's reckless actions were also a factor, a court is likely to rule that the incident was a case of

   a. contrastive negligence

b. contractual negligence

c. contributory negligence

d. immunity

2. For each coach, indicate the coach's approach to risk management, using the following—a: avoiding the risk, b: accepting the risk, or c: transferring the risk

____ Coach Williams takes out an insurance policy to cover herself against legal liability costs in case she is sued.

____ Coach Horiuchi determines that his cross country team can run on a hot day.

____ Coach Allen cancels practice because of extremely muddy field conditions.

3. An athlete who has a disability wants to participate on your team, but you have reservations because you think that the athlete's participation could present a safety risk for other members of your team. What should you do?

a. Let the athlete with the disability play on the team. You don't want to risk a lawsuit.

b. Go with your conscience. The Volunteer Protection Act will shield you from litigation in this circumstance.

c. Discuss the issue with your administrator to consider implications of the Americans With Disabilities Act.

d. Do not allow the athlete to participate if you have any doubts about the effect on your team.

4. To minimize risk, what is the best way to transport your athletes to an event?

a. Arrange for a public carrier.

b. Take them in your own vehicle.

c. Avoid risk altogether by insisting that parents provide transportation.

d. Have the athletes transport themselves and others on the team.

5. If you need to discipline an athlete formally, which of the following is not an example of following due process?

a. Allow the athlete a chance to respond before imposing the penalty.

b. Let the athlete figure out for himself or herself why you are enforcing the discipline.

c. Provide a written record of findings.

d. Make sure that you give the athlete a chance to present his or her side of the situation.

ACTIVITY 21.2

Believe It or Doubt It

Instructions

1. Read the following coaches' statements.
2. For each statement:
   a. If you believe the statement makes sense, check "Believe it."
   b. If you doubt the coach's wisdom, check "Doubt it."

▶ *Believe It or Doubt It* -

1. I have several players on my track team who played football for our school in the fall. They all had a preseason physical at that point, so I don't see a need to make them do it again, just six months later.

   ☐ Believe it

   ☐ Doubt it

2. I let my older players teach the underclassmen about basic techniques. I'll leave them to work with one group while I take another group away to teach them some other skills. This approach saves me time, and I feel that my seniors know this stuff almost as well as I do anyway.

   ☐ Believe it

   ☐ Doubt it

3. I protect myself against potential lawsuits by having my athletes and their parents sign a waiver that releases me from responsibility for any accident that occurs because of participation in the sport. The waiver is a legal contract; so as long as the athletes and parents are willing to sign it, my legal worries are taken care of.

   ☐ Believe it

   ☐ Doubt it

4. When we're doing drills, I don't have a problem matching a sophomore with a senior, as long as they've of similar skill and size.

   ☐ Believe it

   ☐ Doubt it

5. One of my players missed a couple of practices last week because of a minor injury. The injury healed completely by the time she returned, and she didn't show any signs that it would be a continuing problem. In this case, however, you should always fill out an injury report form anyway

because it was serious enough for the athlete to miss a practice.

☐ Believe it

☐ Doubt it

6. Last week we were scheduled to play an away game on a really rainy day. The rain stopped by the time the game was scheduled, but the field was a mess. I've never seen so much mud, and rocks and twigs were strewn all over. I didn't say anything because it's really the home team's responsibility to make sure that the field is safe. Fortunately, someone on their side must have spoken up because they ended up delaying the game.

☐ Believe it

☐ Doubt it

7. We try to do regular checks of all the equipment our players use, but it's nice to know that if something bad happens to a player because of an equipment failure, we won't be the ones that take the heat. The manufacturer is the one who'll get sued.

☐ Believe it

☐ Doubt it

8. I wouldn't be caught dead coaching without liability insurance, and I require my assistants to have it, too. It's just too risky to try to coach in today's world without it.

☐ Believe it

☐ Doubt it

9. Believe me, you've got to watch these kids like a hawk to avoid the chance of legal trouble. I keep close tabs on my athletes wherever they are. I'm always in sight of the athletes in the locker room, and the coaching staff escorts the team off the school grounds after practice.

☐ Believe it

☐ Doubt it

10. It's critical to include a description of risks for injury in the player handbook given out to each athlete to start the season. Our staff also covers this in our parent orientation meeting.

☐ Believe it

☐ Doubt it

11. Sometimes my athletes and I become bored with the same old routines, so I let them try some dives we haven't worked on yet. You've got to be a bit of a daredevil to be a good diver, anyway.

☐ Believe it

☐ Doubt it

ACTIVITY 21.3

Nine Legal Duties

Chapter 20 discussed your nine legal duties as a coach. Clearly you need to be well aware of what these duties are because ignoring them can have some serious consequences. Being well aware means not just knowing what each duty is, but also knowing your responsibilities for fulfilling each duty. That's what this activity is all about.

Instructions

1. Review your nine legal duties listed in the Nine Legal Duties table.

2. Your responsibilities for each duty are described after the table, but *not* in the same order as the duties. Read your responsibilities, and determine which list of responsibilities relates to which legal duty. Write the responsibility letters in column 2 of the table.

3. Read the nine scenarios that follow responsibilities, and determine which scenario relates to which legal duty. Write the scenario numbers in column 3 of the table. The answers for legal duty 1 have been provided to clarify what you need to do.

Nine Legal Duties

Legal duty	Relates to responsibility letter	Relates to scenario number
Duty 1: Properly plan the activity	F	4
Duty 2: Provide proper instruction		
Duty 3: Warn of inherent risks		
Duty 4: Provide a safe physical environment		
Duty 5: Provide adequate and proper equipment		
Duty 6: Match your athletes appropriately		
Duty 7: Evaluate athletes for injury or incapacity		
Duty 8: Supervise the activity closely		
Duty 9: Provide appropriate emergency assistance		

RESPONSIBILITY A

1. Note and remedy hazardous conditions through regular inspections of the playing facility and the warm-up, training, and dressing areas.

2. Develop a facilities inspection checklist for the facilities and equipment used in your sport. Use it regularly, and keep these checklists on file.

3. Change any dangerous conditions that you can; reduce the hazard if you cannot remove it. Warn your players of the hazard and notify the facility manager through written recommendations about correcting the hazard.

4. Give precise rules for using the facility. Post the rules, remind the players of them, and enforce them consistently.

5. Monitor the changing environment and make prudent judgments about continued participation if it becomes hazardous.

RESPONSIBILITY B

1. Buy the best equipment you can afford, considering the age and skill of your athletes.

2. Teach your athletes how to fit, use, and inspect their equipment. Encourage them to return any equipment that does not fit or appears defective.

3. Inspect equipment regularly; the more stress placed on the equipment, the more frequently you should examine it.

4. If players bring their own equipment, you still have a responsibility to inspect it and ensure that it complies with safety standards.

5. Allow only qualified people to install, fit, adjust, and repair equipment. You may want to insist that a manufacturer's representative fit all equipment (e.g., helmets, pads, and mouth guards).

6. Warn players of potentially hazardous equipment, and give verbal and written instructions on using it.

7. Be aware of changes in equipment by keeping current on accepted standards.

RESPONSIBILITY C

1. Keep abreast of current instructional standards for your sport and use them.

2. Teach skills, strategies, and rules in accordance with customary methods of your sport and the developmental level of your athletes.

3. Make your instructions clear, complete, and consistent.

Provide adequate feedback on how your athletes are progressing.

4. If you are a head coach, you must supervise any instruction that you delegate to others.

RESPONSIBILITY D

1. Match players according to size, maturity, skill, and experience as well as age so that they are not placed in situations in which the risk of injury is increased.

2. Enforce eligibility rules; they often are intended to provide equitable competition.

3. Modify the drill or practice structure when mismatches in ability cannot easily be corrected.

4. Be especially alert to mismatches between the sexes, when athletes are recovering from injury, and among athletes with disabilities.

RESPONSIBILITY E

1. Always provide general supervision for all facilities and playing areas your team uses.

2. Provide specific supervision when teaching new skills and when the risk of injury increases.

3. Know your sport so well that you can anticipate potentially dangerous situations and be positioned to prevent them from occurring.

4. Use posters, notices, and signs to support but not replace your supervision.

5. Do not condone reckless or overly aggressive behavior that threatens the safety of any athlete.

RESPONSIBILITY F

1. Develop a season plan using progressions that are appropriate for your athletes.

2. Test players to determine their physical capacity and skill level for your sport.

3. Develop written practice plans that adhere to the recommendations in chapter 12 of *Successful Coaching*.

4. Adapt your plans to the individual needs of your athletes.

5. Don't deviate from your plans without good cause.

6. Keep all records of your planning and testing.

RESPONSIBILITY G

1. Obtain a consent form for each athlete at the beginning of the season.

2. Protect the injured athlete from further harm.

3. Provide appropriate first aid.

4. Attempt to maintain or restore life using CPR when required.

5. Comfort and reassure injured athletes.

6. Activate your emergency plan, transferring the treatment responsibility to trained medical personnel.

7. Complete your injury report form as soon after the injury occurrence as possible.

RESPONSIBILITY H

1. Warn your athletes of the inherent risks of the sport so they know, understand, and appreciate them.

2. Use written notices, releases, videos, and repeated warnings to make certain your athletes understand the risks and are mindful of them.

RESPONSIBILITY I

1. In cooperation with your medical support team, require evidence that all athletes have received preparticipation physical examinations in the past two or three years.

2. Keep a medical history of every athlete on file.

3. Recommend that your medical support team follow the American Academy of Pediatrics guidelines in determining whether and under what conditions persons with special conditions can participate.

4. Follow the NCAA guidelines in seeking to accommodate people with impairments who want to participate on your team.

5. Use extraordinary judgment in identifying athletes who are injured or so ill that they should not participate.

6. Get medical and parental approval before permitting seriously ill or injured athletes to return to participation.

▶ *Scenario 1* -

Bill Edgar, a 16-year-old, was awarded $1.8 million after sustaining permanent paralysis playing baseball. He attempted to score by diving headlong into the catcher. The coach, one of several defendants in the lawsuit, was found negligent for failing to warn Bill that this action could result in serious injury.

▶ *Scenario 2* -

Randy Brooks was a 115-pound (52-kilogram) football player who irritated Coach Jack Bennis with his continual misbehavior and boasting of unfounded ability. After an hour of Randy's provocations one day, Coach Bennis organized a one-on-one tackling drill and matched Randy with Tom McNab, a 205-pound (93-kilogram) tackle and the strongest player on the team. In the drill Randy suffered a serious concussion and was hospitalized. The court found Coach Bennis negligent for his imprudent judgment in matching the players.

▶ *Scenario 3* -

High school basketball coach Sue Emmerling was in a practice session working on speed drills when a student assistant called her to the office for an important telephone call. The team continued to practice but became reckless, and the drill degenerated into horseplay. Two players collided; one broke her jaw and knocked out several teeth. Coach Emmerling was sued and found negligent for failing to fulfill her duty to supervise properly.

▶ *Scenario 4* -

In the second week of practice, first-year wrestling coach John Sterling wanted to impress his team with his knowledge of the sport. He showed them an advanced takedown technique called "souple," in which the wrestler lifts the opponent and then falls back on his neck and shoulder with the weight of the opponent on top of him. Manuel Garcia, a 15-year-old in his first year of wrestling, attempted the takedown and broke his neck, which left him paralyzed. The coach and school district were sued and ruled negligent because Coach Sterling failed to prepare Manuel for this advanced skill with proper strength training and lead-up skills.

▶ *Scenario 5* -

After a short but heavy rain the barren softball infield was too muddy to use for practice, so Coach Ellen Archer moved the team to a large grass field. Kelly Smith stepped in a hole, breaking her leg in three places. The resulting litigation found Coach Archer negligent for not properly inspecting the playing facility.

▶ **Scenario 6** -

Andy Jacobs was knocked unconscious for about 30 seconds when he was slammed to the mat by his opponent in a high school wrestling match. After 15 minutes Andy insisted that he was all right and demanded to continue the match. His coach reluctantly agreed. Andy died 20 minutes after the match from a cerebral hemorrhage. The two physicians who testified at the trial stated unequivocally that the coach should not have permitted Andy to return to the mat. The jury found the coach negligent.

▶ **Scenario 7** -

Robert Bloom thought he was making a good buy when he purchased new plastic face masks for his hockey team. The masks were mounted in the helmets by the school maintenance man, although no instructions were provided on how to do so. Four weeks into the season Brad Kosnick was hit in the mask by a high stick, which shattered the mask and sent a plastic splinter into his left eye. Brad lost the use of that eye, and in the court trial the mask manufacturer, the coach, and the school were found negligent.

▶ **Scenario 8** -

Field hockey player Jill Donovan passed out during practice on a hot, sultry day. Coach Ellis failed to recognize the common symptoms of a heat stroke, and so rather than seeking immediate medical assistance, she instructed Jill to sit under a shade tree while practice continued. Jill slipped into shock and another team member urged Coach Ellis to get help, but the plea fell on deaf ears. The next morning Jill died. Coach Ellis was found negligent in the lawsuit that followed for failing to provide appropriate emergency assistance.

▶ **Scenario 9** -

Spear tackling, a form of tackling in football in which the tackler's head is "speared" into the ball carrier's chest, was the accepted way to tackle in the 1960s. Because many spinal injuries resulted from this technique, however, and several studies demonstrated how vulnerable the spine is in this tackle, the technique was no longer recommended, especially for high school players. Unfortunately, high school coach Mike Douglas did not know that spear tackling was contraindicated. He had learned tackling that way, and so he taught it to his players. Using the technique resulted in quadriplegia for his middle linebacker and a $2.8 million court ruling against Mike and his school.

Unit 21 Solutions

ACTIVITY 21.1

▶ *Chapter 20 Quick Quiz* -

1. c
2. c, b, a
3. c
4. a
5. b

ACTIVITY 21.2

▶ *Believe It or Doubt It* -

1. Believe it. Ensuring that athletes have a preparticipation evaluation is part of your legal duty to evaluate athletes for injury or incapacity. Because this coach's athletes had an exam within the last year, however, he probably doesn't need to demand that they go to the doctor again.

2. Doubt it. This coach could be in hot water if she doesn't supervise the skill instruction that she is designating to others, especially when the techniques being taught could prove hazardous if performed incorrectly. This is one of her legal duties in providing proper instruction.

3. Doubt it. Putting all your trust in waivers to protect you from a lawsuit is not wise. Consider using participation agreements instead, which, unlike waivers, do not attempt to absolve you from all possible negligence but instead establish that you warned the athletes of potential consequences of participating in your sport.

4. Believe it. This coach is trying to fulfill her legal duty to match athletes appropriately.

5. Believe it. Completing an injury report form soon after an injury occurs is part of a coach's legal duty to provide

appropriate emergency assistance. If an injury is serious enough to warrant missing a practice, a report should be filed for your records.

6. Doubt it. The coach should have realized that notifying a facilities manager when conditions are unsafe is part of his legal duty to provide a safe physical environment for athletes.

7. Doubt it. Although an injury because of equipment failure will often be blamed on the manufacturer, you can't consider yourself free from responsibility in this arena.

8. Believe it. Insurance is a key part of managing your risk of litigation. In the unfortunate event that you are taken to court, you'll need help paying for your defense.

9. Doubt it. This coach is most likely going a too far when it comes to her legal duty to supervise activities closely. Athletes need to be supervised at all times, but for situations like getting dressed in the locker room or walking off school grounds after a practice, your supervision can be general (available and alert in case of an emergency).

10. Believe it. This coach is demonstrating how to warn athletes of inherent risks, an important legal duty. Other ways to accomplish this include using written notices, releases, videos, and repeated warnings to make certain that your athletes understand the risks and are mindful of them.

11. Doubt it. Teaching athletes advanced skills before they are ready or because the team is becoming bored is a situation ripe for an accident that could lead to litigation.

ACTIVITY 21.3

▶ *Nine Legal Duties* -

Nine Legal Duties Answers

Legal duty	Relates to responsibility letter	Relates to scenario number
Duty 1: Properly plan the activity	F 1. Develop a season plan using progressions that are appropriate for your athletes. 2. Test players to determine their physical capacity and skill level for your sport. 3. Develop written practice plans that adhere to the recommendations in chapter 12 of *Successful Coaching.* 4. Adapt your plans to the individual needs of your athletes. 5. Don't deviate from your plans without good cause. 6. Keep all records of your planning and testing.	**4:** In the second week of practice, first-year wrestling coach John Sterling wanted to impress his team with his knowledge of the sport. He showed them an advanced takedown technique called "souple," in which the wrestler lifts the opponent and then falls back on his neck and shoulder with the weight of the opponent on top of him. Manuel Garcia, a 15-year-old in his first year of wrestling, attempted the takedown and broke his neck, which left him paralyzed. The coach and school district were sued and ruled negligent because Coach Sterling failed to prepare Manuel for this advanced skill with proper strength training and lead-up skills.

Legal duty	Relates to responsibility letter	Relates to scenario number
Duty 2: Provide proper instruction	**C** 1. Keep abreast of current instructional standards for your sport and use them. 2. Teach skills, strategies, and rules in accordance with customary methods of your sport and the developmental level of your athletes. 3. Make your instructions clear, complete, and consistent. Provide adequate feedback on how your athletes are progressing. 4. If you are a head coach, you must supervise any instruction that you delegate to others.	**9:** Spear tackling, a form of tackling in football in which the tackler's head is "speared" into the ball carrier's chest, was the accepted way to tackle in the 1960s. Because many spinal injuries resulted from this technique, however, and several studies demonstrated how vulnerable the spine is in this tackle, the technique was no longer recommended, especially for high school players. Unfortunately, high school coach Mike Douglas did not know that spear tackling was contraindicated. He had learned tackling that way, and so he taught it to his players. Using the technique resulted in quadriplegia for his middle linebacker and a $2.8 million court ruling against Mike and his school.
Duty 3: Warn of inherent risks	**H** 1. Warn your athletes of the inherent risks of the sport so they know, understand, and appreciate them. 2. Use written notices, releases, videos, and repeated warnings to make certain your athletes understand the risks and are mindful of them.	**1:** Bill Edgar, a 16-year-old, was awarded $1.8 million after sustaining permanent paralysis playing baseball. He attempted to score by diving headlong into the catcher. The coach, one of several defendants in the lawsuit, was found negligent for failing to warn Bill that this action could result in serious injury.
Duty 4: Provide a safe physical environment	**A** 1. Note and remedy hazardous conditions through regular inspections of the playing facility and the warm-up, training, and dressing areas. 2. Develop a facilities inspection checklist for the facilities and equipment used in your sport. Use it regularly, and keep these checklists on file. 3. Change any dangerous conditions that you can; reduce the hazard if you cannot remove it. Warn your players of the hazard and notify the facility manager through written recommendations about correcting the hazard. 4. Give precise rules for using the facility. Post the rules, remind the players of them, and enforce them consistently. 5. Monitor the changing environment and make prudent judgments about continued participation if it becomes hazardous.	**5:** After a short but heavy rain the barren softball infield was too muddy to use for practice, so Coach Ellen Archer moved the team to a large grass field. Kelly Smith stepped in a hole, breaking her leg in three places. The resulting litigation found Coach Archer negligent for not properly inspecting the playing facility.

(continued)

Nine Legal Duties Answers *(continued)*

Legal duty	Relates to responsibility letter	Relates to scenario number
Duty 5: Provide adequate and proper equipment	**B** 1. Buy the best equipment you can afford, considering the age and skill of your athletes. 2. Teach your athletes how to fit, use, and inspect their equipment. Encourage them to return any equipment that does not fit or appears defective. 3. Inspect equipment regularly; the more stress placed on the equipment, the more frequently you should examine it. 4. If players bring their own equipment, you still have a responsibility to inspect it and ensure that it complies with safety standards. 5. Allow only qualified people to install, fit, adjust, and repair equipment. You may want to insist that a manufacturer's representative fit all equipment (e.g., helmets, pads, and mouth guards). 6. Warn players of potentially hazardous equipment, and give verbal and written instructions on using it. 7. Be aware of changes in equipment by keeping current on accepted standards.	**7:** Robert Bloom thought he was making a good buy when he purchased new plastic face masks for his hockey team. The masks were mounted in the helmets by the school maintenance man, although no instructions were provided on how to do so. Four weeks into the season Brad Kosnick was hit in the mask by a high stick, which shattered the mask and sent a plastic splinter into his left eye. Brad lost the use of that eye, and in the court trial the mask manufacturer, the coach, and the school were found negligent.
Duty 6: Match your athletes appropriately	**D** 1. Match players according to size, maturity, skill, and experience as well as age so that they are not placed in situations in which the risk of injury is increased. 2. Enforce eligibility rules; they often are intended to provide equitable competition. 3. Modify the drill or practice structure when mismatches in ability cannot easily be corrected. 4. Be especially alert to mismatches between the sexes, when athletes are recovering from injury, and among athletes with disabilities.	**2:** Randy Brooks was a 115-pound (52-kilogram) football player who irritated Coach Jack Bennis with his continual misbehavior and boasting of unfounded ability. After an hour of Randy's provocations one day, Coach Bennis organized a one-on-one tackling drill and matched Randy with Tom McNab, a 205-pound (93-kilogram) tackle and the strongest player on the team. In the drill Randy suffered a serious concussion and was hospitalized. The court found Coach Bennis negligent for his imprudent judgment in matching the players.

Legal duty	Relates to responsibility letter	Relates to scenario number
Duty 7: Evaluate athletes for injury or incapacity	**I** 1. In cooperation with your medical support team, require evidence that all athletes have received preparticipation physical examinations in the past two or three years. 2. Keep a medical history of every athlete on file. 3. Recommend that your medical support team follow the American Academy of Pediatrics guidelines in determining whether and under what conditions persons with special conditions can participate. 4. Follow the NCAA guidelines in seeking to accommodate people with impairments who want to participate on your team. 5. Use extraordinary judgment in identifying athletes who are injured or so ill that they should not participate. 6. Get medical and parental approval before permitting seriously ill or injured athletes to return to participation.	**6:** Andy Jacobs was knocked unconscious for about 30 seconds when he was slammed to the mat by his opponent in a high school wrestling match. After 15 minutes Andy insisted that he was all right and demanded to continue the match. His coach reluctantly agreed. Andy died 20 minutes after the match from a cerebral hemorrhage. The two physicians who testified at the trial stated unequivocally that the coach should not have permitted Andy to return to the mat. The jury found the coach negligent.
Duty 8: Supervise the activity closely	**E** 1. Always provide general supervision for all facilities and playing areas your team uses. 2. Provide specific supervision when teaching new skills and when the risk of injury increases. 3. Know your sport so well that you can anticipate potentially dangerous situations and be positioned to prevent them from occurring. 4. Use posters, notices, and signs to support but not replace your supervision. 5. Do not condone reckless or overly aggressive behavior that threatens the safety of any athlete.	**3:** High school basketball coach Sue Emmerling was in a practice session working on speed drills when a student assistant called her to the office for an important telephone call. The team continued to practice but became reckless, and the drill degenerated into horseplay. Two players collided; one broke her jaw and knocked out several teeth. Coach Emmerling was sued and found negligent for failing to fulfill her duty to supervise properly.
Duty 9: Provide appropriate emergency assistance	**G** 1. Obtain a consent form for each athlete at the beginning of the season. 2. Protect the injured athlete from further harm. 3. Provide appropriate first aid. 4. Attempt to maintain or restore life using CPR when required. 5. Comfort and reassure injured athletes. 6. Activate your emergency plan, transferring the treatment responsibility to trained medical personnel. 7. Complete your injury report form as soon after the injury occurrence as possible.	**8:** Field hockey player Jill Donovan passed out during practice on a hot, sultry day. Coach Ellis failed to recognize the common symptoms of a heat stroke, and so rather than seeking immediate medical assistance, she instructed Jill to sit under a shade tree while practice continued. Jill slipped into shock and another team member urged Coach Ellis to get help, but the plea fell on deaf ears. The next morning Jill died. Coach Ellis was found negligent in the lawsuit that followed for failing to provide appropriate emergency assistance.

Coaching Principles Self-Study Wrap-Up

LEARNING OBJECTIVES

In this unit you will learn

- about completing the final step in the Coaching Principles Classroom course—taking the Coaching Principles Test.

INTRODUCTION

CONGRATULATIONS! At this point, you should have read *Successful Coaching* and completed the Coaching Principles Classroom course self-study. Now you're ready to take the Coaching Principles Test, which should take about 90 minutes to complete. You should do fine! Just follow the simple steps below.

FIRST

- Get your *Successful Coaching* book and the Coaching Principles Classroom Test Package.
- Take these items out of the Test Package:
    - The Coaching Principles Classroom Test
    - The ASEP Test Answer Form A to record test answers
    - The Coaching Principles Test Instructions

SECOND

- In the classroom portion of this study guide, turn to unit 20, Coaching Principles Wrap-Up, and review Activity 20.4 Testing Procedures.

- In the Coaching Principles Test Instructions, read Step 1: Determine How You Want to Take Your Coaching Principles Test.

- Decide how you will take the test: paper-pencil or online.

THIRD

- If you're going to take the test **ONLINE,** in the Coaching Principles Test Instructions, follow the directions in Step 2: If You Choose to Take the Online Test, and take the test. **REMINDER:** In the class you should have written or learned where to find the following:

    - Your key code. The key code is the 10-digit number printed on the instructions.
    - The instructor's identification number
    - The instructor's last name
    - The organization code (if applicable)
    - The last date of course

- If you're going to take the test **PAPER-PENCIL,** in the Coaching Principles Test Instructions, follow the directions in Step 3: If You Choose to Take the Paper-Pencil Test, and take the test. **REMINDER:** The course code is on the back page of the Coaching Principles Classroom Test, it is four characters long, and it begins with AA followed by two numbers. In the class you should have written or learned where to find the following:

    - Your key code. The key code is the 10-digit number printed on the instructions.
    - The instructor's identification number
    - The instructor's last name
    - The organization code (if applicable)
    - The last date of course

- **REMINDER:** Send your completed test to ASEP. Follow the directions under "Returning Your Completed Paper-Pencil Test to ASEP" in the Coaching Principles Test Instructions.

That's it. You're done. Congratulations, and thanks for taking the Coaching Principles course!

NFHS Coaches Education Program

A New Standard: The Bronze Level

The Bronze Level program represents the most proactive, powerful, and relevant professional development program available today for high school coaches. The curriculum includes **Coaching Principles** (featuring the text, *Successful Coaching, Third Edition*), **Sport First Aid**, and **Coaching [Sport] Technical and Tactical Skills**. The Bronze Level will prepare you for all aspects of coaching and be a recognized and respected credential for all who earn it.

Release of the Bronze Level program represents a shift not only to an upgraded curriculum, but also to the Internet. All three courses are available online, providing unparalleled flexibility, consistency, and reach. For those who prefer face-to-face interaction, traditional classroom courses, led by certified instructors, for *Coaching Principles* and *Sport First Aid* will continue to be offered.

The NFHS Coaches Education Program is supported, developed, and delivered through a partnership with the American Sport Education Program (ASEP), a 20-year leader in the sport education field. The NFHS Coaches Education Program fulfills the coaching education requirements of 35 state high school associations.

To register for these courses, or for more information on course curriculum, call ASEP at 800-747-5698; e-mail asep@hkusa.com; or visit www.asep.com

BRONZE LEVEL